Microsoft® SQL Server™ Express Edition For Dummies

D1098646

SQL Server Management Studio Express — Object Explorer View

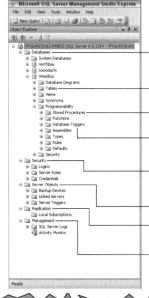

Design your database right from the start. Take a look at Chapter 7 for more.

Find a home for your data. See Chapter 8 for a roadmap.

Store application logic in your database. Chapter 14 has the details.

Make your database smarter. Check out Chapter 15.

Safeguard your system. Chapter 11 tells all.

See how to archive your data in Chapter 13.

Spread the data and the workload. Chapter 6 shows you how.

To get the lowdown on what's up with your database, check out Chapter 5.

SQL Server Management Studio Express — Creating a New Table

Administer your database server with one easy-to-use tool. Chapter 1 shows you how.

Protect your data's integrity. Chapter 8 has more.

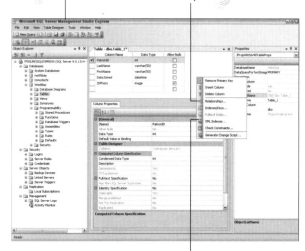

See Chapter 21 to take advantage of the power of XML.

For Dummies: Bestselling Book Series for Beginners

Microsoft® SQL Server™ 2005 Express Edition For Dummies®

Cheat Sheet

Key SQLCMD Parameters

Parameter	Purpose
-S	Specify the server that you want to connect to
-U	Provide your username
-P	Provide your password
-d	Which database to use
-i	The file containing your SQL script

Visual Basic 2005 Express — Integrated Development Environment

Build solutions with no programming.

Quickly create robust, fully integrated applications with Visual Basic 2005 Express. See how in Chapter 19.

Solve any application problems with the powerful debugger.

Design and manage your SQL Server 2005 Express data from within Visual Basic 2005 Express.

For Dummies: Bestselling Book Series for Beginners

Portsmouth
CITY COUNCIL
LEISURE SERVICE   CL-1

WILEY

Wiley Publishing, Inc.

Microsoft® SQL Server™ 2005 Express Edition For Dummies®

Published by
Wiley Publishing, Inc.
111 River Street
Hoboken, NJ 07030-5774
www.wiley.com

Copyright © 2006 by Wiley Publishing, Inc., Indianapolis, Indiana

Published by Wiley Publishing, Inc., Indianapolis, Indiana

Published simultaneously in Canada

For general information on our other products and services, please contact our Customer Care Department within the U.S. at 800-762-2974, outside the U.S. at 317-572-3993, or fax 317-572-4002.

For technical support, please visit www.wiley.com/techsupport.

Wiley also publishes its books in a variety of electronic formats. Some content that appears in print may not be available in electronic books.

Library of Congress Control Number: 2005927727

ISBN-13: 978-0-7645-9927-9

ISBN-10: 0-7645-9927-5

Manufactured in the United States of America

10 9 8 7 6 5 4 3 2 1

1B/QW/QW/QW/IN

WILEY

About the Author

Robert D. Schneider has more than 15 years of experience developing and delivering sophisticated software solutions worldwide. He has provided database optimization, distributed computing, and other technical expertise to a wide variety of enterprises in the financial, technology, and government sectors. Clients have included Chase Manhattan Bank, VISA, HP, SWIFT, and the governments of the United States, Brazil, and Malaysia.

He is the author of *Optimizing Informix Applications, Microsoft SQL Server: Planning and Building a High Performance Database*, and *MySQL Database Design and Tuning*. He has also written numerous articles on technical and professional services topics. He can be reached at Robert.Schneider@Think88.com.

Dedication

In memory of Saul Weiss.

Author's Acknowledgments

The author wants to acknowledge the following people for their invaluable assistance in creating and publishing this work: Nicole Sholly, Tiffany Franklin, Damir Bersinic, Rebecca Senninger, Terri Varveris, Nancy L. Reinhardt, and the folks in Composition Services. And last but certainly not least: Lynn Z. Schneider, Danielle Jolie Schneider, and Nicole Sierra Schneider for their unswerving support and encouragement.

Publisher's Acknowledgments

We're proud of this book; please send us your comments through our online registration form located at www.dummies.com/register/.

Some of the people who helped bring this book to market include the following:

Acquisitions, Editorial, and Media Development

Project Editor: Nicole Sholly

Acquisitions Editor: Tiffany Franklin

Copy Editor: Rebecca Senninger

Technical Editor: Damir Bersinic

Editorial Manager: Kevin Kirschner

Media Development Specialist: Kate Jenkins

Media Development Coordinator: Laura Atkinson

Media Project Supervisor: Laura Moss

Media Development Manager: Laura VanWinkle

Editorial Assistant: Amanda Foxworth

Cartoons: Rich Tennant (www.the5thwave.com)

Composition Services

Project Coordinators: Maridee Ennis, Erin Smith

Layout and Graphics: Carl Byers, Andrea Dahl, Stephanie D. Jumper, Lynsey Osborn

Proofreaders: Laura Albert, Techbooks

Indexer: Techbooks

Publishing and Editorial for Technology Dummies

Richard Swadley, Vice President and Executive Group Publisher

Andy Cummings, Vice President and Publisher

Mary Bednarek, Executive Acquisitions Director

Mary C. Corder, Editorial Director

Publishing for Consumer Dummies

Diane Graves Steele, Vice President and Publisher

Joyce Pepple, Acquisitions Director

Composition Services

Gerry Fahey, Vice President of Production Services

Debbie Stailey, Director of Composition Services

Table of Contents

Introduction

* *

*A*lthough once derided as a provider of relatively low-end relational database products, Microsoft has turned its flagship SQL Server database into a platform that can compete with any database servers on the market. Ironically, the downside of all this power is that some now find SQL Server to be too complex and feature-rich.

In an effort to reclaim the more entry-level segments of the market, Microsoft has created several different versions of SQL Server. Known as *editions*, each of these products addresses a different class of database environment. However, they're all built on the same underlying technology platform, which means that they share many, but not all, of the same features. SQL Server 2005 Express is the most entry-level of these offerings. Even though Microsoft doesn't charge for it, this product has much in common with its more powerful, pricier siblings.

About This Book

This book is designed to help you get productive with SQL Server 2005 Express as quickly as possible. Chances are that you already have enough on your plate, and wading through reams of database architecture and theory before figuring out how to use the product just isn't in the cards.

Here are some of the things you can do with this book:

- ✔ Correctly choose the right version of SQL Server.
- ✔ Quickly install the product in your environment.
- ✔ Rapidly design a database, and then communicate with it.
- ✔ Efficiently monitor, maintain, and protect your important data.
- ✔ Construct a solid, robust application to work with your information.

Foolish Assumptions

You don't need a PhD from MIT to derive value from this book. On the contrary: Any exposure to the items on the following list goes a long way towards helping you make the most from the book. And if you don't currently have any experience, you will soon:

- ✔ **Relational database management systems (RDBMS):** This category includes products such as Microsoft SQL Server 2000, Oracle, DB2, Microsoft Access, and so on.

- ✔ **Relational database design theory:** If you're light in this area, don't worry: I show you how to quickly design your own relational database, as well as some best practices to follow when doing so.

- ✔ **Structured Query Language (SQL):** Even if you're not familiar with SQL, or Microsoft's flavor (Transact-SQL), I show you how to construct queries and data modification statements.

- ✔ **Software development tools:** During the chapter on building SQL Server 2005 Express-based applications, I make the assumption that you have some familiarity with modern software development environments. If you don't, you can still get some good ideas on how to employ tools such as Microsoft Visual Basic 2005 Express and Visual Web Developer 2005 Express in partnership with the database server.

Conventions Used in This Book

As you peruse the book, you'll probably notice several typographical tips along the way. Designed to help you quickly orient yourself, they include **bold** for user entry, `monofont` for code and other computer output, and *italic* for new terms.

What You Don't Have to Read

You don't necessarily need to read this book from cover-to-cover, although I sure hope you want to. The reason that you can skip around is that all the chapters are designed to stand alone: They don't require you to build a foundation of knowledge obtained from other chapters.

However, if you're an absolute newbie with SQL Server who is building a new application, you'll probably want to look at the early chapters on the product's architecture and infrastructure first before moving onto the development section.

Also, if you're not the type of person who pops the hood of your car to see how the motor works, you'll likely find yourself skipping the information called out by the tech stuff icons. Just as your car still runs without you memorizing the workings of its transmission, you can still derive a lot of value from SQL Server 2005 Express even if you don't know its internal architecture.

How This Book Is Organized

Microsoft SQL Server 2005 Express Edition For Dummies is split into eight parts. You don't have to read it sequentially, and you don't even have to read all the sections in any particular chapter. You can use the Table of Contents and the index to find the information you need and quickly get your answer. In this section, I briefly describe what you find in each part.

Part 1: Welcome to SQL Server 2005 Express

This part introduces you to this entry-level, yet very capable database server. I review its features and restrictions, and then show you how to obtain, install, and configure your very own copy. You also see how to determine the right kind of applications to use with this database, as well as how to tell when to upgrade to one of the more feature-rich siblings of SQL Server 2005 Express.

Part 11: Administering a SQL Server 2005 Express System

Don't be fooled by the low (actually, free) price point of SQL Server 2005 Express. Aside from a few capacity and feature restrictions, it works exactly the same as its more powerful siblings. They've all been built on the mainline SQL Server 2005 database platform. However, all this power comes with significant administrative responsibilities. Helping you quickly and effectively perform these managerial tasks is what this part is all about.

Part 111: Adding and Accessing a SQL Server 2005 Express Database

Unless you're the type of person who installs software just for the pleasure of it, you're probably hoping to get some value out of your new SQL Server 2005 Express installation. This part shows you how to create a SQL Server 2005 Express database, and then begin filling it with data. If you're new to relational databases, don't worry: I give you a quick tour of database design theory and SQL Server's internal language, Transact-SQL. On the other hand, if you're a database wizard, you'll want to check out the chapter on advanced Transact-SQL concepts.

Part IV: Keeping Your Data Safe from Harm

Unfortunately, all sorts of nasty problems can afflict your important information, even when it's safely stored in a database like SQL Server 2005 Express. Never fear: You have some powerful tools at your disposal. In this part, I show you how to secure your database from unauthorized manipulation, how to back up your data, as well as how to use transactions to increase the integrity of your information and software applications.

Part V: Putting the Tools to Work: Programming with SQL Server 2005 Express

You may be using SQL Server 2005 Express in conjunction with pre-built applications and office productivity tools; you won't need to do any programming, and you can probably safely skip this part. On the other hand, if you're constructing your own solutions, you can derive a lot of value from seeing how to use stored procedures and functions, interacting with the Common Language Runtime (CLR), as well as gracefully dealing with any errors that might arise along the way.

Part VI: Creating SQL Server 2005 Express Applications

SQL Server 2005 Express is tightly coupled with an entire line of easy-to-use software development technologies from Microsoft. This part shows you how to quickly get productive with programming tools such as Microsoft Visual Basic 2005 Express and Visual Web Developer 2005 Express in conjunction with your new database server. You also find out how to leverage and incorporate XML into your SQL Server 2005 Express-based applications.

Part VII: The Part of Tens

I hope that you find this book contains all that you need to get your work done with SQL Server 2005 Express. However, if you're interested in finding out even more about the product, this part contains a list of ten excellent resources for additional data. Because problem solving comes with the territory with any robust software application, you'll also want to check out the list of ten troubleshooting tips.

Part VIII: Appendixes

This part begins with two migration appendixes. The first helps you decide when to upgrade to a higher capacity version of SQL Server, including an explanation of how to use the excellent Import and Export Wizard to make the migration a snap. The next appendix looks at migration from the point of view of uploading data from Microsoft Access and flat files into your SQL Server 2005 Express database. You also find out how to install the software from the CD that accompanies the book, as well as get a comprehensive list of key relevant SQL Server 2005 Express and relational database terms.

Icons Used in This Book

What's a *For Dummies* book without icons pointing you in the direction of really great information that's sure to help you along your way? In this section, I briefly describe each icon I use in this book.

This icon highlights the new features you find in this latest version of SQL Server Express.

This icon marks a general interesting and useful fact — something that you may want to remember for later use.

When you see this icon, you know that techie stuff is nearby. If you're not feeling very techie, you can skip this info.

The Tip icon points out helpful information that is likely to make your job easier.

The Warning icon highlights lurking danger. With this icon, I'm telling you to pay attention and proceed with caution.

Where to Go from Here

To help you navigate quickly, I list here some common tasks, along with where you can get more details:

Task	Look At
Installation requirements and guide	Chapter 2
Upgrading to SQL Server 2005 Express	Appendix B
Common problems	Chapter 23
SQL Server 2005 Express functionality limitations	Chapter 1
Converting to a more powerful SQL Server version	Appendix A
Pairing the database with the right applications	Chapter 1
Enabling the right network protocols	Chapter 3
Creating databases and tables	Chapter 8
Best practices for database design	Chapter 9
Transact-SQL syntax	Chapter 10
Using XML with SQL Server 2005 Express	Chapter 21
Writing your own stored procedures	Chapter 14
Using views	Chapter 9
Configuring the SQL Server 2005 Express engine	Chapter 5
Integrating transactions to your application	Chapter 12
Taking advantage of replication	Chapter 6
Using SQL Server Management Studio Express	Chapter 4
Intercepting calls to your database	Chapter 15
Protecting your information	Chapter 11
Backing up your database	Chapter 13
Using other languages to build stored procedures	Chapter 16
Graceful error handling	Chapter 17
Building applications with Express editions	Chapters 19 and 20
Reporting services	Chapter 18
Key terms and concepts	Appendix C

Part I

Welcome to SQL Server 2005 Express

The 5th Wave   By Rich Tennant

Fixed Up
DATING SERVICE

"Okay, make sure this is right. 'Looking for caring companion who likes old movies, nature walks, and quiet evenings at home. Knowledge of SQL Server 2005 Express a plus'."

In this part . . .

*B*efore you can start making the most of your SQL Server 2005 Express database server, you need to do a few simple — yet important — tasks. That's what this part is all about: Helping you figure out if SQL Server 2005 Express is right for you, and then getting going as quickly as possible.

First, you find out all about SQL Server 2005 Express, including its major features, as well as where it differs from its bigger (and more expensive) siblings. With that background out of the way, you're ready to see how to get your own, free copy of SQL Server 2005 Express. Next, I tell you about some common situations in which you use this product, as well as some scenarios where you should choose another edition. Finally, the part closes out with some basic steps that you can follow to get your database up and running.

Chapter 1

SQL Server 2005 Express Overview

*F*rom the developer's or user's perspective, SQL Server 2005 Express strikes a nice balance between price (free) and performance (powerful). In this chapter, I offer up some insight into this new product.

To begin, I give you some context to understand how this capable, yet entry-level product came about, along with how it fits in with the rest of the SQL Server product family. Next, you see who the ideal user is for SQL Server 2005 Express, along with a list of some of the product's most compelling features (as well as what's not present). Finally, I show you the kind of tools that you'll want to acquire so you can get started building applications and working with your SQL Server 2005 Express data.

Jumping on Board the SQL Server Express

Once upon a time, if you wanted to store information on a computer, you had to write your own low-level, highly specialized program that organized this data, and also allowed you to update and retrieve the data. This was very cumbersome, time-consuming, and error-prone. Eventually, a host of specialized companies sprang up to provide standardized, industrial-strength products known as databases.

A *database* is a special kind of software application whose main purpose is to help people and programs store, organize, and retrieve information. This frees up application developers to focus on the business task at hand, rather than being responsible for supervising the intricacies of data management.

As more time passed, a new breed of database companies arose. With names like Oracle, Informix, and Sybase, these vendors (and many others) developed a particular kind of database, known as a relational database. *Relational databases* are particularly well designed for storing information in tabular format, which further helped software developers as they built a whole new class of enterprise applications.

Microsoft also entered the relational database fray some years back with the SQL Server database. Once thought of as a relatively lightweight database vendor, Microsoft has continually refined SQL Server to the point where it can compete for the largest and most complicated database-driven applications. Of course, all these capabilities and power have made the SQL Server database platform somewhat intimidating and confusing for many developers and users, especially those that are building and using simpler solutions.

To address this problem, beginning with the SQL Server 2005 product family, Microsoft has created several different versions of SQL Server. Known as *editions*, each of these versions addresses a different class of database environment. Despite this segmentation, all editions are built on the same underlying technology platform. The main difference among the editions is that the simpler, less far-reaching versions don't have all the features and storage capacity that you find in their larger (and more complex) siblings. Here's a list of all the SQL Server 2005 editions:

✔ **Enterprise:** This is the most robust edition of SQL Server 2005. It includes a host of features that make it a good choice for a 24/7, mission-critical database server platform. Just a few of these features include

- Advanced business intelligence analytics
- Robust data transformation logic
- High availability capabilities

This product also has two developer-focused versions, which contain all the Enterprise features but are licensed differently. These are SQL Server 2005 Developer Edition and SQL Server 2005 Evaluation Edition.

✔ **Standard:** With much of the feature set of its big brother, this edition is fine for the vast majority of database applications. The main difference is that this edition is somewhat lighter in both its business intelligence and high availability feature sets.

✔ **Workgroup:** Aimed at smaller, departmental applications, this still-powerful edition of SQL Server 2005 introduces some limitations that are not likely to be issues for these smaller computing environments. Some of these restrictions include

- Hardware and database size constraints
- Diminished high availability
- Reduced business intelligence

✓ **Express:** Now it's time to look at the star of this show. This is the simplest and easiest to use database offering in the SQL Server 2005 product family. On top of that accolade, it's also free to download and redistribute (with some licensing restrictions).

This is the right edition for you if any of the following describe you:

- A software developer (seasoned or brand-new) wanting to learn about relational databases.
- A packaged application provider looking to embed a free, yet sturdy database with your solution.
- An end user with a lot of information to store, but not a lot of cash to buy a database.

To get the lowdown on the differences among each SQL Server 2005 edition, go to

```
www.microsoft.com/sql/prodinfo/features/compare-
                    features.mspx
```

As you evaluate potential uses for SQL Server Express 2005, note that you can use it for all sorts of applications, from traditional, desktop-based rich client software as well as browser-based solutions that are available over the Internet.

SQL Server 2005 Express is just one component of a larger collection of entry-level products aimed at helping developers and hobbyists use Microsoft's technologies to deliver powerful and flexible computing solutions. These products, all of which are part of Visual Studio 2005 Express include the following:

✓ Visual Web Developer 2005 Express

✓ Visual Basic 2005 Express

✓ Visual C# 2005 Express

✓ Visual C++ 2005 Express

✓ Visual J# 2005 Express

All these products work seamlessly with SQL Server 2005 Express. If you're interested in taking advantage of these products, have a look at Chapters 19 and 20.

The SQL Server 2005 Express Environment

Although it's the most junior member of the family, SQL Server 2005 Express has more than enough capabilities and power to support the majority of database-driven applications. You should be aware of these key features — along with some limitations — as you build your solution:

- **Robust technology platform:** SQL Server 2005 Express is built on the same underlying technology platform as all the Microsoft SQL Server products. This significantly increases this product's effectiveness and stability.

- **Interoperability and upgradeability:** Because SQL Server 2005 Express is built on the underlying SQL Server 2005 platform, you can easily develop solutions that work with any SQL Server 2005 edition. In addition, you can straightforwardly migrate from this entry-level edition to a more full-featured edition without changing your database design or altering any application or stored procedure/trigger code.

- **Memory:** With memory costs dropping significantly over time, many administrators now stock their computers with large amounts of RAM. However, regardless of how much memory you have, SQL Server 2005 Express doesn't take advantage of any more than 1GB of RAM.

- **Automatic performance tuning:** This is one feature that SQL Server 2005 Express shares with the other database editions. It lightens the administrative load by automatically updating the database's configuration based on system activities and other profiling data.

However, no automation can free you from the performance implications of an inefficient database or application construction: You are still responsible for designing your database structure and software logic with speed in mind.

- **Database size:** This is probably the most significant limitation of SQL Server 2005 Express, because any given database can't be bigger than 4GB. Although this limitation won't be a problem for many applications, certain data-intensive solutions can test it. Of course, you are free to have multiple databases that are each 4GB.

- **Full security capabilities:** Here's another area where this edition and the more costly versions of SQL Server 2005 basically have no differences. This means that you can take advantage of a broad band of security features as you go about developing your solutions. These range from authentication and auditing all the way through public key management and encryption.

✔ **Multi-processors:** Running a computer with more than one central processing unit (CPU) is a great way to increase performance and throughput. However, SQL Server 2005 Express only takes advantage of one CPU, regardless of how many are available.

✔ **Administrative tools:** Microsoft offers the excellent SQL Server Management Studio Express graphical tool to help you monitor and manage your database. It's available for free download from Microsoft's Web site.

✔ **Visual Studio integration:** Although SQL Server 2005 Express is considered an entry-level product, you're free to use the full power of Microsoft's flagship development platform, Visual Studio. This product is fully integrated with all the SQL Server 2005 database offerings, including Express. Figure 1-1 shows you what this looks like, in the context of building a C# class file.

✔ **Full-text searching:** This feature helps you index and then query large blocks of text-based information. Although it's not present in SQL Server 2005 Express, you will find it in SQL Server 2005 Express with Advanced Services. Regardless of which version you use, your application can still store and work with this kind of information; the method you use might vary, however.

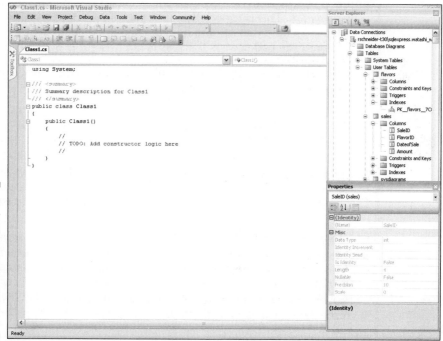

Figure 1-1:
SQL Server
2005
Express
information
available
from inside
Visual
Studio.

✔ **High availability features:** The entire SQL Server 2005 product family offers numerous technologies to help keep your database up and running at all times. However, Express doesn't offer these capabilities, all of which reduce down time or help improve performance:

- Online restore
- Database mirroring
- Partitioning
- Failover clustering
- Online indexing

If you're building a mission critical application and continual uptime is of vital importance to you, you may want to deploy your solution on one of the other SQL Server 2005 editions.

✔ **Rich programming language choices:** The entire SQL Server 2005 product line supports the Microsoft Common Language Runtime (CLR). This means that you can develop internal database logic such as stored procedures and triggers in any one of a number of popular programming languages, rather than in SQL Server's internal programming language: Transact-SQL.

✔ **Analysis services:** The more advanced editions of SQL Server 2005 feature business analytic logic that you can use to help make sense of your information. This is especially true if your environment sports massive volumes of data that need to be crunched to come up with recognizable patterns. The bad news is that this is not present in SQL Server 2005 Express. However, the good news is that chances are that if these kinds of data are found in your organization, you'll have already purchased one of the many third-party business intelligence products.

✔ **Report server:** Users always want more information out of their database. With SQL Server 2005's reporting services, you can set up a wide range of developer-driven and user-driven reports. You can then integrate and deliver these communiqués through a series of different presentation technologies. Happily, you'll find these capabilities present in SQL Server 2005 Express with Advanced Services, which should help please those finicky users. If you're curious about how these features work, take a look at Chapter 18 for the details.

✔ **Integration services:** These features allow you to write powerful integration logic that can take information from a broad range of other data storage locations and then store it inside SQL Server. The same holds true for outbound data. Unfortunately, you won't find these services present in SQL Server 2005 Express. Luckily, this doesn't mean that you can't integrate data among disparate systems; it just means that you may have to do some more work to achieve the same results.

✔ **Notification services:** This refers to the capability, found only in the more feature-rich editions of SQL Server 2005, to build sophisticated publish-and-subscribe applications. Once created, these applications can properly react to a wide variety of events, notifying all interested parties that an event has occurred. SQL Server 2005 Express does let you take advantage of replication, but only as a subscriber.

✔ **Backup/recovery options:** Because backup and recovery are a vital part of any data integrity and reliability plan, SQL Server 2005 offers administrators a choice among several different recovery models, each of which has its own strengths and weaknesses. However, your data-archiving choices are somewhat more reduced for SQL Server 2005 Express. You can still set up a very robust backup and recovery strategy; it's just not as full featured as in the more advanced editions of SQL Server. In particular, because the SQL Server Agent is not present, you won't be able to schedule jobs or configure alerts and operators.

Where Does SQL Server Express 2005 Work Best?

SQL Server 2005 Express brings a lot to the table, but when does it make sense to choose it as your data storage platform? I answer this question in this section.

Small office/Home office (SOHO)

Small offices and home offices (SOHO) are often caught between a rock and a hard place when dealing with software and solutions. Either the technology is underpowered and simplistic, not quite meeting their needs, or it's expensive, overly complex, and resource intensive.

SQL Server 2005 Express strikes a nice balance between simplicity and power, while holding the cost as low as you can possibly get. Plus, because many small businesses one day find themselves morphed (or acquired) into larger enterprises, making this database server the cornerstone of your data storage architecture means that you never outgrow your database: You can easily upgrade to SQL Server 2005 Enterprise.

On top of that, the fact that SQL Server 2005 Express is a true relational database management platform means that you can store and track just about anything in your database. Some particularly good applications include

✔ Inventory details

✔ Sales statistics

✔ Financial metrics

When you have this information safely ensconced in your SQL Server 2005 Express database, you're free to use all sorts of tools and technologies to help make sense of your data. For example, you might store details about all the individual transactions that your organization performs, and then use business intelligence or other data analysis tools to help identify trends from your sales results.

While you're free to store anything you like in your SQL Server 2005 Express database, be aware that any individual database has a maximum storage limit of 4GB for your information. If you find yourself approaching that ceiling, you need to archive some of your older data to make room for newer knowledge.

Distributed enterprise

With the rise of low cost, high-speed Internet connections, many more organizations are realizing benefits from distributed computing. For the distributed enterprise of any size, SQL Server 2005 Express offers a good balance between the low maintenance requirements of an entry-level database like Microsoft Access, and the capabilities of a robust, server-based database.

In addition to these features, you can administer multiple remote SQL Server 2005 Express sites from one location via the SQL Server Management Studio Express.

Another useful capability of SQL Server 2005 Express is its ability to participate as a client in a replication architecture. This means that you could have a single, high-end edition of SQL Server distributing its data among numerous SQL Server 2005 Express clients. These clients could, in turn, support read-only applications like reporting or business intelligence. This type of architecture spreads the processing load across multiple machines, and helps eliminate bottlenecks.

Finally, another good illustration of distributed computing is to use SQL Server 2005 Express as a local database and then aggregate its information to a central server for safekeeping and analysis. For example, suppose that you're building a retail application that will support dozens of locations, none of which will have a database administrator. You could install a traditional, low-end database in each store, but you need to take advantage of a true relational database management system's features, such as advanced security, stored procedures, or triggers. You also need to gather and consolidate this data for reporting purposes. This is a good use for SQL Server 2005 Express: It offers enough power for enterprise-class applications without demanding teams of highly trained administrators for its daily care and feeding.

If you're curious about all that you can do in a distributed computing environment, check out Chapter 6.

Independent Systems Vendor/Original Equipment Manufacturer (ISV/OEM)

ISVs and OEMs have first-hand experience that the cost of embedded technology can eat into profits. That's not a problem with SQL Server 2005 Express: Free generally doesn't have much of an impact on margins. However, don't be fooled by the price: This is a full-featured database, built on the SQL Server platform.

If you base your applications and solutions around SQL Server 2005 Express, you're not locked in: If your customers need extra horsepower and capabilities, they can quickly and painlessly upgrade to a more powerful edition of SQL Server.

The beauty of basing your solutions on a single relational database management product family is that you can do your development on the more advanced editions of SQL Server, using robust tools like Visual Studio, and then easily deploy your application onto the lightweight SQL Server 2005 Express.

As an added benefit to OEMs and ISVs, SQL Server 2005 Express lets you store your data in a single, easily transferred file. Known as an .mdf file, this structure combines the simplicity of a low-end flat file with the power of a true relational database management system. You should note, however, that you have to deploy the SQL Server Express 2005 server, even if you only intend to deploy .mdf files with your solution.

Getting Down to Business with SQL Server 2005 Express

In previous sections, I show you all that you get with your free download of SQL Server 2005 Express Edition. If you're wondering how you can get started using the product, that's what this section is all about. To begin, I point out some things to ponder as you plan and deploy your database. Next, I talk about all the programming tools at your disposal for building a SQL Server 2005 Express-based application. Finally, I show how you can configure and monitor your database.

What happened to MSDE?

For those of you who have followed the entry-level SQL Server database for some time, you're probably wondering what happened to the previous offering from Microsoft.

Known as MSDE (which stands for Microsoft Desktop Engine or Microsoft Data Engine, depending on who answers the phone in Redmond), this database was more complicated to administer, less feature rich, and had smaller capacity than its replacement, SQL Server 2005 Express.

Planning your database

The first thing to keep in mind as you contemplate what to keep in your SQL Server 2005 Express database is that this is not a stripped-down, feature-limited, stand-alone product. It's true that Express does have significant limitations to the amount of information you can store in the database (see "The SQL Server 2005 Express Environment" earlier in this chapter for more details about that), and that certain key high-volume features are not present.

Before you get heavily into using this edition, you should make sure that none of these limitations are showstoppers for you. Remember that the majority of these constraints shouldn't impact you during development; they're only an issue at runtime.

Even though this edition has feature restrictions, SQL Server 2005 Express works with all the same types of information as its more fully featured siblings, and you can easily migrate to a more powerful edition. It also supports all the same application programming interfaces (APIs), as well as the same stored procedure and trigger capabilities.

This means that as a designer, you can build your SQL Server 2005 Express database with confidence, knowing that you aren't painted into a corner by missing capabilities, nor the solution you design is forever consigned to this entry-level database. This works the other way as well: You can design your solution on a more powerful edition of SQL Server 2005, and then deploy it onto SQL Server 2005 Express, as long as it doesn't require any of the features that are only found in the more expensive editions of the product.

One feature that's particularly attractive for distributed application developers and vendors is the Xcopy deployment capability of SQL Server 2005 Express. This lets you easily bundle your application and database (`.mdf`) file and then copy them to another machine. Because everything is already pre-packaged, you don't need to manually configure these other platforms, as long as they have a running instance of SQL Server 2005 Express. When your application launches, the database server automatically attaches the .mdf file to the local instance. This architecture results in an easily implemented portability strategy.

Building SQL Server 2005 Express applications

You have a wide variety of electives when building a solution that stores its information in this database. To begin, as I described earlier in this chapter, Microsoft is making the Visual Studio Express products affordable and easy to use to create database-driven applications. If you're new to application development, checking out these products is definitely worth your while. In fact, take a look at Chapters 19 and 20, which cover Visual Basic 2005 Express and Visual Web Developer 2005 Express, respectively. For a sneak preview, Figure 1-2 shows how closely Visual Basic 2005 Express works with SQL Server 2005 Express.

This tight integration can go a long way toward boosting your productivity. In effect, with these products, Microsoft has broken down the traditional barrier between application and database tools.

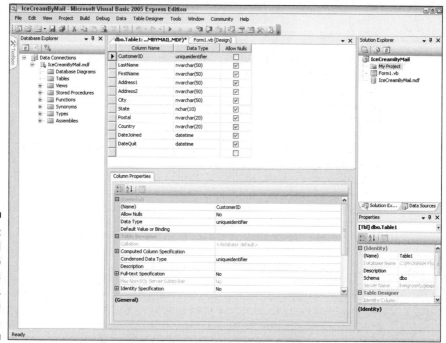

Figure 1-2:
Visual
Basic 2005
Express
and SQL
Server 2005
Express.

If you're more inclined to use heavier-weight, more powerful tools, Visual Studio 2005 makes a lot of sense to employ for application development. It's an extremely potent tool that contains a tremendous amount of functionality. It's also very well integrated with all SQL Server 2005 products, not only the Express edition. Naturally, all this power comes with additional complexity and a somewhat steeper learning curve, so you should decide if your application requires all these capabilities.

Of course, Microsoft isn't the only game in town when it comes to application development technologies. You can use several third-party tools (including open source and shareware) to construct a SQL Server-based solution.

Configuring, managing, and monitoring SQL Server 2005 Express

With your database and application built, it's natural to turn your attention to setting configuration parameters and then monitoring the database. Here again, you have no shortage of options.

To begin, SQL Server 2005 Express snaps into the standard Microsoft Computer Management console. This lets you configure and run your database services, which you can see in Figure 1-3.

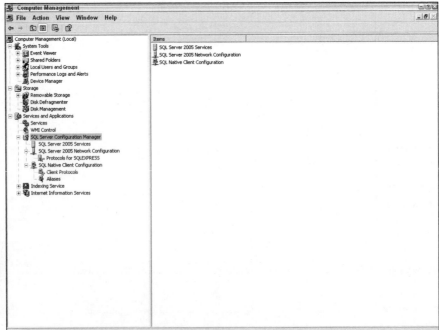

Figure 1-3: Configuring SQL Server 2005 Express services.

For further configuring and managing your SQL Server 2005 Express server, you can choose between graphical and character-based tools. As you might expect, graphical tools provide more intuitive, easy-to-understand information about your server.

When it comes to graphical tools, it's hard to beat Microsoft's free, excellent graphical management environment known as SQL Server Management Studio Express. Figure 1-4 shows a sample of what this product looks like.

SQL Server Management Studio Express can do much more than simply show you tables and run queries. One handy tool is the activity monitor, which opens a window onto all database-related activity for your server. Figure 1-5 shows a sample session; you can monitor a tremendous amount of information using this tool.

For those of you who prefer a character-based configuration and management utility, Microsoft continues to ship the SQLCMD utility, which allows for direct entry of SQL statements. Because you find much of the administrative capabilities for SQL Server embedded in stored procedures, you can run just about any management operation from the rather bland SQLCMD interface.

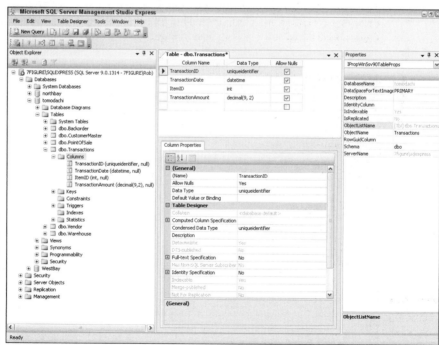

Figure 1-4: Viewing a table in SQL Server Management Studio Express.

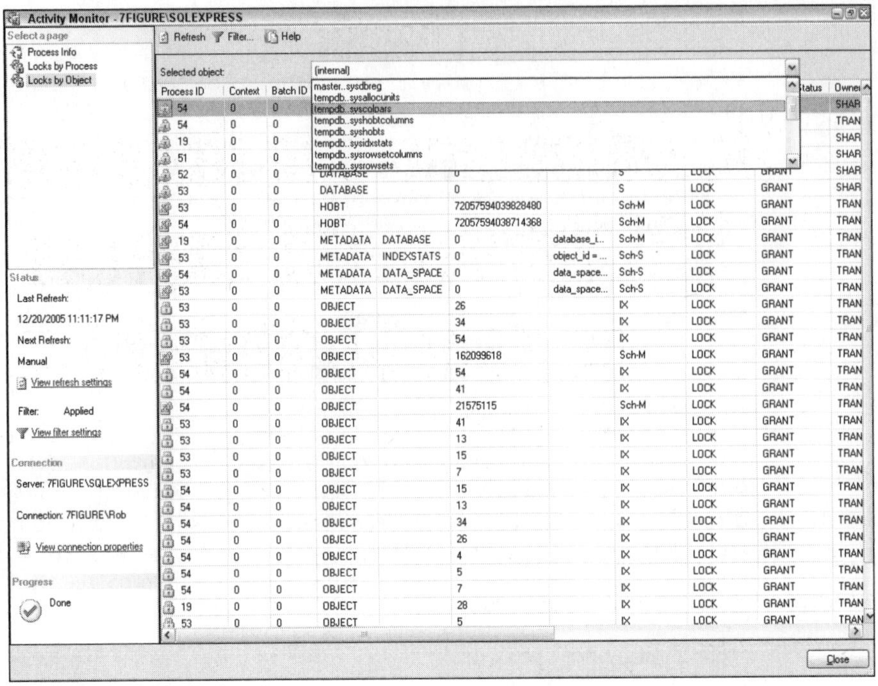

Figure 1-5:
The SQL
Server
Manage-
ment Studio
Express
Activity
Monitor.

Chapter 2

Downloading and Installing SQL Server 2005 Express on Your Computer

In This Chapter

▶ Getting your own copy of SQL Server 2005 Express

▶ Laying the groundwork for installation

▶ Installing SQL Server 2005 Express on your computer

▶ Performing basic tests

*T*raditionally, getting a production-ready copy of a powerful relational database management system has meant pulling out your (or the company's) checkbook and signing on the dotted line. However, this is not the case with SQL Server 2005 Express. Instead, all you need is an Internet connection; you can download the product and get started for free.

In this chapter, you find out what you need to do to get ready for SQL Server 2005 Express, along with how to download, install, and run some basic tests to make sure everything went smoothly. After a successful installation, you still have a few things to do before you can use the product to its fullest potential; I show you those things in Chapter 3. If you have information stored in other locations that you want to entrust to this database, take a look at Appendix B, which describes how to import data into SQL Server 2005 Express.

Getting a Copy of SQL Server 2005 Express

Microsoft has made it easy to get your own copy of SQL Server 2005 Express. Here are just a couple ways that you can get your hands on the product:

✔ **Via the Internet:** If you have a fast Internet connection, you can quickly and easily download SQL Server 2005 Express. Here's all you need to do:

1. **Point your browser to** `http://www.microsoft.com/sql`.

2. **Click the Downloads link.**

   You should now see a link for SQL Server 2005 Express.

3. **Review the System Requirements and Instructions before downloading your product.**

   I describe some of these system requirements in the next section.

You'll be presented with a potentially bewildering array of SQL Server 2005 Express downloads on Microsoft's Web site. Here's a brief overview of each of the available products:

- **Baseline SQL Server 2005 Express:** This is the standalone, entry-level SQL Server database found in `SQLEXPR.EXE`.

- **SQL Server 2005 Express with Advanced Services:** This is the next level up in database power and capability, yet it's still free! If you're interested in enhanced reporting services and full-text searching, this might be the edition for you (see Chapter 18). It's in a file entitled `SQLEXPR_ADV.EXE`.

- **SQL Server Management Studio Express:** This is an excellent, powerful, yet easy-to-use database administration and interaction tool. I strongly recommend getting a copy; you won't regret it.

- **SQL Express toolkit:** If you're interested in developing reports with SQL Server 2005 Express with Advanced Services, the Business Intelligence Development Studio contained in this toolkit is a must-have.

If you can't get to SQL Server 2005 Express via the preceding instructions, just use the Search feature on the Microsoft Web site to find it quickly.

✔ **Via Visual Studio 2005:** SQL Server 2005 Express is part of a larger group of low-priced Microsoft offerings, known as the *Express editions*. These products are aimed at a wide audience of developers that might not have used these types of solutions before, and include

- Visual Basic 2005 Express Edition (which is conveniently on this book's CD)

- Visual Web Developer 2005 Express Edition

- Visual C# 2005 Express Edition

- Visual C++ 2005 Express Edition

- Visual J# 2005 Express Edition

Microsoft also bundles SQL Server 2005 Express with Visual Studio 2005, which is available for purchase either stand-alone or via the Microsoft Developer Network (MSDN).

✔ **Via the CD that ships with this book:** To make things even easier for you, a fully functional copy of SQL Server 2005 Express with Advanced Services is on the CD that comes with this book. You can read more about it in Appendix D.

Before You Install

Although popping in the CD or pointing your browser at the Microsoft Web site and then downloading and installing SQL Server 2005 Express is tempting, you need to make sure that your computer meets some minimal requirements. Otherwise, you could be faced with a long and frustrating troubleshooting session, trying to figure out why things are running poorly (or even not at all!).

Take the time to go through each of these major system readiness categories, making sure that you meet or exceed each of these prerequisites. Also, if you're installing SQL Server 2005 Express on multiple machines, remember that the machine that acts as a central server generally requires faster and better hardware than one that primarily acts as a client. Finally, you need to have administrative privileges on the computer where you're installing SQL Server 2005 Express.

✔ **CPU:** For optimal performance, you want at least a 600 MHZ CPU, although things might be kind of sluggish at that speed. Using a 1GHZ CPU definitely makes things peppier and is recommended.

✔ **Memory:** Because sufficient memory serves as the foundation of any well-performing relational database, make sure that you provide 512MB or more, as recommended by Microsoft. You could probably get away with 192MB (minimum), but you're pushing things at that level. In general, just as you can't be too rich or too thin, you can't provide a relational database with too much CPU or memory, although SQL Server 2005 Express will not use more than 1GB of RAM.

✔ **Disk:** Given that relational databases use disk drives as their primary storage mechanism, recommending a hard-and-fast value for the right amount of available disk capacity is difficult: Every installation is different. Just the product and its related files take up more than 500MB of disk space; you'll likely want to add one or two gigabytes on top of that for your data.

✔ **Operating system:** Microsoft gives you a fairly wide choice of operating systems that can run SQL Server 2005 Express. They include

- Windows Server 2003
- Windows Small Business Server 2003
- Windows XP Home Edition
- Windows XP Media Center Edition

- Windows XP Professional Edition
- Windows XP Tablet PC Edition
- Windows 2000 Advanced Server
- Windows 2000 Professional Edition
- Windows 2000 Server

Be prepared to apply the latest service pack for your operating system; in many cases, SQL Server 2005 Express depends on these patches.

✔ **Supporting software:** Because it's built on top of some of Microsoft's newer technologies, SQL Server 2005 Express requires that you install some additional software technologies, specifically the Microsoft .NET Framework 2.0. You also may be required to deploy the new Microsoft Windows Installer software. In addition to facilitating software installation, this new product also checks whether your Windows software is licensed correctly. Both of these products are free, and available for download from the Microsoft Web site.

✔ If you plan to use the Advanced Services edition, and are interested in its reporting capabilities, make sure that you have Microsoft Internet Information Services installed on your computer.

Installing SQL Server 2005 Express

Kudos to you if you took the time to read the previous section that described the prerequisites for installing SQL Server 2005 Express. And if you didn't, that's okay, too. Now all you need to do is breeze through a few simple steps, and you're ready to start using your new database. Here's how to get SQL Server 2005 Express up and running:

1. **Remove old software.**

   If you've installed any beta editions of SQL Server 2005 Express or the SQL Native Client, you need to uninstall them via the Control Panel's Add and Remove Programs utility.

2. **Back up your system.**

   It may seem a bit excessive, but you'll never regret taking the time to make a backup copy of your important information. If things go wrong, you have a way of restoring your data. And if things go fine (which they probably will), you've still safeguarded your computer.

3. **(Optional) Defragment your disks.**

   This may not seem like the time to defragment your disks, but in fact it's a great opportunity to give SQL Server 2005 Express some nice, clean, well-organized space with which to work. Over time, data on your disk drives gets fragmented, and spreads across the entire disk. This can hurt performance of all applications; SQL Server 2005 Express is no exception. Here's how to defragment your disk:

a. Launch the Windows Disk Defragmenter.

You'll find it via Start➪Programs➪Accessories➪System Tools➪ Disk Defragmenter.

b. Click the Analyze button.

The Disk Defragmenter analyzes your disk and returns a recommendation (see Figure 2-1).

c. If the Disk Defragmenter recommends that you defragment your disk, click the Defragment button.

This may take some time to complete, but be patient: It's worth it.

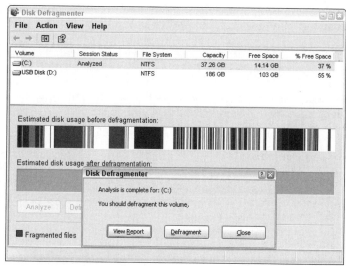

Figure 2-1:
A disk that needs to be defragmented.

4. Install the Microsoft .NET Framework.

This is the foundation on which SQL Server Express was built. You can download it for free from the Microsoft Web site. In fact, you will find a handy link to it right on the SQL Server 2005 Express download page.

5. Run the SQL Server 2005 Express installer program.

If you install SQL Server 2005 Express via the Visual Studio installer, you may have a slightly different set of instructions.

After you launch the installer, you see a screen similar to Figure 2-2.

Once these initial tasks are out of the way, the SQL Server 2005 Express Installation Wizard launches, which is shown in Figure 2-3.

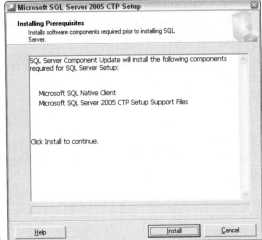

Figure 2-2:
The initial
SQL Server
2005
Express
installation
prerequisite
screen.

SQL Server 2005 Express runs some very sophisticated checks against your system to make sure that the upcoming installation goes smoothly. Each configuration check is flagged as `Success`, `Error`, or `Warning`. You must correct errors; you can get away with ignoring warnings, but things may not run very smoothly if you do so.

Figure 2-3:
The SQL
Server 2005
Express
Installation
Wizard.

For example, Figure 2-4 shows a "close but no cigar" configuration check. This particular machine was a little light on memory; hence the warning. You can even get a report of what the configuration check learned, as shown in Figure 2-5.

Figure 2-4: Results from the SQL Server 2005 Express system configuration check.

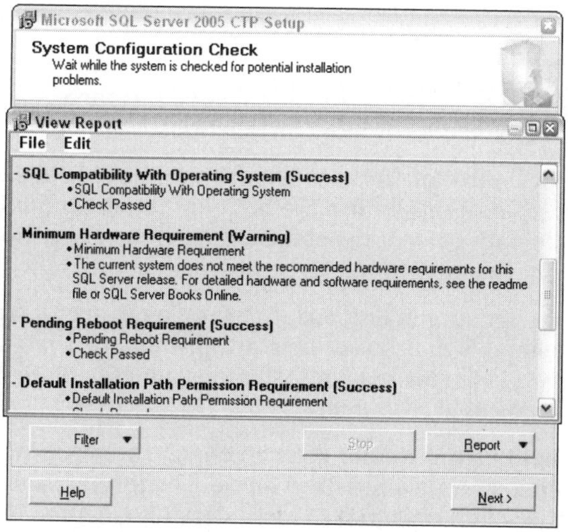

Figure 2-5: Report from the SQL Server 2005 Express system configuration check.

In addition to giving you a place to add your name and company, the next screen, shown in Figure 2-6, lets you elect whether to install SQL Server 2005 Express with its defaults, or customize your site's configuration by unchecking the Hide Advanced Configuration Options check box.

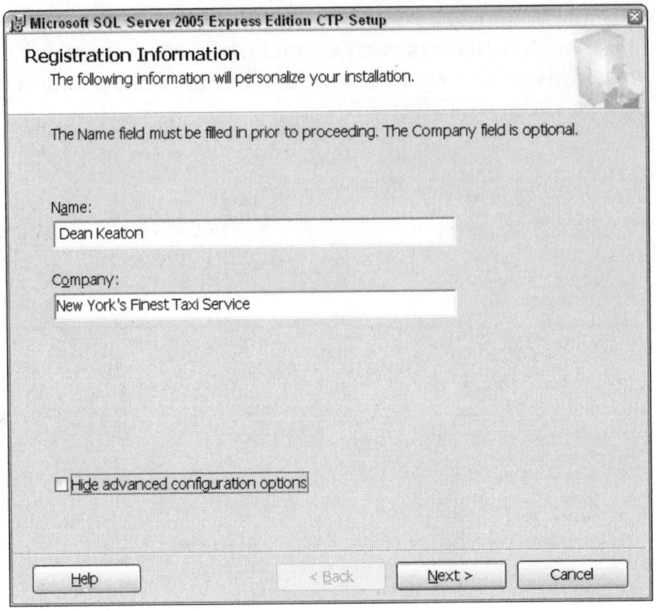

Microsoft SQL Server 2005 Express Edition CTP Setup

Registration Information
The following information will personalize your installation.

The Name field must be filled in prior to proceeding. The Company field is optional.

Name:
Dean Keaton

Company:
New York's Finest Taxi Service

☐ Hide advanced configuration options

[Help]   [< Back]   [Next >]   [Cancel]

Figure 2-6:
Electing to
make
advanced
customiza-
tions for
SQL Server
2005
Express.

For this example, I'll go down the advanced configuration path. In many cases, however, it's wise to just accept the default installation options.

The next few dialog boxes prompt you for some important pieces of information, including:

- **Your instance name:** Choosing the named instance of SQLExpress suffices for most installations.

- **Your service account:** You can choose whether to specify a Windows account or just use the built-in system account. The latter is the path of least resistance. If you're really curious about security, check out Chapter 11.

  The service account dialog box gives you a chance to request that SQL Server and SQL Browser be started when the system starts. This is a good idea for most installations, unless you're really con-strained for system resources.

- **Your authentication mode:** You can choose between Windows Authentication Mode and Mixed Mode. The former is generally a better choice; I discuss that in more detail in Chapter 11.

- **Collation settings:** Here's where you can specify site-specific sort-ing requirements.

• **Error and feature reporting:** You can share, anonymously, information about errors encountered by your SQL Server 2005 Express installation, as well as those database features that you use.

After you finish specifying your site-specific requests, the wizard finishes installing, configuring, and validating SQL Server 2005 Express. Figure 2-7 shows a successful installation.

You can take additional steps to further customize your SQL Server 2005 Express server. I discuss these steps in much more detail in Chapter 3.

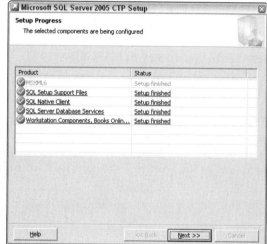

Figure 2-7: A successful SQL Server 2005 Express installation!

 Although it's not mandatory, you would be wise to also download and install SQL Server Management Studio Express from the same place that you obtained SQL Server 2005 Express. It's an excellent (and free!) database administration and query tool that can handle all of your SQL Server management tasks.

Testing Your Installation

Barring any warning messages, system crashes, or other unanticipated problems with your SQL Server 2005 Express installation, you can feel confident that everything is right in your database world. But how can you make sure? In this section, I show you a quick test that you can run to make sure that everything is hunky dory.

The best way to make sure that your installation went well is simply to try to connect to your SQL Server 2005 Express database server and then run some basic database operations. Just follow these steps:

1. **Make sure the SQL Server 2005 Express service is running.**

   Normally, this service is started as part of the installation process. However, making sure that it started correctly is a good idea. Follow these steps to check it:

   a. **Locate the My Computer icon on your desktop or on the Start menu.**

   b. **Right-click it, and choose the Manage option.**

   c. **Expand the Services and Applications folder.**

   d. **Double-click the Services entry in this folder.**

      You see a list of all services (running or not) on your computer, along with whether they're started automatically or manually.

   e. **Scroll down the list of services.**

      Look for the SQL Server (SQLEXPRESS) entry. To see if it's running, look in the Status column. You can also see if it automatically launches by checking the Startup Type column. If it's running, you don't need to go on to the next steps.

   f. **Highlight the SQL Server entry, and then right-click it.**

   g. **Choose the Start option.**

      SQL Server 2005 Express service starts running. If you want to have the service start automatically, choose the Properties option and then select the Automatic option from the Startup Type drop-down menu.

2. **Launch SQL Server Management Studio Express Edition.**

   If you don't have this tool in your environment, I show you how to use the character-based SQLCMD utility in the set of numbered steps following this one.

3. **Connect to your SQL Server 2005 Express database.**

   When you try to connect to your database, you're prompted for a server instance connection string. This can get a little tricky; SQL Server 2005 Express is rather picky about the exact syntax. Assuming you chose the defaults when installing, just specify your string like this:

```
Computer name\sqlexpress
```

So, if your computer is called `Titan`, your server instance connection string would look like this:

```
Titan\sqlexpress
```

4. **Expand the System Databases folder.**

5. **Make sure that the four system databases are present:**

   • master

   • model

   • msdb

   • tempdb

   With these databases in place, you're now ready to create a test database of your own.

6. **Highlight the Databases folder, and then right-click it.**

7. **Choose the New Database option.**

8. **Create a database with any name that you like.**

   You don't need to fiddle with the settings; just choose the defaults. If everything goes well, you see this new database listed under the Databases folder.

9. **Delete the database.**

   Unless you want to keep this database around for real work, you can safely delete it:

   a. **Highlight the new database in the Databases folder, and then right-click its entry.**

   b. **Choose the Delete option from the menu.**

   c. **Confirm that you want to delete this database.**

10. **You can now close SQL Server Management Studio Express.**

    The database server continues running, even if you disconnect.

For those of you with no access to SQL Server Management Studio, here's another way to connect to the database — using the SQLCMD utility — and test your installation.

1. **Open a command prompt.**

   You can do this by choosing Start➪Run, and entering **cmd**. Another way to do this is to choose Start➪Programs➪Accessories➪Command Prompt. After you see the friendly command prompt, it's time to launch SQLCMD.

2. **Type** SQLCMD, **and include the proper parameters.**

   This can get a bit confusing: SQLCMD is rather picky about the exact syntax that it deigns to run. This is not surprising when you realize that it supports over two dozen parameters. This table highlights a small group of key parameters:

Parameter	*Purpose*
-S	Specify the server that you want to connect to
-U	Provide your username
-P	Provide your password
-d	Which database to use

   If you get in hot water, you can always ask SQLCMD for help:

   ```
   SQLCMD /?
   ```

3. **Type the following SQL:**

   ```
   CREATE DATABASE install_test
   GO
   ```

   If you receive another prompt (that is, no error message), then everything is fine. If you want to drop this test database, just type the following SQL:

   ```
   DROP DATABASE install_test
   GO
   ```

That's all you have to do! You now have a working SQL Server 2005 Express database server.

Chapter 3

Setting Up SQL Server Express

● ●

In This Chapter

▶ Completing a successful installation

▶ Deactivating unnecessary database features

▶ Working with the network

▶ Connecting to the database server

● ●

*T*here are many reasons for using a database server like SQL Server 2005 Express. Perhaps you're drawn by its no-cost price, or maybe you're attracted to its rich functionality. Regardless of your motivation, after you install the database server (which I discuss in detail in Chapter 2), you still have a few steps to take before you can take advantage of all that the product has to offer. That's what this chapter is all about.

To begin, I show you what to watch out for during installation, as well as how to use the SQL Server Surface Area Configuration tool to deactivate nonessential features. Finally, you take a quick tour of how to connect to SQL Server 2005 Express from a variety of popular technologies.

Points to Ponder During Installation

SQL Server 2005 Express makes installation rather finicky: Certain key decisions you make while deploying the product are difficult to reverse.

To begin, you should carefully consider what communication protocols, features, and security capabilities you'll need. The installation wizard gives you the chance to make these features part of your environment from the very start. Although in many cases you can add them after the fact, conscientiously planning your installation is a good idea.

When in doubt, install all capabilities from inception. You can't easily add certain features later. The next sections describe how to configure them after you pass the installation stage.

Keeping a Low Profile

In the previous section, I advise you to install as many protocols and features as you believe that you'll ever possibly need. Now you need to disable some of those protocols and turn off the features you don't need via the SQL Server Surface Area Configuration utility. By letting you easily close any open doors to your database server and shut down extraneous features, this tool helps boost both security and server performance.

Don't be in too much of a rush to start removing features and closing off protocols: Spend a little time examining your current and planned database usage patterns before uprooting capabilities.

You can get to the SQL Server Surface Area Configuration utility in two ways. The first lets you manage the database connectivity services and protocols; the second is aimed at regulating available features.

Configuring surface area for services and connections

As a security precaution, SQL Server 2005 Express ships with remote connectivity disabled. To let other computers communicate with your database server, just follow these simple steps.

1. **Launch SQL Server Surface Area Configuration.**

   You can find it by choosing Start⇨All Programs⇨Microsoft SQL Server 2005⇨Configuration Tools⇨SQL Server Surface Area Configuration.

2. **Connect to the computer you want to administer.**

   By default, the utility points at the local server.

3. **Click the Services and Connections link.**

4. **Expand the SQLEXPRESS folder (or whatever you named your database server), followed by the Database Engine.**

5. **Click the Remote Connections entry.**

   You can now choose whether your database will only accept local connections, or whether it will participate in conversations with remote computers. You can also select whether you want to enable TCP/IP, named pipes, or both kinds of connectivity, as shown in Figure 3-1.

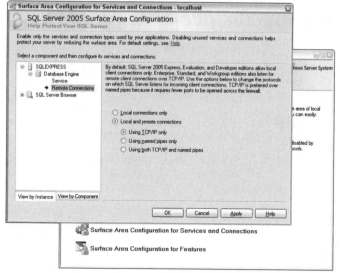

Figure 3-1:
Configuring
services
and
protocols.

After you configure the protocols, your next duty is to administer the SQL Server Browser service. This Windows service allows client computers to locate your SQL Server 2005 Express database server.

If you plan on using only the default instance of SQL Server 2005 Express, or your clients know the name of your server and instance details, you don't need to enable the SQL Server Browser service.

If you're already running the SQL Server Surface Configuration utility, you can skip Steps 1 through 3.

1. **Launch SQL Server Surface Area Configuration.**

   You can find it by choosing Start⇨All Programs⇨Microsoft SQL Server 2005⇨Configuration Tools⇨SQL Server Surface Area Configuration.

2. **Connect to the computer you want to administer.**

   By default, the utility points at the local server.

3. **Click the <u>Services and Connections</u> link.**

4. **Expand the SQL Server Browser folder.**

5. **Pick one of the options from the Startup Type drop-down menu.**

   If you want the service to be enabled, you can choose Automatic or Manual. The former is preferable if remote connectivity is a part of your normal processing; otherwise opting for Manual is fine. On the other hand, if you don't want this service to run at all, just choose the Disabled option.

Configuring surface area for features

After getting your protocols and services squared away, you now can change gears and take a look at the features you'll be running in your SQL Server 2005 Express environment. You can use the SQL Server Surface Configuration utility to enable or disable a number of key features, including the following:

- ✔ **Ad-hoc remote queries:** This feature allows OLE-DB to contact remote data sources and process queries.

- ✔ **CLR integration:** This stands for Common Language Runtime, and enabling it lets you use other programming languages to write internal database routines.

- ✔ **Native XML Web Services:** This technology allows your database server to communicate with client applications via the Simple Object Access Protocol (SOAP).

- ✔ **Object Linking and Embedding (OLE) Automation:** This lets your SQL Server 2005 Express instance use OLE-aware custom objects.

- ✔ **Service Broker:** This feature enables different SQL Server instances to communicate, using a reliable and secure protocol.

- ✔ **xp_cmdshell:** This capability lets you launch operating system-level commands from within your SQL Server 2005 Express environment.

After you decide what features you want to enable, it's easy to express your wishes to SQL Server 2005 Express. Here's how to make enable features:

1. **Launch SQL Server Surface Area Configuration utility.**

   You can find it by choosing Start⇨All Programs⇨Microsoft SQL Server 2005⇨Configuration Tools⇨SQL Server Surface Area Configuration.

2. **Connect to the computer you want to administer.**

   By default, the utility points at the local server.

3. **Click the <u>Services and Connections</u> link.**

4. **Expand the SQLEXPRESS folder (or whatever you named your database server), followed by the Database Engine folder, as shown in Figure 3-2.**

5. **Check the boxes for each service that you want enabled.**

6. **After you're done, click OK to save your changes.**

Don't be afraid that disabling a feature will permanently damage your server; you can usually enable most features later.

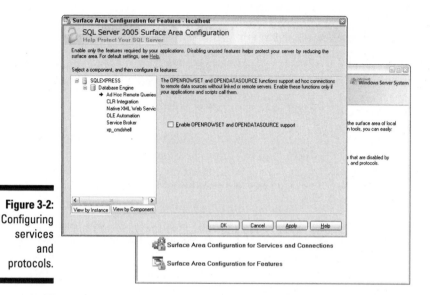

Figure 3-2:
Configuring
services
and
protocols.

Is Anyone Out There?

Your database server is a social animal: It happily chats with other users and computers, but only if you let it. In this section, I show you how to enable and configure the various protocols that can make these conversations possible.

To begin, understanding what purpose a communication protocol serves is a good idea. These standards allow disparate database servers and clients to speak and understand each other. A multitude of protocols are out there; here are the ones that can work with SQL Server 2005 Express:

- **TCP/IP:** This is, by far, the most popular communication protocol out there. In fact, it's the foundation of the Internet. Whenever you open a browser and connect to a Web site, TCP/IP is the underlying standard that makes it all possible, and is probably the best choice for your database communication protocol.

- **Named Pipes:** Generally used for both intra-machine and client/server communication, this protocol is less frequently found on Internet-based conversations. They are also somewhat less secure than TCP/IP.

- **Virtual Interface Adapter (VIA):** As a protocol that is reliant on specialized hardware, the odds are you won't likely encounter VIA as often as TCP/IP or named pipes.

✔ **Shared memory:** As you would guess from its name, this protocol relies on a fast, dedicated section of memory that SQL Server 2005 Express uses for communication between the database and any clients that wish to work with it. However, shared memory has one gotcha: Client applications and processes must reside on the same computer as the database server, making this protocol somewhat irrelevant in a highly distributed environment.

Now that you're a wiz with SQL Server's myriad protocols, it's time to see how to enable or disable any of the ones I just listed:

1. **Launch SQL Server Configuration Manager.**

   You have two ways to make this happen:

   • Choose Start➪All Programs➪Microsoft SQL Server 2005➪ Configuration Tools➪SQL Server Surface Area Configuration. The SQL Server Configuration Manager window opens (see Figure 3-3).

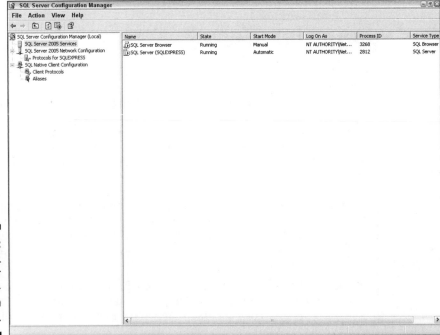

Figure 3-3: The SQL Server Configuration Manager.

• Right-click My Computer, select Manage, and then expand the Services and Applications folder. The Computer Management window opens (as shown in Figure 3-4).

Notice how the user interface is the same in both cases: The only difference is that in the former you're running the utility stand-alone, while the latter displays it as part of Computer Management.

You have three paths to follow from here:

• **SQL Server 2005 Services:** Here is yet another way to start, stop, and disable your database services.

• **SQL Server 2005 Network Configuration:** This is where you enable, configure, or disable any of the four services I just listed, for inbound connections. I discuss Network Configuration in this section.

• **SQL Native Client Configuration:** Here is where you can specify how you want outbound (that is, from your database to other databases) protocols to work.

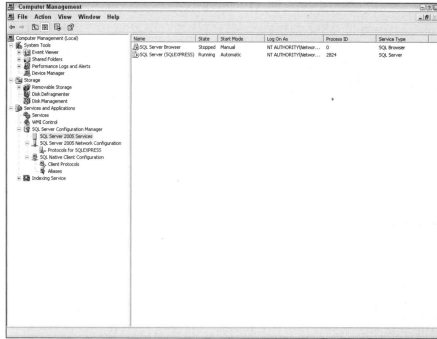

Figure 3-4:
The SQL Server Configuration Manager via Computer Management.

2. **Click the entry for SQLEXPRESS (or whatever you named your database server).**

   On the right side, you see entries for each of the protocols.

3. **Right-click any protocol that you want to configure.**

   Figure 3-5 shows the TCP/IP protocol properties.

   As you can see, you have several properties at your disposal, including

   - **Enabled:** This property asks a very simple question: Do you or don't you want this service to run?

   - **Keep Alive:** Aside from taking up space on your screen, this property doesn't do anything, so you can safely ignore it.

   - **Listen All:** This setting controls how SQL Server 2005 Express, your network, and your computer's network cards all work together. You can also switch to the IP Addresses tab for further configuration.

   - **No Delay:** Just like Keep Alive, this property is just there for show; you can disregard it.

4. **When you're done, click OK to save your changes.**

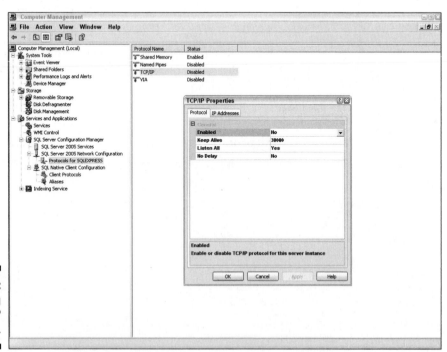

Figure 3-5:
Configuring
TCP/IP
properties.

Connecting to Your Server

You would be forgiven for assuming that after you complete all the tasks necessary to set up your SQL Server 2005 Express database server, getting a conversation going with it would be a cinch. As it turns out, the last step in establishing a connection can often be the most frustrating. Try as you might, you just can't seem to hook up with your database.

Helping you get around this annoying obstacle is what this section is all about. I give you an inventory of the major types of applications that you need to connect to your server, along with what you need to do to help them "find" your database.

Connecting with SQLCMD

This all-purpose, character-based utility lets you connect to your SQL Server 2005 Express database and perform all sorts of work.

When you're wrestling with a particularly tough connection problem, going back to the basics is a good idea: Use SQLCMD as your test bed as you try things out. Once SQLCMD works, you can then apply your results to the other tools that I describe in this section.

SQLCMD has been around for quite a while, and consequently offers a wide variety of different options. You can get a list of all these options with these steps:

1. **Open a command prompt.**

   Choose Start⇨Run, and enter **CMD**. A command prompt comes up.

2. **In the command prompt window, type** SQLCMD -? **and press Enter.**

   Figure 3-6 shows all the parameters that you can supply.

```
C:\WINDOWS\system32\cmd.exe                                        _ □ ×

C:\>SQLCMD -?
Microsoft (R) SQL Server Command Line Tool
Version 9.00.1314.06 NT INTEL X86
Copyright (c) Microsoft Corporation.  All rights reserved.

usage: Sqlcmd            [-U login id]          [-P password]
  [-S server]            [-H hostname]          [-E trusted connection]
  [-d use database name] [-l login timeout]     [-t query timeout]
  [-h headers]           [-s colseparator]      [-w screen width]
  [-a packetsize]        [-e echo input]        [-I Enable Quoted Identifiers]
  [-c cmdend]            [-L[c] list servers[clean output]]
  [-q "cmdline query"]   [-Q "cmdline query" and exit]
  [-m errorlevel]        [-V severitylevel]     [-W remove trailing spaces]
  [-u unicode output]    [-r[0|1] msgs to stderr]
  [-i inputfile]         [-o outputfile]        [-z new password]
  [-f <codepage> | i:<codepage>[,o:<codepage>]] [-Z new password and exit]
  [-k[1|2] remove[replace] control characters]
  [-y variable length type display width]
  [-Y fixed length type display width]
  [-p[1] print statistics[colon format]]
  [-R use client regional setting]
  [-b On error batch abort]
  [-v var = "value"...] [-A dedicated admin connection]
  [-X[1] disable commands, startup script, enviroment variables [and exit]]
  [-x disable variable substitution]
  [-? show syntax summary]

C:\>_
```

Figure 3-6: Available parameters for SQLCMD.

Yikes! Look at all those parameters. Don't worry — you don't need to stay up all night experimenting with the dozens of different options at your disposal. Actually, when simply connecting to SQL Server 2005 Express, you only need to concern yourself with a handful of these variables:

- ✔ **-U:** The login ID of the user who is trying to connect to the database.

- ✔ **-P:** The password for the user specified with the -U parameter.

  If you omit the -U and -P parameters, SQLCMD tries to log in using your Windows login.

- ✔ **-S:** The server name, with the instance name as an optional appendage. In many cases, just using *ComputerName*\SQLEXPRESS (where *ComputerName* is the name of your server) works. Optionally, you can substitute either localhost or . for *ComputerName*.

- ✔ **-E:** Try to use a trusted connection, which happens to be default behavior for SQLCMD. Just like its name implies, this type of connection bypasses some of the security safeguards; if you try to pass a login and password, SQL Server 2005 Express reports an error.

Connecting with SQL Server Management Studio Express

If the thought of using the character-based SQLCMD utility to manage your SQL Server 2005 Express server leaves you cold, try SQL Server Management Studio Express instead. It's a graphical tool that offers database administration as well as data interaction capabilities. Here's how you can connect to your server, using this tool:

1. **Launch SQL Server Management Studio Express.**

2. **Choose File➪Connect Object Explorer.**

3. **Enter the name of your server and, optionally, an instance name.**

   The Connect to Server dialog box appears, as shown in Figure 3-7.

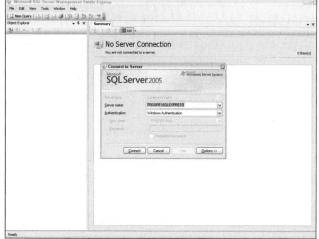

Figure 3-7:
The SQL
Server
Manage-
ment Studio
Express
connection
dialog box.

After you successfully connect, you should see a window similar to Figure 3-8.

For much more about using SQL Server Management Studio Express, check
out Chapter 4.

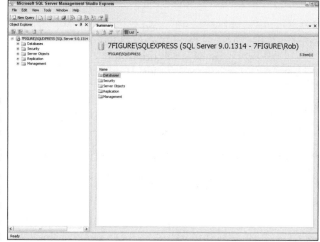

Figure 3-8:
A success-
ful SQL
Server
Manage-
ment Studio
Express
connection.

Connecting with ODBC

Over the past decade, Open Database Connectivity (ODBC) has become the preferred method that most software vendors use to interact with information repositories such as SQL Server 2005 Express. If you're using one of these tools, you need to set up an ODBC connection. Just follow these steps and you'll be all set:

1. **Choose Start⇨Control Panel⇨Administrative Tools⇨Data Sources (ODBC).**

2. **Click either the User or System DSN tab.**

   Selecting the System DSN tab (which is shown in Figure 3-9) is generally a good idea; your data source is then visible to other users on your computer.

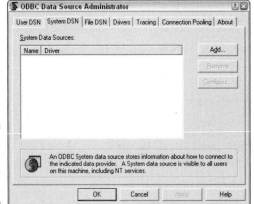

Figure 3-9: The ODBC System DSN dialog box.

3. **Click Add.**

   The Create New Data Source dialog box appears, as shown in Figure 3-10.

4. **From the list of drivers, pick either the SQL Native Client or the SQL Server driver.**

   The SQL Native Client is the more current connectivity client, so I recommend that you select this option.

Figure 3-10:
Choosing
an ODBC
driver.

5. **Click Next.**

   The Create a New Data Source to SQL Server dialog box appears, as
   shown in Figure 3-11.

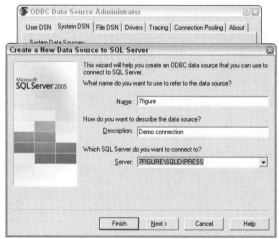

Figure 3-11:
Selecting a
database
server.

6. **Enter the name and description of your connection, pick the server,
   and click Next.**

7. **Choose the authentication method you want and click Next.**

8. **Choose your default database and click Next.**

9. **Fill in the final settings (shown in Figure 3-12) and click Finish.**

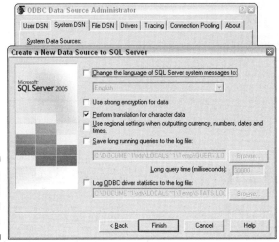

Figure 3-12:
Final ODBC
settings
dialog box.

10. **Test your new ODBC connection.**

The SQL Native Client offers a handy test feature to help validate that your connection was set up correctly. Just click Test to launch the verification utility, as shown in Figure 3-13. Figure 3-14 shows a verification of a successful connection.

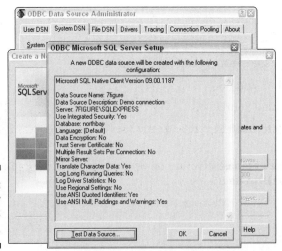

Figure 3-13:
Summary
of ODBC
settings.

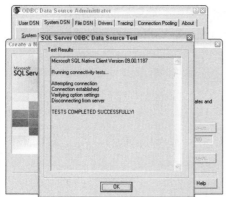

Figure 3-14:
A successful connection.

Connecting with Visual Studio Express

In an effort to increase its market share and mind share with the hobbyist and entry-level developer audience, Microsoft has released a suite of development products that are tightly coupled with SQL Server 2005 Express. Together, these are part of the Visual Studio Express product family, and cover many popular programming languages:

- Visual C# Express
- Visual Basic Express
- Visual C++ Express
- Visual Web Developer

Connecting any of these products to SQL Server 2005 Express is a snap; for example, here's how to do it with Visual Basic Express:

1. **Launch the Visual Studio Express product.**
2. **Choose Tools⇨Connect to Database.**

   The Choose Data Source dialog box opens, shown in Figure 3-15.

3. **Choose the Microsoft SQL Server Database File option, and click Continue.**
4. **Browse to the database file you want to use, and click the Open button in the Browse dialog box.**

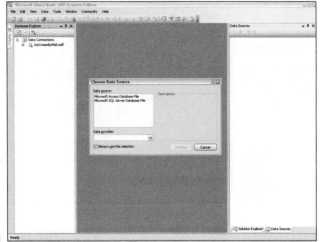

Figure 3-15:
Choosing
SQL Server
Express.

5. If you want to set any advanced connection variables, click Advanced.

Figure 3-16 shows some of these more advanced settings.

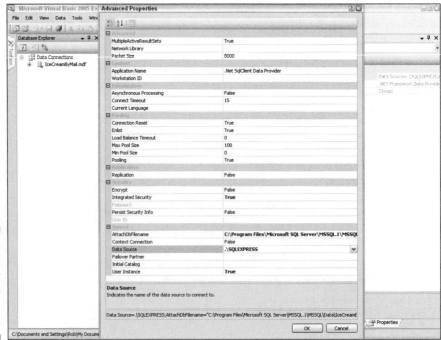

Figure 3-16:
Advanced
SQL Server
Express
connection
settings.

6. Click Test to ensure that your connection is configured correctly.

If all goes well, you receive a message stating that the connection worked.

7. Click OK to complete the connection.

You now see your SQL Server 2005 Express database within the Database Explorer window, as shown in Figure 3-17.

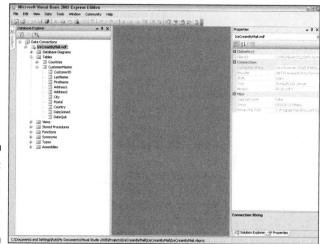

Figure 3-17:
A suc-
cessful
database
connection.

Part II

Administering a SQL Server 2005 Express System

The 5th Wave   By Rich Tennant

"So far he's called up a cobra, 2 pythons, and a bunch of skinks, but still not the file we're looking for."

In this part . . .

A database administrator's work is never done. In a single day, you can witness a collection of disparate challenges requiring intervention, ranging from halting runaway queries to satisfying new development requests to setting up additional servers. But you don't need to go it alone.

First, I give you some ideas of how to plan for the future of your SQL Server 2005 Express, as well as how you can use some handy tools to look after your information. Next, you discover some tips and tactics for monitoring and managing your server's performance. Finally, because no database is an island, I show you how to take advantage of replication and other techniques for accurately and safely spreading your data across multiple servers.

Chapter 4

Putting SQL Server 2005 Express to Work

. . . .

In This Chapter

▶ Growing with SQL Server 2005 Express

▶ Deciding when to upgrade

▶ Choosing a database administration tool

▶ Creating databases, tables, and logins

. . . .

Don't make the mistake of equating the zero-cost price point of SQL Server 2005 Express with limited capabilities. On the contrary: This product offers a rich feature set that will likely suffice for most of your data storage needs. With that said, you should understand that there are some restrictions that might affect you in the future.

In this chapter, I show you how to weigh any constraints that come with SQL Server 2005 Express and decide when the time is right to upgrade. Although many of you will never need to migrate, all of you should select a database administration tool. Choosing and using the right administrative technology is also a big part of this chapter.

Planning For Tomorrow as Well as Today

After going to the trouble of downloading, installing, and configuring your SQL Server 2005 Express server, you're probably ready to get started developing or deploying your database-driven solution. After all you've been through you're certainly entitled to that. But this is also a good point to take a step back and estimate how you expect to use your SQL Server 2005 Express database, as well as what kind of growth is likely to happen over time.

This is more than just an academic exercise. As I show a little later in this section, a time may come when you decide that you've outgrown your database server, and that it's time to upgrade. Two factors usually drive this decision: database usage and growth, which I describe now, and feature restrictions, which is the highlight of the next part of this section.

Estimating database usage and growth

A database grows, often significantly, over time. Some of the drivers for this expansion include the following:

- ✔ **More data:** Like a drawer that becomes over packed, databases have a tendency to accumulate more and more stuff over time. Archive and purge as often as you like, but you'll still probably notice your database continuing to grow. As you see in the next section, this growth may pose a problem when you approach 4GB of information in a single database. Fortunately, you can create multiple databases that can each hold up to 4GB of information.

- ✔ **Additional users:** Set up a database with interesting information, and the world will beat a path to your door (or at least to your database). Fortunately, SQL Server 2005 Express has no built-in user restrictions, so you should be able to gracefully support new users. Keep in mind that if you want to support remote users, you need to enable and configure a protocol such as TCP/IP or named pipes. Chapter 3 has more details about these protocols.

- ✔ **Additional applications:** Just as the amount of data and number of users typically grow over time, you'll (or people that work with you) naturally discover new uses for SQL Server 2005 Express. You can confidently build these new applications as long as you keep the product's built-in restrictions in mind. And if you do find that you've outgrown SQL Server 2005 Express, you can easily move your application and database onto a more feature-rich version of SQL Server 2005.

Deciding when to graduate

SQL Server 2005 Express runs on the same technology platform as its larger, more powerful SQL Server 2005 siblings. However, SQL Server 2005 Express has a number of limitations that aren't present in these other versions. In this section, I point out these restrictions, with an eye toward helping you determine when the time is right to move to a more feature-rich version.

If you find that your needs outstrip the capabilities of SQL Server 2005 Express, you're probably on the upgrade path. On the other hand, these restrictions may not be an issue for your installation. In that case, you can look forward to running on SQL Server 2005 Express for a long time to come.

- ✔ **Database size:** This is probably the most significant limitation of SQL Server 2005 Express. An individual database can't exceed 4GB. This is not a problem for many applications, but it might be for yours.

- ✔ **Memory:** Even if your system is stuffed with memory, SQL Server 2005 Express only takes advantage of 1GB. This limitation typically hurts applications with large numbers of users or big data storage requirements.

- ✔ **Multiple CPUs:** One way to boost performance is to run your database server on a multiple CPU computer. Unfortunately, an additional CPU won't help a SQL Server 2005 Express installation. If you find that performance is too sluggish, you can't take advantage of this feature.

- ✔ **Full-text searching:** Modern database-driven applications can store a tremendous variety of information. A significant portion of this data is often kept in the form of large blocks of text. Full-text search, which is not entirely available in SQL Server 2005 Express, takes advantage of sophisticated indexes to speed up retrieving this data. If your application needs to speedily search and manipulate large volumes of this kind of information, you want to consider upgrading. Luckily, SQL Server 2005 Express with Advanced Services does offer full-text search capabilities; this product is also available as a free download from Microsoft. Check out Chapter 18 for the details about using this feature.

- ✔ **Analysis services:** In the past few years, an entire technology segment has sprung up around business intelligence. These products help users mine and analyze large blocks of data, which then produces meaningful results that drive business activity. SQL Server 2005 now incorporates its own collection of business intelligence features, which are known collectively as Analysis Services. If you deal with hefty quantities of information that you want to slice-and-dice directly via the database engine, consider moving to a more feature-rich version of SQL Server 2005.

If you're already using a third-party business intelligence product, you probably won't need to upgrade your database. Instead, these third-party products can likely work with SQL Server 2005 Express to produce high quality data analysis.

- ✔ **Integration services:** No database is an island; this rule also applies to SQL Server 2005. Most organizations have information spread among all sorts of databases and applications. Eventually, you might need to load this data into a SQL Server database, or vice-versa. Previously, integrating would require you to develop or purchase software to map and possibly transform the data so that it could correctly be placed into, or extracted from, your database.

However, with SQL Server 2005, Microsoft has developed a collection of robust transformation technologies in an effort to ease the often painful process of synchronizing information. If you're likely to need far-reaching data conversions, you'll probably benefit from moving to a more full-featured edition.

✔ **Reporting services:** This group of capabilities makes it easy to securely share information from your SQL Server database with users both inside and outside your organization. It isn't offered in the baseline SQL Server 2005 Express Edition, but it is part of other versions, including SQL Server 2005 Express with Advanced Services.

✔ **Notification services:** This feature lets you take advantage of sophisticated publish and subscribe capabilities. For example, you could build an application that would register interest in a particular database or XML file event. Once that event occurs, the SQL Server 2005 Notification Service would contact your application, which could then take appropriate action. You can still build this kind of application in SQL Server 2005 Express, but it requires much more time, as well as custom code.

✔ **High availability:** If you're running mission-critical, 24/7 applications, the more feature-rich editions of SQL Server 2005 offer a collection of technologies that make life easier for you and your users. These include capabilities like the following:

- Partitioning

- Online restore

- Online indexing

- Database mirroring

- Failover clustering

Even if you're running SQL Server 2005 Express, you can increase the chances that your database server remains available by taking advantage of hardware-based and other redundancy technologies. However, if this solution isn't enough, consider upgrading to a higher grade of SQL Server 2005.

Administering Your SQL Server 2005 Express System

Spend a little time with any Microsoft SQL Server product, and you'll quickly come to the conclusion that you can navigate several possible avenues to do just about any task. What's true for the most powerful edition of SQL Server 2005 is also true for Express. This is especially noticeable with common database administration tasks. In this section, I show you two of the more popular ways to handle the database administration tasks that are sure to come your way.

To begin, I raise the important point that you can use a character-based utility such as SQLCMD for nearly any tasks that you can tackle with the other choice: SQL Server Management Studio Express. Next, I dive into that technology to show you how easily you can carry out any of the everyday administrative jobs that you're likely to encounter when using SQL Server 2005 Express.

Using character-based utilities

For any number of perfectly understandable reasons, many administrators have never taken a shine to the new-fangled graphical tools that have become so prevalent with Microsoft technologies. Luckily for these folks, Microsoft continues to support the SQLCMD utility, which you can run from any command prompt. Because Microsoft also ships hundreds of built-in stored procedures, chances are that you can handle any administrative task that comes your way. For example, Figure 4-1 shows output from an administrative stored procedure run via the SQLCMD utility.

Although useful, trying to make sense of this data might cause you to reach for the aspirin. If you'd like your information in a more palatable form, read on.

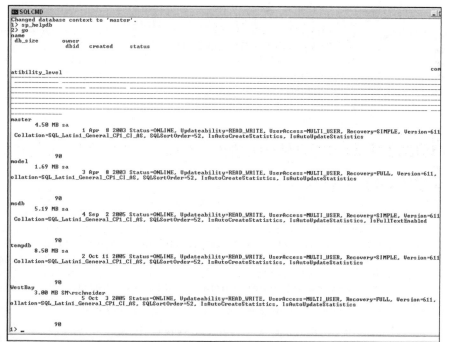

Figure 4-1:
The
SQLCMD
utility.

Using SQL Server Management Studio Express

If you're an administrator who believes a picture is worth a thousand words, you'll probably want to use a graphical tool to get your job done. One of the best tools on the market is SQL Server Management Studio, which is available from Microsoft. A full-featured version ships with the more expensive editions of SQL Server, but you can still use the Express Edition of this product to get the job done for SQL Server 2005 Express.

Here are just a few uses you can find for SQL Server Management Studio Express:

- ✔ Database administration
- ✔ Creating tables
- ✔ Adding users
- ✔ Granting permissions
- ✔ Running queries

Using third-party database administration tools

Many an enterprising, innovative software company has been started to fill in the gaps in the Microsoft product line. In particular, a number of vendors specialize in database management and administration. If you find that none of the tools I describe earlier in this section are right for you, many of these third-party products are available for trial download via the Internet. I also list a few of these tools in Chapter 22.

Creating a Database and Table

Here's how you would use SQL Server Management Studio Express to create a database:

1. **Launch SQL Server Management Studio Express.**

2. **Connect to the appropriate SQL Server Express instance.**

   If you don't see any germane connections, you can create one by clicking the Connect Object Explorer icon.

3. **Expand the connection's entry in the Object Explorer.**

4. **Highlight the Databases folder.**

5. **Right-click this folder, and choose New Database.**

The New Database dialog box appears, as shown in Figure 4-2. You specify some key information for the new database:

- **Database name:** You can name your database just about anything you like. You'll notice that as you key in the database name, the data and log file entries are updated to reflect your choice.

- **Database owner:** As you might suspect, this is where you identify the login that has primary ownership of the database.

- **Data file information:** When you create a database, SQL Server 2005 Express generates two types of files. The first, of type *Data*, holds your database's information: tables, indexes, and so on. The second, of type *Log*, stores information that the server uses to protect your database's integrity and make data archiving and restoration possible.

One handy SQL Server 2005 Express feature is its ability to gracefully and automatically manage database expansion. It does this via the autogrowth feature, which you can control by clicking the ellipses button in the Autogrowth column of the New Database dialog box. When enabled, SQL Server 2005 Express uses the guidelines that you specify to control how the database grows, and when it stops growing. Figure 4-3 shows the parameters you can control for database growth.

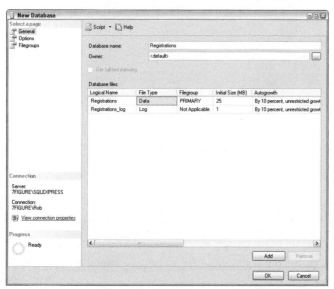

Figure 4-2:
The New
Database
dialog box.

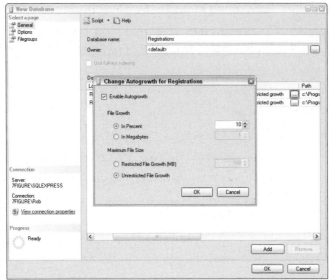

Figure 4-3:
Setting
autogrowth
policies.

In addition to the database naming and sizing parameters, you also have all sorts of other settings to tinker with. You find them on the Options page (shown in Figure 4-4).

In most cases you can leave these set to their default values.

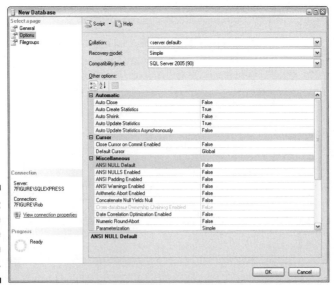

Figure 4-4:
The
database
creation
options.

6. **After you're done filling in details for all relevant prompts, click OK.**

   SQL Server 2005 Express now takes your requests and creates the database. Once complete, you can see it in the Object Explorer, as shown in Figure 4-5.

After the database is in place, here's how you can create a table. If you left SQL Server Management Studio Express running, you can skip Steps 1 and 2.

1. **Open SQL Server Management Studio Express.**

2. **Connect to the appropriate SQL Server Express instance.**

   If you don't see any germane connections, you can create one by clicking the Connect icon.

3. **Open the Databases folder.**

4. **Expand the folder for your database.**

5. **Highlight the Tables folder.**

6. **Right-click this folder, and choose New Table.**

   This brings up a tab where you can enter information about your table, its columns, and their properties. In this case, I'm creating a table to hold transaction details. Figure 4-6 shows what this looks like.

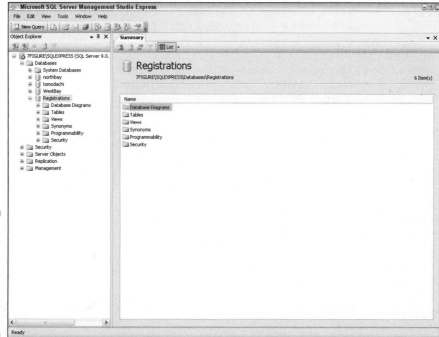

Figure 4-5:
A newly created database as it appears in the Object Explorer.

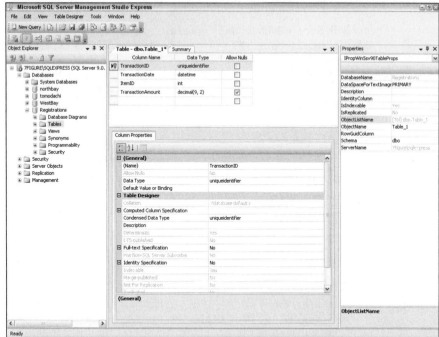

Figure 4-6:
Designing
a table.

Check out Chapter 8 for much more about how to design and build your own tables.

7. After you're ready to create the table, click the Save icon.

This generates the table, making it ready to receive information. You can check the Object Explorer to see if things turned out the way you wanted; Figure 4-7 shows what a completed table looks like.

After your tables are in place, SQL Server Management Studio Express has some handy features dedicated to making interaction with your database more straightforward. One helpful feature is its ability to generate SQL script that you can plug into your applications. This automatically created SQL script covers a wide variety of operations:

- Create
- Update
- Insert
- Delete
- Drop
- Alter
- Execute

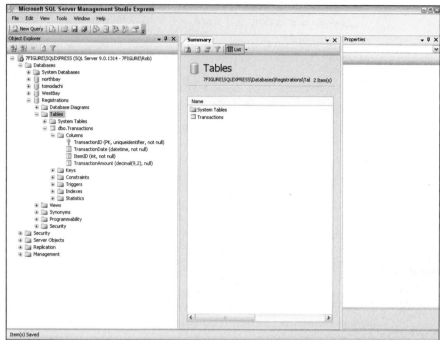

Figure 4-7:
Viewing a
completed
table in the
Object
Explorer.

Note that depending on the database object in question, some of these commands may not be available. Nevertheless, automatically generated SQL scripts are a great way to jumpstart your database development.

Here's all that you need to do to get started. (If you left SQL Server Management Studio Express running from the earlier examples in this chapter, you can skip Steps 1 and 2.)

1. **Open SQL Server Management Studio Express.**

2. **Connect to the appropriate SQL Server Express instance.**

   If you don't see any germane connections, you can create one by clicking the Connect icon.

3. **Open the Databases folder.**

4. **Highlight any object in the Object Explorer.**

   For example, if you want to generate a table creation script for a given table, you would simply highlight that table. On the other hand, if you want SQL Server 2005 Express to generate SQL for reading from a specific view, just highlight that view.

5. **Right-click the object you want to see, choose Script...As, and then choose the action you want.**

   Depending on context, you have a range of options to choose from. Don't be afraid to experiment: This is a great way to figure out how to write correct SQL statements. In this example, I've asked SQL Server 2005 Express to generate a SELECT statement for a table.

6. **Choose the output method:**

   - New Query Editor Window

   - File

   - Clipboard

   If you choose New Query Editor Window, Figure 4-8 shows what you see.

Even though SQL Server Management Studio Express is extremely powerful and flexible, you might want to check out one of the many third-party, independent database administration tools available on the market.

For all its benefits, SQL Server Management Studio Express has its limitations. Some times you'll probably wish that it did more, and that you didn't have to drop into Transact-SQL so often. If that describes you, never fear: You have alternatives.

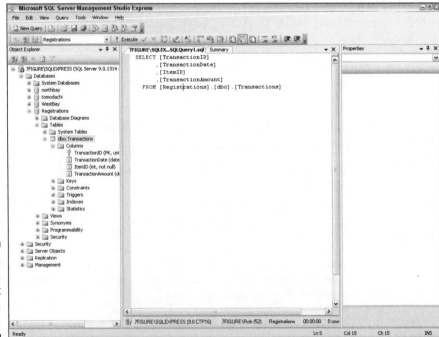

Figure 4-8:
Output from the Script Table As command.

Creating databases and tables is just a small part of what you can get done
with SQL Server Management Studio Express. As its name implies, you can
also handle all sorts of administrative tasks. For example, here's how you
would create a new database login. (If you left SQL Server Management
Studio Express running from the earlier examples in this chapter, you can
Skip Steps 1 and 2.)

1. **Open SQL Server Management Studio Express.**

2. **Connect to the appropriate SQL Server Express instance.**

   If you don't see any germane connections, click the Connect icon to
   create one.

3. **Expand the Security folder.**

4. **Expand the Logins folder.**

   This gives you a list of everyone who is registered to work with your
   database server.

5. **Right-click the Logins folder, and choose the New Login option.**

   Figure 4-9 shows you what this form looks like.

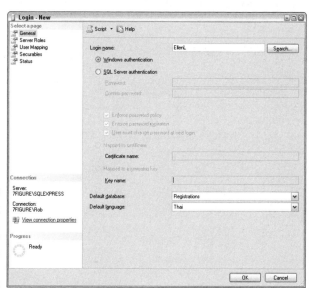

Figure 4-9:
Creating
a new
database
server login.

6. **Fill in the values for all the relevant settings for your new user.**

   There are five properties pages of information that you can provide:

   - **General:** Here's where you tell SQL Server 2005 Express the new login user's name, choose a security method, and request a default database and language.

   - **Server Roles:** Using this page, you can associate this new database user with a set of predefined security profiles.

   - **User Mapping:** Here's where you associate a database user with one from the Windows operating system.

   - **Securables:** This is where you can set up highly specific security criteria.

   - **Status:** Here's where you can set high level permissions, such as whether the user can connect to the database, as well as whether the login is enabled or not.

7. **Click OK to complete the operation.**

   Your database login is now ready to go. If you're curious about security, check out Chapter 11.

Chapter 5

Maintaining a SQL Server 2005 Express System

In This Chapter

▶ Taking advantage of user instances

▶ Customizing your database server's operation

▶ Monitoring and improving performance

*A*lthough SQL Server 2005 Express comes with an attractive price (free!), and a truthful promise of low maintenance requirements, you're still not completely off the hook with your babysitting responsibilities. In this chapter, I show you how to get these chores done with the least amount of effort.

To begin, you find out how SQL Server 2005 Express allows you to easily run separate user instances, thereby granting normal database users extra powers within their own workspace. With that out of the way, I show you how to configure the database server, followed by some helpful performance tips.

Master of the Database Domain

User instances are a handy feature offered by SQL Server 2005 Express that let regular users run their own, separate instance of the database server. When you request a user instance, the primary SQL Server 2005 Express service spawns a unique process containing the user instance.

Even though these users are not administrators, within the context of their own instance they have much higher privileges. However, because they're in their own instance, they can't damage or otherwise disrupt the parent instance of SQL Server 2005 Express. You enable user instances by setting a configuration parameter, a task that I describe in the next section.

Setting SQL Server 2005 Express Parameters

You may be tempted to think of SQL Server 2005 Express as a monolithic, unchanging application. That would be the wrong assumption, however. In fact, dozens of settings control all sorts of engine behavior, from the number of user connections allowed to how the database interacts with different programming languages to how it deals with remote connections. As an administrator, you have the power (in most cases) to change these settings at will. In this section, I describe some common parameters, along with how you can easily modify them.

The database engine automatically tunes many of the SQL Server 2005 Express parameters. In some cases, you know better than the engine; in most cases, you're better off leaving the parameters alone and letting the server do its job. To keep things clear and prevent inadvertent changes, very few of the parameters I describe are self-tuning.

How to configure your server

Like so many of the Microsoft products, SQL Server 2005 Express offers several alternate paths to achieving your goal; in this case, setting database server configuration values. Here are three of the most commonly used options:

- **The SQL Server Surface Area Configuration utility:** This tool, which is available by choosing Start⇨All Programs⇨Microsoft SQL Server 2005⇨ Configuration Tools⇨SQL Server Surface Area Configuration, lets you decide which protocols and features to expose. Although it's traditionally used just after you install the product, you could also put it to work when you're in production.

- **SQL Server Management Studio Express:** You can use this powerful and flexible database management utility (available via download from Microsoft) for all sorts of useful tasks, including configuring and customizing your server. Figure 5-1 shows a list of all the pages at your disposal for viewing and setting database properties. In this case, I've selected the Memory page.

- **The sp_configure system stored procedure:** No matter what your database configuration, you should have access to the character-based SQLCMD utility. SQLCMD — and sufficient permission — is all you need to run this stored procedure. Because all installations have the ability to run this stored procedure, I focus on it for the balance of this section.

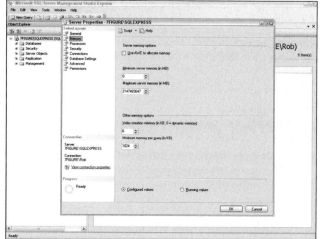

Figure 5-1:
Setting
memory
options with
SQL Server
Manage-
ment Studio
Express.

First, a word or two about how to launch `sp_configure`. Just follow these steps and you'll be ready to make your changes:

1. **Launch SQL Server Management Studio Express.**

   You can get things going by choosing Start⊅All Programs⊅Microsoft SQL Server 2005⊅SQL Server Management Studio Express.

2. **Connect to your database server.**

3. **Click the New Query icon on the Standard toolbar.**

4. **Run the `sp_configure` stored procedure.**

   You need to pass in parameters that indicate the setting you're modifying, along with the value that you want. For example, here's how to allow remote access:

   ```
   sp_configure 'remote access', '1'
   go
   ```

   This setting is binary: Either remote access is on, or it's off. On the other hand, here's how to change the numeric value for the remote query timeout setting, expressed in seconds:

   ```
   sp_configure 'remote query timeout', '300'
   go
   ```

   If you run `sp_configure` without any parameters, you get a list of all changeable settings.

5. **After you run the `sp_configure` stored procedure, run the `RECON-FIGURE` command for the change to take effect.**

Depending on the setting you've changed, you may need to restart your database server for the alteration to take effect. SQL Server 2005 Express sends a message telling you what to do next.

Common server parameters

Here are some of the more frequently modified database server parameters. You should note that for most installations, the default values are just fine; you should plan on tuning only if you're experiencing poor performance or other suboptimal behavior.

Before you embark on your database configuration adventure, note that SQL Server 2005 Express considers some parameters to be advanced, which means that you need to run `sp_configure` before even attempting to make any alterations. I describe how to run this stored procedure in the preceding section. Here's what you need to do to gain access to these advanced parameters:

```
sp_configure 'show advanced options', '1'
go
```

That's it: You're now ready to view and change advanced configuration options. With these options now showing, you can now turn your attention to customizing SQL Server 2005 Express to your liking. Here are some of the major functional areas that you can control:

- ✔ **User instances:** As I describe earlier in this chapter, user instances let non-administrators have their own running copy of a SQL Server 2005 Express database. In this instance, the user has full privileges. To turn on this feature, be sure that the User Instances Enabled option is set to 1, which is its default.

- ✔ **User connections:** If you're intent on overriding the automatically tuned User Connections parameter, you can use it to stipulate the upper limit of concurrent user connections to your SQL Server 2005 Express database server.

- ✔ **Tracing database activity:** If you're the curious type, you can command SQL Server 2005 Express to trace events that happen in your database. These events are then written into a log file. I describe log monitoring in the upcoming "Monitoring performance" section; for now, you can request log file updates by setting Default Trace Enabled to 1.

- ✔ **Configure trigger behavior:** In Chapter 15, I show you how to employ triggers to enforce business rules, protect your data, and provide other application customizations. Depending on how you've written your triggers, they might return a *result set* (that is, a set of rows generated by the trigger). If your application isn't equipped to handle the results, you may experience unanticipated (and unwanted) behavior. To prevent these results from gumming up the works, set the Disallow Results from Triggers option to 1.

✔ **Control process behavior:** Usually, all your applications that work with SQL Server 2005 Express get along just fine. Occasionally, however, two or more processes find themselves in conflict for the same resource at the same time. If you want to be notified when this quarrel happens, try tuning the blocked process threshold setting. Measured in seconds, it can range from 0 all the way up to 86,400.

✔ **Allow other programming languages:** In Chapter 16, you see how to use Microsoft's Common Language Runtime feature to leverage additional programming languages to build your stored procedures, functions, and triggers. However, you need to set the CLR Enabled parameter to 1.

✔ **Configure remote access settings:** If your SQL Server 2005 Express instance is like many others, you probably have remote users and processes connecting to your database server. You have several tunable options at your disposal. Three of the more interesting options are remote access (which determines whether non-local users and processes can connect to your server), remote login timeout (which specifies the number of seconds to wait before aborting a login attempt from another computer), and remote query timeout (which sets a delay threshold before SQL Server 2005 Express aborts a query from a remote user or process).

✔ **Set user options:** You can control the default behavior for users' SQL Server 2005 Express sessions either individually with the SET option or globally via the User Options setting. You compose this numeric value by adding unique integers, producing a distinct value. Table 5-1 lists all the user option parameters.

How do you use these numbers? An illustration can make things much clearer. Suppose that you want all users to have the following behavior in their sessions:

- Close open cursors when a transaction commits.

- Don't report the number of rows affected by any statements.

- Rollback a transaction if an error happens.

It's actually quite simple. For each of these three requirements, consult Table 5-1 and determine the numeric value for that setting. Then, add the three numbers together (4 + 512 + 16384 = 16900 in this case) and run the sp_configure stored procedure as follows:

```
sp_configure 'user options', '16900'
```

Unless you want to change the default behavior for all users, you never need to make these types of requests. In fact, most environments can simply use the out-of-the-box settings offered by SQL Server 2005 Express.

Table 5-1	Key User Configuration Parameters
Value	*Purpose*
1	Check constraints right now, rather than waiting
2	Enable default transactions for certain types of connections
4	Close open cursors when a transaction commits
8	Follow the ANSI standard when warning users about truncation
16	Follow the ANSI standard when padding a fixed-length variable
32	Follow the ANSI standard when encountering a NULL
64	Halt a query should a divide-by-zero occur
128	Return NULL should a divide-by-zero occur
256	Decide on whether to use a single or double quote
512	Don't report on the number of rows affected by a statement
1024	Unless otherwise specified, let new columns accept NULL values
2048	Unless otherwise specified, don't let new columns accept NULL values
4096	Respond with NULL if you attempt to combine NULL with a string
8192	Respond with an error if a math expression loses precision
16384	Rollback a transaction should an error occur

Picking Up the Pace

No matter how fast your database server and applications may be, your users will probably always want things to run more quickly. In this section, I offer you an assortment of recommendations to help squeeze some additional speed out of your SQL Server 2005 Express database.

Monitoring performance

Before you can even start on your journey, taking stock of where you are is a good idea. Several tools are at your disposal to help you get a good idea of database and system activity and response levels. These tools belong to two main classes: Operating system and database-specific utilities.

Operating system performance tools

The Windows operating system offers two very helpful utilities that you can use to measure what's happening on your computer.

- ✔ **Windows Task Manager:** If you've ever tried to figure out an unexplained system slowdown, I bet you're already on good terms with this utility. You can launch it by either right-clicking the taskbar and choosing Task Manager, or by pressing the famous Ctrl+Alt+Delete key sequence and clicking the Task Manager button in the dialog box. Figure 5-2 shows the kinds of details that it reports. In this example, I'm tracking the CPU's workload over time.

- ✔ **Microsoft Management Console (MMC) Performance Snap-in:** Unless you're a professional system administrator or just naturally curious, you probably don't even know that this utility exists. A general-purpose management application, you can launch its performance-centric view by choosing Start⇨Control Panel⇨Administrative Tools⇨Performance.

  It offers hundreds of indicators for all sorts of system information. Figure 5-3 shows the SQL Server metrics alone. Each performance object offers its own set of statistics.

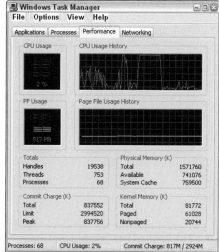

Figure 5-2:
The
Windows
Task
Manager.

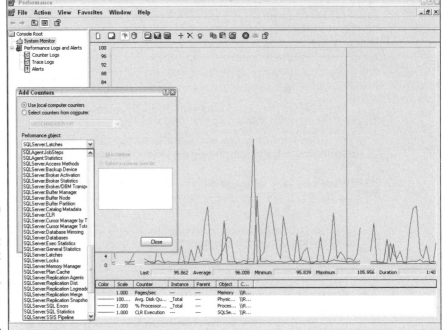

Figure 5-3:
Microsoft
Management
Console's
SQL Server
performance
objects.

Curious administrators should explore this great example of statistical gathering software in depth. Because you're merely gathering information, you can experiment to your heart's content, secure in the knowledge that you won't negatively impact your system.

Database performance tools

You can take advantage of the built-in Activity Monitor from SQL Server Management Studio Express. It reports on all kinds of important performance information:

- ✔ Databases in use
- ✔ Active commands
- ✔ Applications

✔ Memory utilization

✔ Locks

✔ Object access

To access the Activity Monitor, just follow these simple steps:

1. **Launch SQL Server Management Studio Express.**

2. **Expand the Management folder.**

3. **Double-click the Activity Monitor icon.**

Figures 5-4 and 5-5 give you an idea of what you can learn from the Activity Monitor.

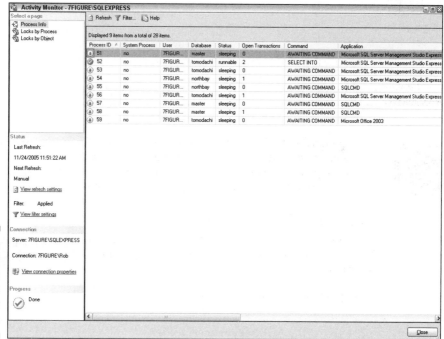

Figure 5-4:
Viewing
user actions
in the
Activity
Monitor.

Figure 5-5:
Viewing
locks in the
Activity
Monitor.

Process ID	Context	Batch ID	Type	Subtype	Object ID	Description	Request Mode	Request Type	Reques
52	0	0	OBJECT		13		IX	LOCK	GRANT
52	0	0	OBJECT		15		IX	LOCK	GRANT
52	0	0	OBJECT		26		IX	LOCK	GRANT
52	0	0	OBJECT		34		IX	LOCK	GRANT
52	0	0	OBJECT		41		IX	LOCK	GRANT
52	0	0	OBJECT		54		IX	LOCK	GRANT
52	0	0	HOBT		72057594045333504		Sch-M	LOCK	GRANT
52	0	0	METADATA	DATA_SPACE	0	data_space_id = 1	Sch-S	LOCK	GRANT
52	0	0	METADATA	INDEXSTATS	0	object_id = 7436...	Sch-S	LOCK	GRANT
52	0	0	OBJECT		743673697		Sch-M	LOCK	GRANT
52	0	0	OBJECT		5		IX	LOCK	GRANT
52	0	0	OBJECT		4		IX	LOCK	GRANT
52	0	0	OBJECT		7		IX	LOCK	GRANT
52	0	0	DATABASE		0		S	LOCK	GRANT
53	0	0	DATABASE		0		S	LOCK	GRANT
54	0	0	DATABASE		0		S	LOCK	GRANT
55	0	0	DATABASE		0		S	LOCK	GRANT
56	0	0	DATABASE		0		S	LOCK	GRANT

If SQL Server Management Studio Express isn't to your liking, copious third-party database monitoring and management tools are on the market. Most of these offerings include their own views of performance management. If you're curious about some of these interesting products, have a look at Chapter 22 for more.

SQL Server 2005 Express also does a good job of tracking system activity over time. You can view its logs to get a better idea of what's been happening on your database server. To launch the log viewer, follow these steps:

1. **Launch SQL Server Management Studio Express.**

2. **Expand the Management folder.**

3. **Expand the SQL Server Logs folder.**

   You see a collection of log files, both current and archived.

4. **Double-click any of these log files to launch the viewer.**

Figure 5-6 shows a sample of what's contained in a log file.

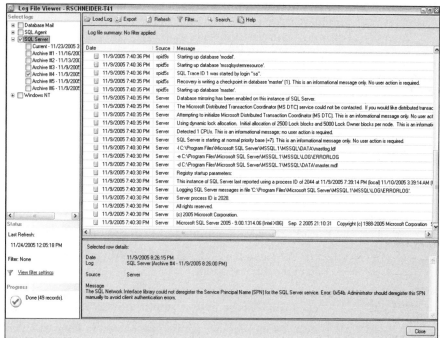

Figure 5-6:
Viewing
log files.

Enhancing your computer

To squeeze some additional throughput from your database server, try any of these suggestions:

- **Upgrade to a faster CPU:** Computers continually get faster; just about anyone who has bought a new computer soon faces the depressing realization that the shiny new box is practically obsolete. What's true for a personal computer is also true for database servers. If you have the budget, one of the fastest ways to quicker performance is simply to upgrade to a newer and peppier CPU.

  Before breaking out the credit card, remember two important caveats:

  - SQL Server 2005 Express can only leverage one CPU; installing multiple CPUs within the same computer won't gain much performance.

  - A slightly faster computer won't yield tremendous response improvements. Typically, you won't see dramatically faster computers hit the market for two or three years.

✔ **Add memory:** Because so much database work takes place in memory, providing more of this valuable, yet relatively inexpensive commodity helps augment performance.

Trees don't grow to the sky, and unlimited memory doesn't shorten your applications' response time to nanoseconds. A point comes where diminishing returns set in, so it's best to take an evolutionary approach when increasing memory.

✔ **Adjust virtual memory:** The Windows operating system uses the page file as a disk-based substitute for memory. This virtual memory comes in handy when the processing load on your system overwhelms the available physical memory. However, this virtual memory operates at about one-tenth of the speed of true memory. In most cases, Windows automatically manages this setting. If you're inclined to tinker with it, just follow these simple steps:

1. **Right-click My Computer and choose Properties.**

2. **On the Advanced tab, click the Settings button within the Performance section.**

3. **On the Advanced tab of the Performance Options dialog box, click the Change button within the Virtual Memory section.**

4. **Adjust your memory settings (as shown in Figure 5-7) and click OK.**

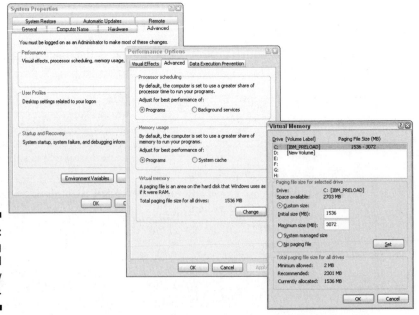

Figure 5-7: Changing virtual memory settings.

You may need to restart your computer for these alterations to take effect.

✔ **Defragment your disks:** Like your closet and desktop, over a period of time your disk drives become cluttered and disorganized. The damage here is not aesthetic: A disorderly disk drive hurts performance by forcing your computer to jump around to locate necessary information. Luckily, Windows includes a handy disk defragmenter that you can use to set things right again. Here's how to use it:

1. **Launch the Windows Disk Defragmenter by choosing Start⇨ Programs⇨Accessories⇨System Tools⇨Disk Defragmenter.**

2. **Click the Analyze button.**

   The Disk Defragmenter analyzes your disk and returns a recommendation. If you're lucky, you won't even need to move on to Step 3.

3. **If the Disk Defragmenter recommends that you defragment your disk, click the Defragment button.**

   This step may take some time to complete, but be patient; it's worth it.

✔ **Leverage multiple computers:** If you find that your database server is overloaded, consider bringing additional computers into the picture. Although SQL Server 2005 Express doesn't have the full distributed computing capabilities of its more expensive siblings, you can still gain benefits by offloading work onto ancillary processors. If you're curious about using SQL Server 2005 Express in a distributed environment, take a look at Chapter 6.

Speeding up the database

While you may not have any control over your hardware platform, chances are you can make some improvements to your SQL Server 2005 Express database and its related applications. Try any of the following to coax more performance out of your database server software:

✔ **Efficient table design:** Just as you can't construct a solid house on quicksand, you can't create an optimal database application on top of a bad design. Take the time and get this vital activity right. Flip ahead to Chapter 8 for a detailed review of best practices when creating a new database.

✔ **Optimal indexing:** Many times, the fastest and easiest way to decisively enhance performance is to introduce better indexes into your database. The reason for an index is simple: In the absence of an index, SQL Server 2005 Express is often forced to wade through vast quantities of extraneous information, desperately searching for the correct results. On the other hand, a proper index can cut out hundreds of thousands of extra steps, often locating the right data in one read. Don't be afraid to experiment with indexes. If you want more guidance on this topic, see Chapters 9 and 10.

✔ **Database statistics:** When you ask SQL Server 2005 Express to locate or modify information, the database engine must often choose among several different paths. At first glance, each tactic appears to be an equally qualified candidate. However, this is usually not the case: One path is often much faster than its peers. To help the database server arrive at a good decision, SQL Server 2005 Express has the ability to track statistical details about the data that makes up each index. You can use the following commands and stored procedures to determine the database server's statistics-gathering behavior.

- **Collecting statistics:** If you want to fine-tune the statistical accumulation process, use the CREATE STATISTICS command. On the other hand, if all you want to do is gather information across a broad range of tables, simply use the sp_createstats system stored procedure.

- **Monitoring statistics:** When statistics are in place, you can learn more about them by invoking the DBCC SHOW_STATISTICS command.

- **Maintaining statistics:** You can refresh your statistical sample by running either the UPDATE STATISTICS command, or invoking the sp_updatestats system stored procedure.

✔ **Better bulk operations:** These tasks, which involve moving large blocks of information in or out of your database, can often consume tremendous amounts of system resources. You would be wise to consider the optimal time to run these operations, as well as steps you can take to reduce their effect on your server. Chapter 9 discusses bulk operations, including the bcp utility, in more detail.

✔ **Use stored procedures, functions, and triggers:** These centralized bits of application logic stored in your database help protect your information while standardizing and enforcing business rules. As a side benefit, in certain cases, this concentration can also augment system responsiveness. Check out Chapters 14 and 15 to get a better picture of these objects.

✔ **Efficient applications:** It may sound obvious, but even the best, most effectively structured database can collapse under the load of a badly designed, improperly programmed software application. While you may not win any friends among your developer compatriots, you need to implore them to write their application code as economically as possible.

Chapter 6

Distributing Your Data with Replication

*W*ith hardware costs plummeting, network bandwidth charges dropping like a stone, and free software (such as SQL Server 2005 Express) all the rage, chances are that you might have two or more networked computers at your disposal. Even though it's a free product, SQL Server 2005 Express has many features that can help you leverage this extra horsepower to build database applications that are faster, cheaper, and more reliable.

In this chapter, you discover how to take advantage of the SQL Server 2005 Express replication features, which enable you to spread your information and processing load across multiple servers.

Replication is one of those topics that can overwhelm you with its nuances and complexities. Luckily, it doesn't have to. Simply stated, SQL Server's replication is an easy-to-implement, automated set of processes for distributing data among multiple machines. These computers can be in the same physical location, or they may be spread across the world and connected via the Internet. Regardless of your unique computer distribution, replication helps keep your SQL Server 2005 Express database in sync with other database servers.

Determining When and Why to Replicate

Replication makes a lot of sense in two common types of circumstances.

- ✔ **Reporting/data warehouse:** In this scenario, your goal is to distribute information from your primary database servers onto secondary computers. These additional processors are then available to serve up reports, business intelligence, or any other query-intensive service. Some of these reports may be interactive, while others may be generated as part of a daily, weekly, or monthly scheduled job.

  By using replication, you can automate the potentially cumbersome task of keeping these database servers in sync; you also greatly reduce the chance for errors and other synchronization problems to sneak their way into your environment.

- ✔ **Information archiving/backup:** Backing up or otherwise archiving your valuable SQL Server 2005 Express-based information is one way to improve the health and happiness of any database administrator. While replication is not intended to replace standard database backups per se, it's often used as an adjunct to this vital system administration task.

Given these common scenarios, replication offers many benefits for those database administrators who take the time to implement a solid data distribution strategy. Here are some of its most compelling advantages:

- ✔ **Shared workload:** Spreading information among multiple computers means that you can let users on those machines work with local copies of their data, rather than forcing a central database server to shoulder the entire workload.

  In many cases, these other computers have ample capacity to process just about any kind of database-related task. This helps lighten the load on your primary database server.

- ✔ **Safeguarded data:** When combined with a stringent backup strategy, data replication offers additional protection for your important data. Simply put, distributing your information among many different database servers greatly reduces the likelihood of a complete loss of data, even if the core database server is damaged or otherwise made unusable.

- ✔ **Reduced costs:** Replication is one way to put more client computers to work, which helps reduce the amount of processor-intensive labor on the part of your central database server. This can often spell the difference between using this principal server as-is, or being forced into an expensive hardware upgrade.

Discovering the Types of Replication

Each of the three major flavors of replication is useful for different situations and architectures:

- **Transactional:** For this type of replication, your SQL Server 2005 Express server receives data modifications nearly instantaneously. If you need to know every alteration as soon as it happens, this architecture is probably right for you. On the other hand, if your data doesn't change that often, or if you have a slow network connection, you'll likely want to employ one of the following two replication blueprints.

- **Snapshot:** Just as you might surmise from its name, this type of replication copies a full image of your database to the remote servers. It's a good choice when you don't need up-to-the minute updates, or when your data doesn't change that often. The downside is that subscribers may miss out on a data alteration until the next snapshot.

- **Merge:** This replication architecture makes the most sense when you expect multiple database servers to be modifying the same underlying information at the same time. For example, you might distribute portions of your master customer database to multiple subscribers. Each subscriber is free to make alterations to this database; alterations can't happen with the two other scenarios. Merge replication, as its name suggests, is SQL Server's way of blending this data to preserve accuracy and information cohesion.

Understanding Replication Limitations

By now, you're probably wondering if all this great functionality comes without any strings attached. Alas, replication has some restrictions, at least when dealing with SQL Server 2005 Express. The good news is that replication works just fine for the two major scenarios (reporting/data warehouse and information archiving/backup) that I describe earlier in the section "Determining When and Why to Replicate"; the bad news is that all the following are factors to consider with this entry-level database product:

- **No publications; subscription only:** This limitation means that any data that you create or modify on your SQL Server 2005 Express server can't in turn be published for other database servers to consume. However, this restriction doesn't have a major impact on the two primary replication cases I describe earlier because both examples describe situations where SQL Server 2005 Express is the final destination for replicated information.

✔ **Server-based, push-only subscriptions:** Because there is no agent present in SQL Server 2005 Express, you may not initiate a subscription request from a computer running this edition. Instead, you must first configure subscriptions on the remote server; only then can you request access to this information from the computer running SQL Server 2005 Express.

✔ **Ease-of-use:** Until the release of SQL Server Management Studio Express, setting up subscriptions on your SQL Server 2005 Express database server meant rolling up your sleeves and diving into either Transact-SQL or programming to the Replication Management Objects (RMO) guidelines. Fortunately, this graphical tool makes replication an easily obtainable reality in your environment.

✔ **SQL Server-only subscriptions:** Although SQL Server is a solid, industrial-strength database server, other types of information repositories are out there. Unfortunately, although the more expensive editions of SQL Server support directly subscribing to alternate sources of information such as Oracle, you don't have this option with SQL Server 2005 Express. However, you could use one of these higher-level SQL Server editions as a proxy for a different brand of database server; it could manage a subscription, and then publish the results to which you can subscribe.

Now that the fine print is out of the way, it's time to look at all the replication components and architecture.

Replication Concepts

At its heart, SQL Server replication consists of interaction among several components, and each has an important role to play. To make things clearer, I segregate them by whether they play a role in publishing or subscribing. I also list them from the smallest objects to the largest.

Components for publishing

✔ **Article:** This unit of information is the smallest that you can replicate. It typically consists of data from a table, stored procedure, view, and so on.

✔ **Publication:** This grouping consists of at least one, and possibly many more articles. An identifiable relationship is usually among all the articles in a given publication.

✔ **Publisher:** This database server offers up publications (which in turn consist of articles) for other database servers to subscribe.

✔ **Distributor:** Much like the middleman who facilitates transactions in the real world, the distributor is an instance of SQL Server that is responsible for managing all the replication details of one or more publishers. In fact, the distributor and publisher commonly work together on one machine.

Components for subscribing

✔ **Subscription:** Just as you can subscribe to your favorite magazine, you can set up a subscription to a publication. Unlike magazine subscriptions, however, you can configure when it should arrive, and how it should be sent to the subscriber.

✔ **Subscriber:** This database instance serves as the destination for subscriptions. It's important to note that publishers and subscribers can reside on the same machine, although they're typically found on separate computers.

Setting Up Replication

If you've read through the chapter to this point, you're probably itching to get started with replication. If so, this section is for you. Here's what you need to do to make replication a reality in your environment. To begin, I use the transactional style of replication; you can easily choose one of the other flavors if it's more appropriate for your environment.

When setting up publications and subscriptions, you can elect to use a combination of Transact-SQL and stored procedures, or you can put your effort into SQL Server Management Studio. The graphical tools are so much easier to use that for this example, I place all the focus on them.

Your first task is to set up the publication and articles on the publisher.

SQL Server 2005 Express lacks the capabilities to publish information: It can only serve as a subscriber. This means that you need to run the next few steps on a version of SQL Server 2005 (such as Workgroup, Standard, or Enterprise) that supports information publication.

Here's how to publish data:

1. **Launch SQL Server Management Studio.**

2. **Connect to the database server that will publish the data.**

3. **Expand the Replication folder.**

4. **Right-click the Local Publications folder, and choose the New Publication option.**

   The New Publication Wizard launches, which walks you through all necessary steps to get your data published.

5. **Fill in all the relevant details in each dialog box.**

   Pay particular attention to the Articles dialog box (shown in Figure 6-1), which is where you select those objects for publication.

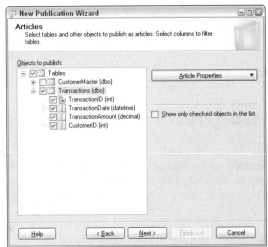

Figure 6-1:
Choosing
objects
to be
published.

After you identify the objects to publish, you can also specify any filtering criteria that you want applied to help reduce the number of items sent for replication.

6. **Decide if you want to create an immediate snapshot.**

   If you're replicating to an empty database, choosing this option is a good idea.

7. **After you finish, review the publication's properties, and click Finish (as shown in Figure 6-2) to complete your work.**

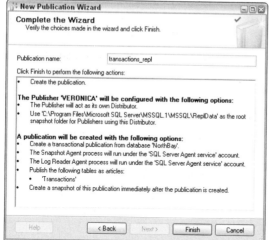

Figure 6-2:
Reviewing
details
about the
publication.

That's the publisher's perspective on things. Here's what to do on the subscriber side:

1. **Launch SQL Server Management Studio or SQL Server Management Studio Express.**

2. **Connect to the database server that will receive the data.**

3. **Expand the Replication folder.**

4. **Right-click the Local Subscriptions folder, and choose the New Subscription option.**

   The New Subscription Wizard launches, which walks you through all necessary steps to subscribe to an existing publication.

5. **Fill in all relevant details in each dialog box.**

   Pay particular attention to the database that you want to receive the subscription. You don't even need to have created a table; the initial synchronization takes care of that if you want.

6. **When you finish, review the subscription's properties and click Finish to get things going.**

   Figure 6-3 shows a summary of a new subscription. Note that for this example, the publisher and subscriber are on the same machine. Obviously, they can also be on separate machines (and usually are).

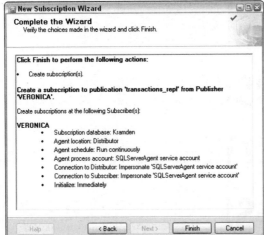

Figure 6-3:
Summariz-
ing a new
subscription.

That's all you need to do. Depending on how you configured your publications and subscriptions, information should begin flowing around your network. And the best part is that SQL Server is doing all the work. If you want to observe the data movement, you can launch the replication monitor by right-clicking the Replication folder in SQL Server Management Studio, and choosing the Launch Replication Monitor option.

Part III

Adding and Accessing a SQL Server 2005 Express Database

The 5th Wave

By Rich Tennant

@RICHTENNANT

"Your database is beyond repair, but before I tell you our backup recommendation, let me ask you a question. How many index cards do you think will fit on the walls of your computer room?"

In this part . . .

After downloading, installing, and configuring your SQL Server 2005 Express database server, you're ready to start putting it to the test: storing, retrieving, and managing information. For that reason, in this part I discuss important design concepts that you should keep in mind as you plan your relational database.

From there, I move on to showing you how to create important objects, such as databases and tables, and explaining the SQL Server 2005 Express database access language (Transact-SQL). Finally, I demonstrate a few nifty advanced techniques for pushing Transact-SQL to the limits.

Chapter 7

Planning Your Database

. . . .

In This Chapter

▶ Deciding what you want to store in your database

▶ Building an entity relationship model

▶ Migrating from your entity relationship model to a relational model

▶ Following good relational database design practices

. . . .

Chances are that you went through all the work involved in acquiring and then installing SQL Server 2005 Express so that you could store and manage information, rather than just admire your server from afar. In this chapter, I give you a good idea of how to set up your database to handle whatever kind of data you throw at it.

As you go about creating your database, understanding the differences between your logical and physical database design is important, as well as how to take advantage of some of the best relational database design practices discovered over the years.

Finally, SQL Server Management Studio Express, available for free download from Microsoft, offers some very handy tools for designing and relating SQL Server 2005 Express tables, so I spend some time at the end of this chapter showing you how to make your own diagrams.

What Can You Store in a Database?

Over the years, databases have become more and more flexible with regard to what they let you keep in them. While you can't store tasty snacks, car keys, or Christmas presents in a relational database (yet), Table 7-1 shows all the data types that you can place in SQL Server 2005 Express.

Table 7-1	SQL Server 2005 Express Data Types
Data Type	*Holds*
bigint	Integers between –9.22 billion and 9.22 billion
binary	Fixed-length binary data, up to 8000 bytes in size
bit	A one or a zero (also known as TRUE or FALSE)
char	Fixed-length non-Unicode character data, up to 8000 bytes long
datetime	A timestamp between January 1, 1753 and December 31, 9999
decimal	Numbers with fixed precision and scale, ranging from –10^38 to 10^38
float	Floating-point data; can have an enormous range
image	Variable length binary data; can be up to 2GB in size
int	Integers between –2.1 billion and 2.1 billion
money	Decimal numbers between –922 trillion and 922 trillion
nchar	Fixed-length Unicode character data, up to 4000 bytes long
ntext	Variable-length Unicode data; can be up to 2GB in size
numeric	Numbers with fixed precision and scale, ranging from –10^38 to 10^38
nvarchar	Variable-length Unicode character data; can be very large if space permits
real	Floating-point data; can have an enormous range
smalldatetime	A timestamp between January 1, 1900 and June 6, 2079
smallint	Integers between –32,768 and 32,768
smallmoney	Decimal numbers between –214 thousand and 214 thousand
text	Variable-length non-Unicode data; can be up to 2GB in size
timestamp	Generates automatic, unique binary numbers
tinyint	Integers between 0 and 255

Data Type	Holds
uniqueidentifier	Creates a system-wide unique identifier (GUID)
varbinary	Variable-length binary data; can be very large if space permits
varchar	Variable-length non-Unicode character data; can be very large if space permits
XML	Up to 2GB of XML-based data

If all these data types aren't enough for you, you can even create your own specialized data types via the SQL Server 2005 Express user-defined type feature.

You can use the CREATE TYPE statement to define your own, personalized alias data types. This statement essentially creates a synonym for the data type, which can be very useful when building your database.

For example, suppose your project has multiple database designers, and that each of them is responsible for building some tables that will track addresses. Furthermore, imagine that you want to standardize all your address fields as variable length and character-based fields that hold up to 60 bytes (VARCHAR(60)).

You could rely on each designer to adhere to your request, but you're likely to be sorely disappointed. The odds are that each designer will implement his or her own interpretation of what an address should be. Some will choose fixed character fields, while others will use the VARCHAR type, but set it at a different length than the 60 you require.

Using the CREATE TYPE statement as your guide, here's how to enforce consistency for these fields:

```
CREATE TYPE ADDRESS FROM VARCHAR(60) NOT NULL
```

Now, your designers can use ADDRESS whenever they create a table that needs to track address information:

```
CREATE TABLE shipping_info
(
    ShippingID INT PRIMARY KEY NOT NULL,
    StreetAddress ADDRESS,
...
)
```

When SQL Server 2005 Express reports on your table, it helpfully provides both the ADDRESS alias, as well as the fact that this alias translates to a VARCHAR(60).

Designing Your Database

After you familiarize yourself with all the categories of information that you can store in a database, you can come up with a good design. Although each database design project is different, they typically begin at the logical design level, where you model the relationships among all the major data that you want to track. After you nail down the logical design, your next job is to translate that model into the physical elements and tables that you'll create in SQL Server 2005 Express.

Logical design

Building a logical design is quite simple. All you need to do is identify the major entities, itemize any of their attributes, and determine how they relate to other entities. *Entities* are specific, real-world objects that exist in your database. *Attributes* are characteristics of each entity.

Although end-users can be picky and a real drag to deal with, interviewing the eventual users of your database to see what they want you to build is the only way to build a good database. As a bonus, they probably have a good idea what real-world entities exist, as well as how the entities relate to each other. By including the user in the design process, you can go a long way toward building something of value and quality.

Here's an example of a logical design. Suppose that you're building a system to track ticketing and seating for sporting events. In this case, you would quickly classify several entities, along with key attributes. These include

- ✔ The ticket
  - Ticket holder's name
  - Price paid for ticket
  - Date and time ticket was purchased
- ✔ The seat
  - Seat location
  - List price
- ✔ The event
  - Date of the event
  - Time of the event

After you categorize all the major entities, all you need to do now is figure out how they relate. Armed with that intelligence, you can then build your *entity relationship model.* In fact, many tools on the market make drawing your entity relationship model a breeze. Figure 7-1 shows a nice example of a simple entity relationship model from the ticketing scenario. I used Microsoft Visio to draw this diagram.

Figure 7-1:
A basic
entity
relationship
diagram.

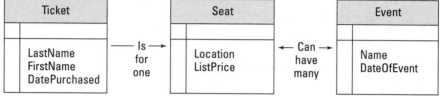

Ticket		Seat		Event
LastName FirstName DatePurchased	— Is → for one	Location ListPrice	← Can → have many	Name DateOfEvent

As you build your entity relationship diagrams, try to use natural language to describe their relationships. This goes a long way toward helping you design a database that works in the real world.

Physical design

A database's physical design refers to concrete, real-world, database-oriented objects. These include

- Tables
- Columns
- Relationships
- Indexes

Now that your logical design is done, the last step to building a working, real-world relational database is to convert the logical database into a physical database.

Although exceptions always abound, the general rule is to take each major entity and turn it into a table. In turn, all attributes for each entity become a column. If a many-to-many relationship exists between two tables, you probably need to create a third table to serve as a storage area for the attributes that identify the relationship.

Make sure that you're not turning an attribute into its own table. For example, if you're tracking information about a customer, the phone number is usually an attribute of the customer entity, which means that it would belong as a column in the `Customer` table. However, if you expect to track variable quantities of phone numbers for a customer, you could consider making the phone number its own entity and giving it a dedicated table.

When you define your tables and columns, your next step is to use the relationships from your entity relationship diagram to help you figure out what kind of indexes and keys you need to build. I discuss relationships among tables, including primary and foreign keys, in much more detail in Chapters 8 and 10.

Using Database Diagram Tools in SQL Server Management Studio Express

SQL Server Management Studio Express offers some nifty database diagramming tools. Not only do they give you a good picture of your database, they can also save you from having to write extensive Data Definition Language (DDL) code. Here's how to get started:

1. **Launch SQL Server Management Studio Express.**

   Make sure you can see the Object Explorer. If it's not visible, you can open it by choosing View➪Object Explorer.

2. **Connect to the appropriate server.**

   If you don't see any connections, now is a good time to add one. Just click the Connect Object Explorer icon. When you finish, you can proceed to Step 3.

3. **Expand the specific database that you want to diagram.**

4. **Right-click Database Diagrams and choose New Database Diagram.**

   A new, blank diagram is created. You may first be asked if you approve creating objects to enable diagramming. Answer Yes to any of these requests.

5. **Highlight one or more tables that you want to include in the diagram, and then click Add followed by Close.**

   The tables are placed on the palette. If any relationships are already defined for the tables, they show up here.

6. **After making any necessary changes, make sure to save your work by clicking the Save icon or choosing File➪Save Diagram.**

What kinds of changes can you make to a table after placing it on a diagram? As it turns out, quite a few:

- Rename the table.

- Enter some descriptive text about the table.

- Change the schema to which the table belongs.

- Set a variety of other table properties.

- Update any of a wide selection of properties for any of the columns present in the table.

    You can even add a new column if you forgot to include it earlier.

All this is great, but suppose that all you want to do is add a new table and relate it to one of the other tables already on your palette. Simply follow these steps:

1. **Right-click anywhere on the diagram and choose Add Table.**

2. **Select the table you want to add, and then click Add followed by Close.**

    With the table on the palette, you're now ready to create the relationship.

3. **Click the column that will serves as your join key, and draw a line to its partner.**

    Figure 7-2 shows a simple database diagram that has a foreign key relationship defined between two tables. Of course, you can easily construct much more robust, intricate diagrams.

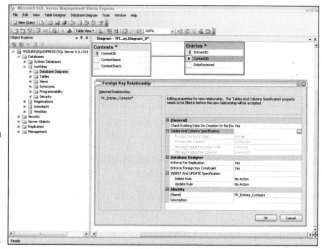

Figure 7-2:
The Visual Studio database diagram tool.

Normalization

After you define your tables and columns, making sure you conformed to the best practices and rules of relational database design is a good idea. One of the best-known rules is normalization, which I discuss throughout the rest of this chapter.

While you might think that *database normalization* means that you're forced to clean up your information and remove any eccentric, troublemaking, or otherwise wacky data, it's actually just a collection of increasingly rigid principles and guidelines that you can use to conceive a well-designed relational database.

In this section, you find out about the three major normalization rules, including when you should use them. And because all rules are made to be broken, the next section clues you in on some situations when you can side-step these regulations.

First normal form

As the most lenient data normalization rule, the first normal form simply requires that a table not have any repeating fields. Taking a shortcut and violating this rule is very tempting, but you'll probably regret doing so in the long run. For example, suppose that you're building an employee management database, and want to keep track of the names of your employees' dependents. Table 7-2 is one way that you could design a table to store this information.

Table 7-2		Employee Dependents		
Name	*Dependent1*	*Dependent2*	*Dependent3*	*Dependent4*
Flint	Wilma	Pebbles	Barney	Derek
Newhart	Larry	Darryl	Darryl2	
Sanford	Lamont	Esther		

So far, so good. But what happens when Mike Brady joins the firm? He has six children, a wife, and a maid, which — in addition to being an insurance nightmare — means that you must now change this table's structure. That's a risky move, one that could break applications that were built with the original table in mind. Here's where the first normal form comes to the rescue.

Tables 7-3 and 7-4 can handle employees with zero, one, or many dependents; no changes are necessary to cope with more dependents.

Table 7-3	Employees
Name	
Flint	
Newhart	
Brady	
Sanford	

Table 7-4	Employee Dependents
Name	*Dependent*
Flint	Wilma
Flint	Pebbles
...	
Brady	Alice
Brady	Robert

Now the Bradys can have ten children if they like, and your database and applications can handle these joyous events without any extra work for you.

Second normal form

Things get a little sterner with the second normal form. This rule requires that each column in a table is functionally dependent on the primary key. A *primary key* is one or more columns that, when taken together, serve to uniquely identify a particular row. There can be no duplicate primary key values in a given table.

In this case, suppose that you have built a database to track heating and air conditioning work that your company delivers. Table 7-5 shows a small sample list of these procedures.

Table 7-5	Maintenance History	
Customer	*ServiceDate*	*Procedure*
ScrapCo	10/17/2006	Clean refrigeration units, change filters
Ivanhoe Paper	12/30/2006	Install and tune heating coils
High Hat Airways	6/10/2007	Clean refrigeration units, change filters

For this table, assume that the primary key is the combination of the `Customer` and `ServiceDate` columns, while the `Procedure` column contains a fixed set of services offered by your firm. Storing this text in this table violates the second normal form; it is not functionally dependent on the primary key. It would be a better design if you separated these procedures into their own table, and placed an identifier in the maintenance history table. Tables 7-6 and 7-7 make this clear.

Table 7-6	Procedure List
ProcedureID	*Procedure*
118	Clean refrigeration units, change filters
119	Install and tune heating coils
120	Remove old equipment, replace grating

Table 7-7	Maintenance History, Now Supporting the Second Normal Form	
Customer	*ServiceDate*	*ProcedureID*
ScrapCo	10/17/2006	118
Ivanhoe Paper	12/30/2006	119
High Hat Airways	6/10/2007	118

This design is cleaner and more efficient. For one thing, if you decide to change the exact wording of a procedure, you need to change it in one place only. You reduce the chance for errors, and help improve consistency. You also store substantially less data in the `Maintenance History` table, because the `ProcedureID` column now holds a simple number, rather than a long set of text.

Third normal form

Now you're in the land of the database professors. The third normal form takes the second normal form, and adds even more regulations: No transitive dependencies are allowed. A *transitive dependency* exists when a table has a specific column that is not designated as a key, but it still defines other columns. Extending the maintenance example from before, suppose that you added another column to the Maintenance History table (Table 7-7), as shown in Table 7-8.

Table 7-8	Maintenance History, with Additional Data		
Customer	*ServiceDate*	*ProcedureID*	*Outstanding Balance*
ScrapCo	10/17/2006	118	$1783.33
Ivanhoe Paper	12/30/2006	119	$0.00
High Hat Airways	6/10/2007	118	$27,601.00

Although it's not obvious, this table violates the third normal form. The `Customer` column is not the primary key (although the combination of it plus the `ServiceDate` column is). However, it does define the `Outstanding Balance` column, which really belongs in a master table, rather than in this set of detailed data. To get in line with the third normal form is pretty easy in this case, as you can see in Tables 7-9 and 7-10.

Table 7-9	Customer Master, Containing Additional Header Information	
Customer	...	*Outstanding Balance*
ScrapCo	...	$1783.33
Ivanhoe Paper	...	$0.00
High Hat Airways	...	$27,601.00

Table 7-10	Maintenance History, in Compliance with the Third Normal Form	
Customer	*ServiceDate*	*ProcedureID*
ScrapCo	10/17/2006	118
Ivanhoe Paper	12/30/2006	119
High Hat Airways	6/10/2007	118

Now all the header information is contained in the `Customer Master` table (Table 7-9), and the detailed maintenance records are in the `Maintenance History` table (Table 7-10). It can be tricky to figure out when you break any of these rules. As you'll see in a moment, sometimes breaking a rule is smart.

When not to normalize

Sometimes, the three normal forms are just too restrictive and harsh. Fortunately, your computer won't crash and the world won't end if you decide to bend the rules a little bit. This section points out a couple of occasions when you are perfectly justified in violating strict normalization rules.

Historical data

Imagine that you're processing millions of rows a month. These rows are stored in one main transaction table. In most cases, customers are only interested in recent transactions — those that have happened in the past two months.

For situations like this, splitting your data into at least two tables is okay: current and historic information. These tables would have an identical structure, but would contain fresh and old data, respectively. Every month, you could move records from the current table into the archive table, perhaps as part of a large batch processing operation.

Calculated values

In most cases, permanently storing any calculated values (sums, averages, and so on) in your database is not wise. Instead, you're better off calculating them at runtime. This avoids problems with stale data, especially if the underlying detail data changes often. In some cases, however breaking this rule and keeping these calculated values in your database makes sense. This usually happens with massive amounts of data to process, and very little time to do it.

For example, suppose that you're maintaining a distributed retail management system. Your company is doing very well; you have tens of thousands of customers each day, which yields hundreds of thousands of transactions each month. What if your users want to run queries that summarize these transactions in a number of different ways? If you try to calculate these answers at runtime, you run the risk of performance degradation. In this type of scenario, maintaining a lookup table that contains commonly requested calculated values makes sense. You could then update this table during times when there isn't much activity. Table 7-11 is an example of a summary table.

Table 7-11	Transaction Summary		
Region	*Average Sale*	*Number Customers*	*Maximum Sale...*
Northeast	81.30	18,302	199.85
Midwest	79.14	22,099	287.15
West	84.92	21,142	309.11

Now, when users need to get calculated summary data, they can consult this table instead of launching fishing expeditions through the main transaction table.

When you're faced with a massive data table that you want to split up and denormalize, and you've chosen to upgrade to a more feature-rich edition of the SQL Server product family, consider using the *partitioning feature*. This feature lets you break up a table and spread its load across your environment. Three types of partitioning are available:

- **Hardware:** This style of partitioning leverages fast hardware devices such as the CPU and multiple disk drives to help even out your information processing.

- **Vertical:** When you apply vertical partitioning to a table, SQL Server divides one table containing the entire set of columns into two or more tables, each containing just a subset of the original columns.

- **Horizontal:** This kind of partitioning creates identical copies of a table, and then spreads the data among all the tables. The criteria for distributing the data are usually determined by a database designer or administrator. A good example would be to instruct SQL Server to distribute a table based on last names: A-F goes to one location, G-K to another, and so on. The databases are responsible for sending the information to its rightful place after you specify the distribution rules. Note that this type of partitioning is only available in SQL Server Enterprise Edition.

Chapter 8

Creating Databases, Tables, and Relationships

*W*hen you want to store information in SQL Server 2005 Express, your first responsibility is to define a database that will serve as a container for your records. Your next job is to create the tables where the actual data will reside, along with any restrictions on what you can place in these tables. Finally, by defining relationships among your information, you help SQL Server 2005 Express ensure good data integrity and protect your business rules.

In this chapter, you see how to accomplish all these tasks. To begin, you get the hang of using the handy (and free) SQL Server Management Studio Express tool, which lets you do all the database management tasks I describe throughout the chapter. Because you may have other preferences when working with a data management tool, I also show you some different approaches you can take to achieve the same results.

Using SQL Server Management Studio Express

SQL Server Management Studio Express packs a lot of features into a small (and free!) package. You can use it to

- ✔ View the structure of your SQL Server 2005 Express instance, including databases, tables, views, stored procedures, and so on.
- ✔ Connect to other SQL Server instances.
- ✔ Perform many administrative tasks.
- ✔ Run queries and other data access jobs.
- ✔ View results, or export them to text files.

Not bad for a free tool! You can download it from the Microsoft Web site (www.microsoft.com/sql/editions/express/default.mspx); installation is a snap. Here's a brief tour through the product, highlighting those features that you're most likely to use right away.

First, launch SQL Server Management Studio Express by choosing Start➪ All Programs➪Microsoft SQL Server 2005➪SQL Server Management Studio Express. You're prompted with a dialog box that lets you specify which server you want to connect, as well as your login details.

Depending on how you've configured your environment, you'll notice that the user interface is divided among several components. One of the most important of these entities is the Object Explorer, which I describe next.

The Object Explorer

The Object Explorer in the SQL Server Management Studio Express user interface is responsible for listing, in tree format, the following vital bits of information:

- ✔ **The connection:** This portion of the tree tells you about the connection, including the names of the computer and SQL Server 2005 Express instances.
- ✔ **Database details:** If you expand the Databases folder, you're treated to a collection of really important system folders. These include a list of system databases, as well as an inventory of your own databases.

Expand any of your database folders and you see details broken out as follows:

- **Database Diagrams:** Here's where you can get a graphical view of your information, including the relationships you've defined among objects in your database.

- **Tables:** The contents of this folder are divided between system tables, which are provided for and looked after by SQL Server 2005 Express, and user tables. Each table further breaks down into columns and indexes.

- **Views:** Views are virtual tables, composed of information from one or more "real" tables. If you expand this folder, you see a list of both system and user-defined views. Opening a particular view yields a list of the columns that make up the view.

- **Synonyms:** These are substitute names for objects in your database.

- **Programmability:** Here's where you can get a list of all your system and user-defined stored procedures, including their input and output parameters. You can also find out about your functions via this tree entry.

- **Security:** This folder itemizes all the users who have access to your database.

✔ **Security:** The Security folder contains all the login names for people who are authorized to use your database server, along with the server roles and credentials you've set up. Note that this folder is different than the Security folder within a database. The latter simply lists all those already authorized database server users who also have access to that database.

✔ **Server Objects:** This folder holds details about those devices that you've defined for backup purposes, as well as any servers linked to this database server, and any triggers that have been defined on the server.

✔ **Replication:** SQL Server 2005 Express offers the ability to subscribe to data feeds from other SQL Server instances. This folder cites any active subscriptions.

✔ **Management:** You can view a collection of your SQL Server logs, including current and archived versions. These are excellent sources of diagnostic information about your database server.

Figure 8-1 is an example of the SQL Server Management Studio Express Object Explorer, with many of its folders expanded.

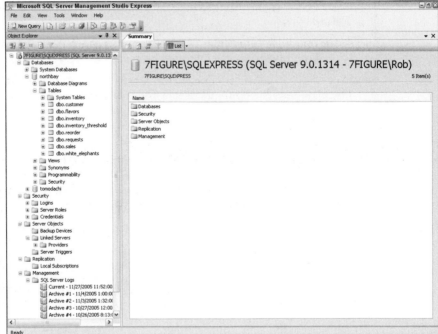

Figure 8-1:
The SQL
Server
Management
Studio
Express
Object
Explorer.

To get the latest-and-greatest view of everything about your SQL Server 2005 Express instance, right-click anywhere on the Object Explorer tree and choose Refresh.

The Query window

The Query window is where you and SQL Server 2005 Express get to know each other, up close and personal. The workspace contains input windows (described as the *Query Editor*) for queries and other data interaction. You can also elect to have your output show up at the bottom of the screen in the area (described as the *Output window*). You can create as many Query Editor windows as you need simply by clicking the New Query icon on the Standard toolbar.

When you're comfortable working in the workspace, you can decide how and where you want your results to appear. You have three options; click one of these icons at the top of the window:

✔ **Text:** This formats your output into simple text, and places it in the Output window.

✔ **Grid:** This option provides more attractive results, placing them into a grid at the bottom of the Output window.

✔ **File:** This is the "to-go" option for your queries. SQL Server 2005 Express takes the results and nicely places them in a text file.

Creating Key Database Objects

In this section, I show you how to use a combination of graphical and text tools to create and maintain major database objects.

Databases

Creating, altering, and deleting databases are significant events in the life of your SQL Server 2005 Express environment. However, none of these tasks requires much heavy lifting, as you'll now see.

Creating a database

To create a database, just follow these steps:

1. **Launch SQL Server Management Studio Express.**

2. **Connect to the appropriate SQL Server 2005 Express instance.**

3. **Expand the connection's entry in the Object Explorer.**

4. **Highlight the Databases folder.**

5. **Right-click this folder, and choose New Database.**

   The New Database dialog box appears (as shown in Figure 8-2) that lets you specify the new database's name, as well as a collection of properties about the new database.

6. **Enter values for these prompts (as shown in Figure 8-3), and click OK.**

   In many cases, you can safely accept the default values from the Options page.

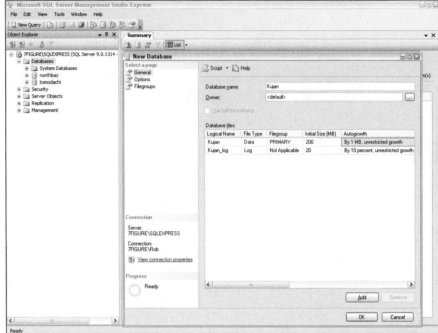

Figure 8-2:
Creating a
database in
SQL Server
Management
Studio
Express.

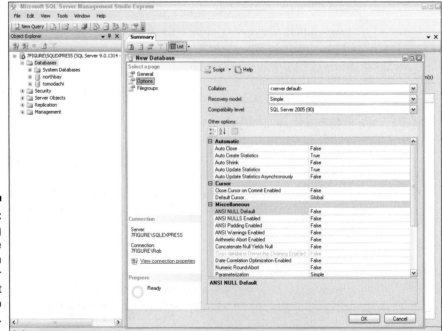

Figure 8-3:
Setting
database
properties in
SQL Server
Management
Studio
Express.

Renaming a database

After you have a database in place, renaming it is easy:

1. **Launch SQL Server Management Studio Express.**
2. **Connect to the appropriate SQL Server 2005 Express instance.**
3. **Expand the connection's entry in the Object Explorer.**
4. **Expand the Databases folder.**
5. **Right-click the database whose name you want to change, and choose the Rename option.**
6. **Enter a new name of your choice for the database, and press Enter to save your modification.**

Deleting a database

When the time comes to say goodbye to a database, all you need to do is follow these steps:

1. **Launch SQL Server Management Studio Express.**
2. **Connect to the appropriate SQL Server 2005 Express instance.**
3. **Expand the connection's entry in the Object Explorer.**
4. **Expand the Databases folder.**
5. **Right-click the database that you want to remove, and choose the Delete option.**
6. **Click OK in the confirmation dialog box.**

Renaming and dropping databases can be hazardous to your applications' health. Creating a backup is a good idea before making changes of this magnitude. The sanity you save may be your own. Check out Chapter 13 for more about archiving your information.

Tables

Tables are where the rubber meets the road in a database: they dutifully store your vital information. I show you how to create and maintain these important structures.

Creating a table

After you decide that you want to create a new table, bringing it into existence is easy. You have two major routes that you can follow: SQL/application code versus a graphical tool. In the following list, I describe the advantages and drawbacks of each:

- ✔ **SQL/application code:** Choosing this route means that you directly enter, via either SQL or an application programming language, the exact syntax that you want to create your table. This approach has some very compelling advantages:

  - **Power and flexibility:** You can specify exactly what you want to happen; a graphical tool may not be able to specify all the nuances that you can in SQL.

  - **Repeatability:** You can group your table creation statements into a script or program that you can run again and again. This is much less tedious than having to manually create the table in a graphical tool.

  - **Automation:** If you're shipping a self-installing application to external locations or need other automation features, creating your tables with SQL or application code is the only way to go. You definitely don't want to burden your users with the responsibility of using a graphical tool to manually create your tables.

  The main drawback to this approach is that it does require more understanding of SQL or the programming language of your choice.

- ✔ **Graphical tool:** This is the flip side of SQL. Using a graphical tool might just mean that you can escape all the vagaries of the `CREATE TABLE` statement. This is a laudable goal, so if your table designs are simple, and you don't want to learn any SQL, use the graphical tool of your choice to create your table.

  Many graphical tools on the market can create SQL Server 2005 Express tables. Figure 8-4 is an example of SQL Server Management Studio Express creating a table.

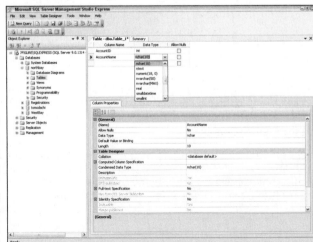

Figure 8-4:
Creating a table with SQL Server Management Studio Express.

If you change your mind, and suddenly become very curious about the CREATE TABLE statement, many of these graphical tools can generate the SQL for you, as well as show you what SQL they used to create your table.

Here's how to build tables, using SQL or another programming language:

1. **Open SQL Server Management Studio Express.**

2. **Open the Databases folder.**

3. **Expand the folder for your database.**

4. **Click the New Query button.**

5. **Type your SQL.**

   Here's a snippet of SQL that creates a basic table:

   ```
   CREATE TABLE partner
   (
       partner_id INTEGER PRIMARY KEY,
       partner_name VARCHAR(30),
       partner_area VARCHAR(10)
   );
   ```

6. **After you're ready to create the table, click the Execute button.**

7. **Check the results to make sure things ran correctly.**

   If they did, you receive a message like this:

   ```
   Command(s) completed successfully.
   ```

8. **If things ran successfully, save the code by clicking the Save button.**

   Make sure that you're in the Query window and not the results window before clicking the Save button.

You now have a table that's ready to be filled with important data, plus the actual code that built the table. How can you run this code again? You can run the code in at least two ways. First, you can simply open the file in SQL Server Management Studio Express, and click the Execute button to launch the SQL. Alternatively, you can use the SQLCMD tool to run the script from the command line.

SQLCMD is a very helpful utility that allows both batch and interactive access to SQL Server 2005 Express. Follow these steps to use SQLCMD:

1. **Open a command prompt.**

   Choose Start➪Run and enter **cmd**. Or choose Programs➪Accessories➪ Command Prompt. When you see the friendly command prompt, it's time to launch SQLCMD.

2. **Run SQLCMD, passing the proper parameters.**

   This can get a bit confusing: SQLCMD is rather picky about the exact syntax that it deigns to run. This is not surprising when you realize that it supports over two dozen parameters. Table 8-1 highlights a small group of key parameters.

   If you get in hot water, you can always ask SQLCMD for help:

   ```
   SQLCMD /?
   ```

3. **Run your script.**

   Here's an example of how I ran SQLCMD, along with the parameters I provided:

   ```
   SQLCMD -S dbserver -U Nicole -P Sierra -d WestBay -i
          build_abc.sql
   ```

Make sure that your script file is in the right directory; SQLCMD can't find it otherwise. Alternatively, provide a full path to the file.

Table 8-1	Key SQLCMD Parameters
Parameter	*Purpose*
-S	Specify the server that you want to connect to
-U	Provide your username
-P	Provide your password
-d	Which database to use
-i	The file containing your SQL script

Modifying a table

If you made a mistake when you created a table, don't despair! Modifying the table to your liking is no big deal. You can choose from several approaches when amending an existing table. The right approach is largely dependent on what kind of modification you're making.

If you're only renaming a table, here's the simplest way to make it happen:

1. **Open SQL Server Management Studio Express.**

2. **Open the Databases folder.**

3. **Expand the folder for your database.**

4. Expand the Tables folder.

5. Position the cursor on the table you want to rename, and click once.

6. Rename the table as you like, and press Enter.

That's all renaming takes! Now, if you want to make more complex changes, you'll probably need to use straight SQL or a more robust graphical tool. This is true for any of these kinds of adjustments:

✔ Adding a column

✔ Changing a column's data type

✔ Removing a column

✔ Changing default values, constraints, and so on

This is just a partial list; several other types of alterations require a visit to SQL land. Luckily, the SQL for these kinds of modifications is quite easy. Here's how to proceed:

1. Back up your table.

Mistakes happen to the best of us. To help recover from the slight possibility of catastrophic error, creating a backup is always a good idea before undertaking any kind of major database change.

2. Launch SQL Server Management Studio Express, and click on the New Query button.

Using SQL Server Management Studio Express makes the most sense; it's free, and provides great functionality. You can see your table's structure, which helps reduce the chance of any inadvertent SQL errors.

3. Type your SQL statement, or make the changes graphically.

I describe the SQL approach; however, when given the choice, you can opt for the graphical approach.

The ALTER statement is very flexible, and is generally the right choice for making table modifications. Of course, you need to make sure that you have permission to use this statement. After you have permission, here are some examples of ALTER in action. First, here's the original CREATE TABLE statement:

```
CREATE TABLE partner
(
    partner_id INTEGER PRIMARY KEY,
    partner_name VARCHAR(30),
    partner_area VARCHAR(10)
);
```

- **Dropping a column:** When you realize a certain column is no longer necessary, you can easily remove it:

```
ALTER TABLE partner DROP COLUMN partner_area;
```

  - **Adding a new column:** After dropping a column , you may want to bring it back. Fortunately, you only need to run the ALTER statement to re-create the column:

```
ALTER TABLE partner
ADD partner_area VARCHAR(10)
```

    - **Creating a default value constraint:** SQL Server 2005 Express lets you set up restrictions on your tables. These are known as *constraints*, and I discuss them a little later in this chapter. For now, here's a simple default value constraint for the partner_area column:

```
ALTER TABLE partner
ADD CONSTRAINT partner_area_unassigned
DEFAULT 'unassigned' FOR partner_area ;
```

4. **Run your statement.**

5. **Check for any problems.**

   If things work out okay, you receive a message like this:

```
Command(s) completed successfully.
```

   If you receive an error message, try modifying your SQL statement to correct the problem.

Removing a table

Getting rid of tables you no longer need is very easy. Just follow these simple steps.

1. **Back up your data.**

   Unless you're sure that you'll never need to set eyes on this data again, consider making a backup. Even if you don't need the data, you might need to re-create the table's structure at some point later.

2. **Choose the method you want to use.**

   You have numerous tools at your disposal when you create a table. The same holds true when dropping a table. Of all your choices, however, SQL Server Management Studio Express is the safest: Because you can see all your tables, you more than likely won't delete the wrong table.

3. **Drop the table.**

The SQL syntax for deleting a table is very simple:

```
DROP TABLE SoonToBeGone;
```

You don't need to first delete any of the table's data or remove any of its indexes or relationships: The DROP statement takes care of all cleanup.

Relationships

In terms of SQL Server 2005 Express, relationships do not mean how well your data gets along with its friends, co-workers, or neighbors. Instead, relationships describe the interdependencies among the data stored in different tables. Relationships have three main classes:

✔ **One-to-one:** A one-to-one relationship means that a row in Table A has one (and only one) corresponding row in Table B. For example, you might track client information such as name, address, and so on in a Customers table. At the same time, you might want to follow details about each client's credit rating in a secondary CreditStatus table.

These two tables have a one-to-one relationship. A client can have one and only one credit rating; a credit rating can belong to one and only one client.

✔ **One-to-many:** A one-to-many relationship exists whenever rows from Table A can have many related rows in Table B, yet Table B's rows can only be related back to one row in Table A. Continuing with the previous example, suppose that you want to track order information for each client. These details reside in an Orders table. A customer can have many orders, but each order belongs to one and only one customer.

✔ **Many-to-many:** This kind of relationship exists when a row in Table A can have many related rows in Table B, and vice-versa. This kind of relationship is very common in relational databases, and generally requires that you create an intermediate table to store both sides of the relationship. Continuing with the previous customer and order examples, suppose that you're tracking the items that each customer has ordered. You keep your master item list in an Items table. A customer can order many items; an item can be ordered by many different customers.

In this case, you need to create a table to store an identifier for each customer who has ordered an item, and the identifiers for this item. These kinds of tables usually take the names of both sides of the relationship, so CustomerItems is a good choice. Using this intermediary table, you can then construct useful queries from both perspectives. You can ask SQL Server 2005 Express for a list of all customers who purchased an item, as well as all the items purchased by a given customer.

Enforcing relationships

As a database designer or developer, you specify relationships when you create the table. You can also add them after the fact, by creating or altering tables. But after you create your relationships, how do you enforce them? Thankfully, enforcement in SQL Server 2005 Express doesn't require guilt or the threat of force. Instead, all you need to do is use a combination of indexes and your table definition syntax.

Primary keys and relationships

A *primary key* is made up of one or more columns that serve to uniquely identify a row in a table. By defining a primary key, you're telling SQL Server 2005 Express not to allow two or more rows in the table to have the same value in the primary key column(s). For example, you may decide that your `Customer` table has a primary key called `CustomerID`. No two rows in this table may have the same value in that column, which helps in enforcing relationships. Without the primary key rule, you could inadvertently create two customers with the same `CustomerID`, which breaks the one-to-one and one-to-many relationships.

Foreign keys and relationships

A *foreign key* establishes a relationship between two tables. When you define a foreign key, you tell SQL Server 2005 Express to prevent rows from being added or altered in a given table unless another table has a corresponding row. A good example is what happens when you want to add an order to the `Orders` table I cite in the previous section, "Relationships." To do it right, you must first make sure that no record of this customer is already present in the `Customers` table. If it doesn't exist, then you need to create it. Only then can you safely add the order.

If, for some reason, the order gets added without a corresponding customer, then your relationships have been damaged. Foreign keys help you make sure that SQL Server 2005 Express automatically enforces these rules.

Constraints

Primary and foreign keys actually belong to a large class of database rules known as *constraints*. There are two other constraints, both of which keep your data nice and clean, and your database applications running smoothly:

- ✔ **UNIQUE:** This constraint tells SQL Server 2005 Express not to allow two or more rows to have the same values for a given column or group of columns. This is very similar to the primary key constraint, but the `unique` constraint does allow null values in a column.

✔ **CHECK:** This is a very interesting and useful constraint. Basically, it tells SQL Server to prevent any violations of business or data rules that you specify when you create the table. For example, you might define a column to hold age information, and require that any values placed into this column range between 0 and 110. With this constraint in place, SQL Server 2005 Express carefully monitors activity related to this column. Any attempts to violate the constraint results in an error, and Express rejects the invalid data.

I describe these constraints in more detail in Chapter 10.

Creating a relationship

Ideally, you'll create all your relationships when you define your tables. However, what happens if you forget to set up an important relationship, such as a foreign key relationship? Never fear — you can never be too late in building good relationships among your data.

For this example, I show you how to use the SQL Server Management Studio Express data diagramming tool to create a foreign key relationship. Assume that you're building a system to track sweepstakes entries. A Contests table, which holds information about all your contests, and an Entries table, which holds details about each entry for a given contest, are the two most important tables. Here's a portion of each of these two tables:

```
CREATE TABLE Contests
(
    ContestID INTEGER PRIMARY KEY NOT NULL,
    ContestName VARCHAR(30) NOT NULL,
    ContestStarts DATETIME NOT NULL
)

CREATE TABLE Entries
(
    EntrantID INTEGER PRIMARY KEY NOT NULL,
    ContestID INTEGER NOT NULL,
    DateReceived DATETIME NOT NULL
)
```

After you create the tables, you suddenly realize that you need to set up a foreign key relationship between the two tables. Here's how to fix things:

1. **Open SQL Server Management Studio Express.**

2. **Choose View⇨Object Explorer.**

3. **Open a connection to your favorite database server.**

   If you don't see any valid connections, click the Connect Object Explorer icon.

4. **Once connected, expand the entry for your database, right-click Database Diagrams, and choose Add New Diagram from the menu.**

   You may be asked if SQL Server 2005 Express can set up internal objects to support diagrams. Answer Yes to any of these questions. Once these objects are in place, a list of candidate tables for your database diagram appears.

5. **Highlight the tables that you want to relate, and click Add.**

6. **After SQL Server Management Studio Express places the tables on the diagram, click Close in the Add Table dialog box.**

7. **Draw a line between the two columns that you want to serve as the relationship.**

   In this case, it's the `ContestID` column in both tables. After you draw the line, SQL Server Management Studio Express brings up several important dialog boxes, as shown in Figure 8-5.

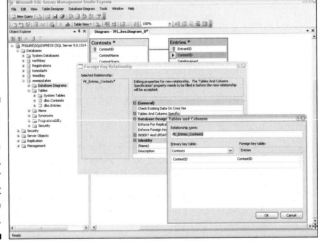

Figure 8-5:
Setting up a relationship with SQL Server Management Studio Express.

The first one is the Tables and Columns dialog box. It generates an automatic name for the relationship, as well as displays the columns and tables that make up the relationship.

8. **Assuming that you built your diagram correctly, click OK in this dialog box.**

   The Tables and Columns dialog box closes, and the Foreign Key Relationship dialog box opens.

9. **Feel free to make any additional changes to the data in this dialog box.**

   For example, you may want to set up a rule about what should happen when you delete a row in the primary table, which is what's happening in Figure 8-6.

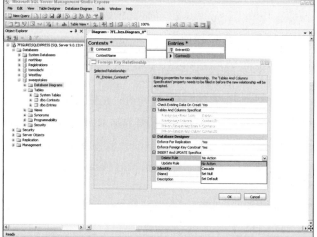

Figure 8-6:
Defining behavior for
DELETE
with SQL
Server
Management
Studio
Express.

10. **After you make your changes, click OK.**

11. **Save the diagram by clicking the Save icon, or choosing File⇨Save.**

    SQL Server Management Studio Express gives you one last chance to change your mind. If you choose Yes, you are prompted for a name for the diagram; your tables are also updated with this new relationship.

    That's all there is to setting up a relationship — you now have defined a foreign key relationship, plus gotten a nifty diagram as a side benefit.

Changing or removing a relationship

In most cases, you can easily change your SQL Server 2005 Express database settings simply by launching SQL Server Management Studio Express and making your requests. However, implementing alterations to existing relationships is more complex, and requires some planning on your part. The main reason for this is that relationships exist to protect your database's integrity and changing or removing one can have far-reaching implications.

Before tinkering with or removing a relationship, spend a little time looking at your database structure and data, and visualize the impact of your planned change.

To change or remove a relationship, just follow these steps:

1. **Open SQL Server Management Studio Express.**

2. **Choose View➪Object Explorer.**

3. **Open a connection to your favorite database server.**

   If you don't see any valid connections, click the Connect Object Explorer icon.

4. **Expand the appropriate Database folder, followed by its Tables folder.**

5. **Right-click the relevant table, and choose the Modify option.**

   A window opens that shows how you set up the table.

6. **Right-click anywhere on the screen, and choose the Relationships option.**

   The Foreign Key Relationships dialog box opens, shown in Figure 8-7.

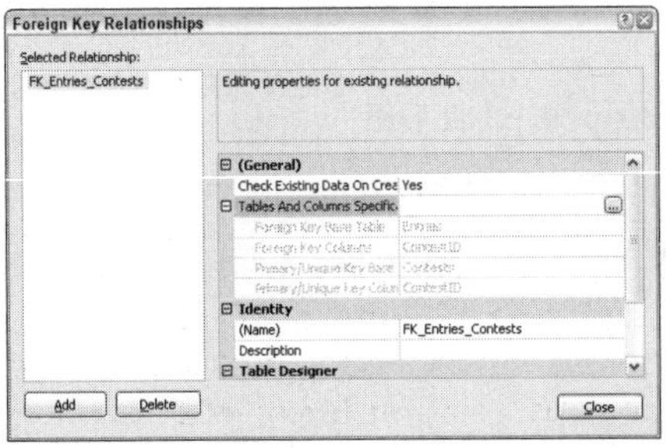

Figure 8-7:
The Foreign
Key Rela-
tionships
dialog box.

7. **Highlight the relationship you want to alter or remove.**

8. **After you make your changes, click the Close button.**

Chapter 9

Talking to a SQL Server

*M*ore so than with most other advanced information storage technologies, you can use loads of tools and products to communicate with your SQL Server 2005 Express database. In this chapter, I point out some of the more common pathways that you can follow to have a meaningful relationship with your database, and — more importantly — with the data that you entrust to its care.

To begin, I tell you all about the SQL standard, along with Microsoft's flavor of it, known as Transact-SQL. The next part of the chapter dives into a brief overview of the various types of tools at your disposal for easy communication with SQL Server 2005 Express. Finally, I show how you can use SQL to straightforwardly create, modify, and remove information in your SQL Server 2005 Express database.

What Is Transact-SQL?

Like many people new to SQL Server 2005 Express, you probably keep hearing of "Transact-SQL," and you wonder what it is. Another question you may be pondering is what the difference is between Transact-SQL and plain old SQL. Not to worry: In this section, I answer these and many other questions.

SQL: The start of it all

SQL stands for *Structured Query Language*. It was originally developed by IBM way back in the 1970s, as a standardized way to talk to a relational database. Unlike many innovations from that era (disco, wide ties, polyester shirts, and leisure suits), SQL has survived to this day and remains the de-facto language for accessing database information.

The American National Standards Institute (ANSI) is the organization charged with defining and maintaining the SQL language standard. By and large, it's done a good job of coming up with a useable data access language. However, significant gaps exist between the SQL standard and the real-world demands of database-accessing applications. Because nature abhors a vacuum, a large market has grown and matured around this standard: Many vendors now provide relational database products, including IBM, Oracle, MySQL, and Microsoft.

In an effort to overcome the deficiencies in SQL, each of these vendors has made proprietary extensions to the standard. These extensions enable application developers to build powerful database-driven solutions. Typical extensions include

- ✓ **Error handling:** Standard SQL provides no way to easily determine if an error has happened. More importantly, it doesn't offer a way to recover from an error condition. Because faults and flaws are unavoidable, this presents a problem.

- ✓ **Variables:** Application variables provide local storage within a program. This storage is necessary for many different reasons, and is not part of standard SQL. Without variables, writing a program that can hold temporary information is very difficult.

- ✓ **Conditional logic:** Standard SQL offers no programmatic conditional logic statements. These kinds of statements let you build intelligent programs that can choose a processing path based on logical conditions.

Transact-SQL: SQL on steroids

Originally developed by Sybase, Transact-SQL is a powerful extension of standard SQL. It offers all the extensions I describe in the preceding bulleted list, plus many more. You can bundle Transact-SQL code into a wide variety of software applications

- ✓ Web pages
- ✓ Application code, such as Visual Basic, Visual C#, and so on

✔ Scripts that can be run from the SQLCMD utility

✔ Packaged enterprise applications

Here's an example of some basic, standard SQL for inserting a record into a table:

```
INSERT INTO inventory (part_number, part_name, part_count)
VALUES (1811, 'Gasket', 12)
```

With this code, you can't easily recover from a problem. Many kinds of problems can derail even a simple INSERT statement such as this one. These include referential integrity violations, data type issues, permission problems, and so on.

Transact-SQL handles problems much easier. Here's a small example of Transact-SQL doing the same kind of work:

```
BEGIN TRY
    INSERT INTO inventory (part_number, part_name,
            part_count)
    VALUES ('Gasket',1811,12);
END TRY
BEGIN CATCH
    SELECT ERROR_NUMBER() as ErrorNumber,
    ERROR_MESSAGE() as ErrorMessage;
END CATCH;
```

In this case, notice the error handling logic. Gracefully handling a problem is much easier. This particular INSERT statement is erroneous; the part_number and part_name fields are reversed. Transact-SQL provides great diagnostics to help resolve the problem:

```
245
Conversion failed when converting the varchar value 'Gasket' to data type int.
```

You can add logic to check the error number and take appropriate action based on the kind of error that you run into. By chaining these kinds of error handlers together, you can build more sophisticated and robust database applications.

Accessing Information

After you master the history of SQL and its powerful progeny, Transact-SQL (refer to the earlier sections of this chapter), you can use the SQL Server 2005 Express database for what it does best: store, manage, and retrieve information.

Your first decision is to pick one or more tools to get access to your data. The market abounds with choices:

- ✔ **SQL Server Management Studio Express:** Available for free download from Microsoft, this tool provides interfaces for managing and maintaining your database, along with a workspace for entering SQL. For most database interactions, it's hard to beat this free tool. Figure 9-1 shows a Query window within SQL Server Management Studio Express.

- ✔ **Data access tools:** The market abounds with choices to help you make the most of your SQL Server 2005 Express data. These include reporting tools, business intelligence products, and simple application development platforms. Figure 9-2 shows one of the more popular platforms, Microsoft Access, caught in the act of importing data from two SQL Server 2005 Express tables.

- ✔ **Office productivity tools:** Even if you're not a sophisticated software developer, you can still get value from your SQL Server 2005 Express database. Most modern office productivity tools have database access features that allow you to connect and work with your SQL Server 2005 Express installation. Figure 9-3 illustrates how Microsoft Excel can serve as a front-end to your database. In this case, I'm using Microsoft Query to first identify the data that I want to return to my spreadsheet.

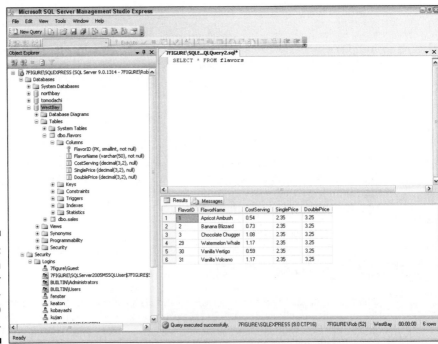

Figure 9-1:
A query in SQL Server Management Studio Express.

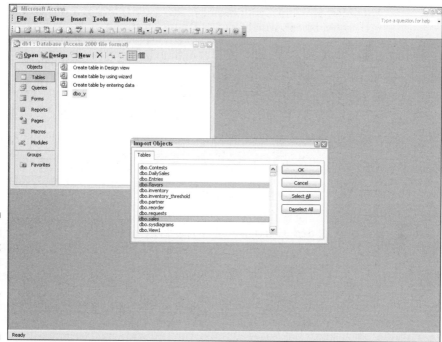

Figure 9-2:
Microsoft
Access
working
with SQL
Server 2005
Express.

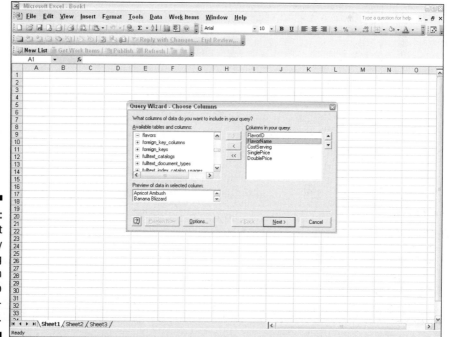

Figure 9-3:
Microsoft
Query
identifying
information
to return to
a spread-
sheet.

After you make your request, Microsoft Query returns data to your spreadsheet, which is what Figure 9-4 shows.

✔ **Application development platforms:** Professional application developers use these technologies to build robust, powerful database-driven applications. Figure 9-5 shows Microsoft Visual Studio interacting with a SQL Server 2005 Express database. In this case, a window shows all the tables for a given database, along with an active Query window for a particular table.

✔ **Packaged enterprise applications:** Many of today's enterprise applications embed a relational database to store their information. Usually, the application vendor does not broadcast this reality. In fact, certain vendors hide the database from anyone who wants to access its information without going through the packaged application. In many cases, you can use one of the tools that I mention in this section to work with your embedded SQL Server 2005 Express database.

✔ **Homegrown applications:** This final category refers to any database-accessing applications that may have been built for you, or by you. In fact, you may be developing your own database application right now. In any case, just like clothing that's made to measure, these applications are tailored for your organization's specific data processing needs.

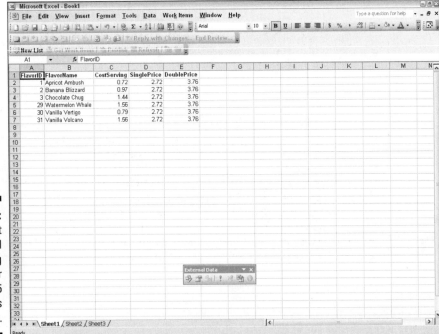

Figure 9-4:
Microsoft Excel displaying SQL Server 2005 Express data.

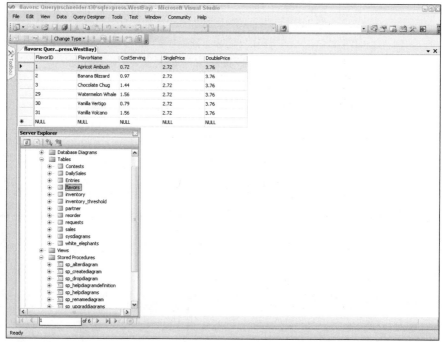

Storing Information in Your Database

After you choose one or more data access technologies, your next task is to start using your database. Because a vacant database is quite boring to explore, the first thing I do here is show you how to insert information into your SQL Server 2005 Express tables. To keep things straightforward, I use SQL Server Management Studio Express as the tool for direct database access in the examples for the rest of this chapter.

For the purposes of these next sections, imagine that you're starting the first premium ice cream stand of a chain. You use these few simple tables to help track vital information about your growing business.

Because an ice cream store without any products wouldn't be much use, Table 9-1 tracks details about your exciting flavors.

Table 9-1	Flavors			
FlavorID	*FlavorName*	*CostServing*	*SinglePrice*	*DoublePrice*
1	Apricot Ambush	0.54	2.35	3.25
2	Banana Blizzard	0.73	2.35	3.25
3	Chocolate Chug	1.08	2.99	3.99
...				
29	Watermelon Whale	1.17	2.35	3.25
30	Vanilla Vertigo	0.59	2.35	3.25
31	Vanilla Volcano	1.11	2.35	3.25

Here's the SQL that creates this table:

```
CREATE TABLE Flavors
(
    FlavorID SMALLINT PRIMARY KEY NOT NULL,
    FlavorName VARCHAR(50) NOT NULL,
    CostServing DECIMAL (3,2),
    SinglePrice DECIMAL (3,2),
    DoublePrice DECIMAL (3,2)
)
```

The PRIMARY KEY instruction in this SQL tells SQL Server 2005 Express to make sure that no duplicates are in the FlavorID column. Primary keys help keep the information you store in your database accurate.

Next, your business will melt faster than a Mr. Softee cone in August if you don't have any sales, so you use Table 9-2 to keep an eye on your revenue.

Table 9-2	Sales		
SaleID	*FlavorID*	*DateOfSale*	*Amount*
1	5	12/30/2006	5.75
2	31	12/30/2006	11.25
...			
2902	2	1/8/2007	3.25

Here's the SQL that creates this table:

```
CREATE TABLE Sales
(
    SaleID INTEGER PRIMARY KEY NOT NULL,
    FlavorID SMALLINT NOT NULL REFERENCES
            Flavors(FlavorID),
    DateofSale DATETIME NOT NULL,
    Amount DECIMAL(4,2) NOT NULL
)
```

The REFERENCES section of the preceding SQL is known as a foreign key constraint: It prevents any records being entered into this table that do not have a corresponding flavor in the Flavors table.

Without foreign keys, the quality of information in your database could become damaged very quickly. For example, think about what would happen if you deleted flavors without removing their corresponding sales records. You would essentially have sales information that has been orphaned; its vital, related records have been deleted. Foreign keys prevent these mistakes from happening.

With your tables now ready for business, you can start filling them with data. You can use the INSERT statement for this job. First, you insert data into the Flavors table:

```
INSERT INTO Flavors VALUES (1, 'Apricot Ambush', 0.54, 2.35, 3.25)
INSERT INTO Flavors VALUES (2, 'Banana Blizzard', 0.73, 2.35, 3.25)
INSERT INTO Flavors VALUES (3, 'Chocolate Chug', 1.08, 2.35, 3.25)
```

After you put information into the Flavors table, you're now ready to add data to the Sales table:

```
INSERT INTO Sales VALUES (1, 3, 6/10/2006, 5.75)
```

This statement means that on June 10, 2006, you sold $5.75 worth of Chocolate Chug. You could simply key in the flavor name in the Sales table, but doing so would be redundant; using a numeric code that you can use to look up the name in the Flavors table is for the best.

What happens if you try to insert a row in the Sales table without a corresponding row in the Flavors table? Because I thoughtfully put a foreign key constraint on the Sales table, any attempt to violate this referential integrity directive causes an error:

```
The INSERT statement conflicted with the
FOREIGN KEY constraint
"FK__sales__FlavorID__412EB0B6". The conflict
occurred in database
 "WestBay", table "flavors", column 'FlavorID'.
The statement has been terminated.
```

In addition to the foreign key constraint you just saw, SQL Server 2005 Express has other capabilities that help protect your information. For example, see what happens if you try to insert a row with a duplicate primary key in the Sales table:

```
INSERT INTO Sales VALUES (1, 3, 6/10/2006, 5.75)
...
INSERT INTO Sales VALUES (1, 31, 6/11/2006, 6.75)
```

```
Violation of PRIMARY KEY constraint 'PK__sales__403A8C7D'.
Cannot insert duplicate key in object 'dbo.Sales'.
The statement has been terminated.
```

These kinds of protection are very important. Without it, you could easily end up with duplicate or otherwise damaged information — causing you to make incorrect decisions.

Bulk Inserts

Many applications require you to load large quantities of information into your database at one time. SQL Server 2005 Express offers two helpful tools that simplify and speed this previously challenging task. You can use the BULK INSERT statement from SQL, or the bcp utility from the command line.

The BULK INSERT statement

The BULK INSERT statement is very useful when you have a file that you want to insert all at once, and you want to use direct SQL entry to launch the insert operation.

For example, imagine that your cash registers generate a large file (called Register.txt) at the end of the day, and that you want to load this file into your Sales table. Suppose that the raw file looks like this:

```
3422,3,6/10/2007,9.00
3423,8,6/10/2007,3.50
3424,1,6/10/2007,2.75
3425,15,6/10/2007,12.25
3426,22,6/10/2007,10.00
3427,30,6/10/2007,18.00
```

Loading this file requires a simple SQL statement:

```
BULK INSERT Sales FROM 'C:\Register.txt'
WITH (DATAFILETYPE = 'char', FIELDTERMINATOR = ',')
```

This command loads the information found in the file, and reports on the number of rows it processed:

```
(114 rows processed)
```

Pay attention to the layout of your raw data files. Getting confused about the exact character that separates each field is very easy. The fields themselves may be in the wrong order, which causes no end of aggravation as you try to decipher what's happening when you insert information.

The bcp utility

Just as the BULK INSERT statement allows you to take a text file and load it into SQL Server 2005 Express via the SQL interface, the bcp utility does the same from the command line. Here's how you invoke bcp to load the sales information into your database:

```
C:\>bcp Westbay.dbo.Sales in Register.txt -S
DBSERVER\sqlexpress
```

A lot can go wrong with a bulk insert process. Problems can range from syntax errors, data issues, and so on. Test this type of operation with a small data file before attempting a massive upload. Otherwise you may potentially damage your database, which is not much fun.

Format file

Ideally, your raw data files exactly match the layout of your tables. Unfortunately, things are rarely this simple in the real world. Significant differences likely exist between what you're given and what you need. Fortunately, you can create a format file that tells SQL Server 2005 Express exactly what to expect from these data files.

To easily generate a format file, just run the bcp utility as I show here. SQL Server 2005 Express walks through the specified table and file, and gives you the option to create a format file at the end:

```
C:\>bcp Westbay.dbo.Sales in Register.txt -S
DBSERVER\sqlexpress
Password:

Enter the file storage type of field SaleID [int]:
Enter prefix-length of field SaleID [0]:
```

```
Enter field terminator [none]:

Enter the file storage type of field FlavorID [smallint]:
Enter prefix-length of field FlavorID [0]:
Enter field terminator [none]:

Enter the file storage type of field DateofSales
        [datetime]:
Enter prefix-length of field DateofSales [0]:
Enter field terminator [none]:

Enter the file storage type of field Amount [decimal]:
Enter prefix-length of field Amount [1]:
Enter field terminator [none]:

Do you want to save this format information in a file?
        [Y/n]
Host filename [bcp.fmt]:
```

After you finish defining this file, you can use it for all future bcp runs.

Finding Information in Your Database

Now that you have information in your tables, you may be wondering how you can retrieve it. As I show you earlier in this chapter (in the "Accessing Information" section), you have many software tools at your disposal. However, no matter what technology you use, chances are that it uses SQL (or Transact-SQL) as its data access language, so I focus on the combination of SQL and SQL Server Management Studio Express as the means to getting at your information.

In this section, you get the hang of using SQL to write powerful queries to make sense of what's in your database. For clarity's sake, I continue with the ice cream store example.

The SELECT statement

Saying that the SELECT statement is at the heart of any relational database system — SQL Server 2005 Express included — is not an exaggeration. In a nutshell, SELECT allows you to retrieve data. To make it work, you need to provide only a few pieces of information, and SQL Server 2005 Express dutifully reports on what's stored in the database.

To build a SELECT statement, just follow these simple steps:

1. **Choose an access method.**

   In the earlier section, "Accessing Information," I show you the many tools to choose from to enter a query. For these steps, I use SQL Server Management Studio Express.

2. **Open a Query window.**

   You need a place to type your query. For SQL Server Management Studio Express, all you need to do is click the New Query icon, which opens a new Query window.

3. **Choose a table that you want to view and expand the entry to see the list of columns.**

   I discuss multiple table queries in the "Joining Tables" section. For now, just pick one table. Using SQL Server Management Studio Express, you can get a list of tables by expanding the Databases entry, expanding your database, and then opening the Tables folder.

    If you want to see all columns, just use an asterisk wildcard (*).

4. **Choose the columns that you want to view.**

5. **Type your query, using the table and column names that you want to see.**

   At its most basic, all you need is to combine the SELECT keyword with the names of the columns you want to view from the target table, along with the FROM keyword and table name.

6. **Click the Execute button to launch the query.**

For example, imagine that you want to get a list of all the flavors that you sell. Here's what your query looks like:

```
SELECT * FROM Flavors
```

This information is the minimum amount that you can provide to the SELECT statement. Here's a small segment of its results:

FlavorID	FlavorName	CostServing	SinglePrice	DoublePrice
1	Apricot Ambush	.54	2.35	3.25
2	Banana Blizzard	.73	2.35	3.25
3	Chocolate Chug	1.08	2.35	3.25
...				
...				
29	Watermelon Whale	1.17	2.35	3.25
30	Vanilla Vertigo	.59	2.35	3.25
31	Vanilla Volcano	1.17	2.35	3.25

Because you provide a wildcard, this query returns all columns and all rows. But what if you only want the name of the flavors, and no other columns? A simple change to the query does the trick:

```
SELECT FlavorName FROM Flavors

FlavorName
---------------------------
Apricot Ambush
Banana Blizzard
Chocolate Chug
...
...
Watermelon Whale
Vanilla Vertigo
Vanilla Volcano
```

If you mistakenly enter a non-existent table or column name, SQL Server sets you straight:

```
SELECT sorry_not_here FROM this_table_does_not_exist
Invalid object name 'this_table_does_not_exist'.
```

```
SELECT sorry_not_here FROM Flavors
Invalid column name 'sorry_not_here'.
```

If you want to see multiple columns, just put commas between their names:

```
SELECT FlavorName, SinglePrice FROM Flavors

FlavorName                              SinglePrice
--------------------------------------- -----------
Apricot Ambush                                 2.35
Banana Blizzard                                2.35
Chocolate Chug                                 2.35
...
...
Watermelon Whale                               2.35
Vanilla Vertigo                                2.35
Vanilla Volcano                                2.35
```

You can change the output order of the columns by simply moving them around in the SQL statement.

Filtering your results

As you can see from the previous query, you're still getting all rows back from your query. But what if you're only interested in a subset of this data, perhaps only those flavors that cost less than $1 to make? That's where the WHERE clause comes in. Its job in life is to filter results for your queries, so that you get only the data you want. Here's what a filtered query looks like:

```
SELECT FlavorName, CostServing FROM Flavors
WHERE CostServing < 1.00

FlavorName                                     CostServing
------------------------------------------     -----------
Apricot Ambush                                         .54
Banana Blizzard                                        .73
Vanilla Vertigo                                        .59
```

You can get fancier with filters. Here's a query with two filters:

```
SELECT FlavorName, CostServing FROM Flavors
WHERE CostServing < 1.00 AND FlavorName LIKE 'Vanilla%'
```

This query returns all your low-cost vanilla-named flavors. The AND keyword does just what it says — it tells SQL Server 2005 Express to combine the two parts of the WHERE clause. In this case, both sides must be true to return a row: The row must have a CostServing less than 1.00, and a FlavorName that begins with Vanilla. If only one of these is true, SQL Server 2005 Express doesn't return that row.

You can build very rich filters that combine multiple criteria in a single statement. You can use AND, OR, and NOT to construct various combinations of filter conditions. These are known as *Boolean searches*. Here's an example of a more complex Boolean search:

```
SELECT * FROM Flavors
WHERE (FlavorName NOT LIKE ('Vanilla%')AND CostServing > 1.00)
OR (FlavorName LIKE ('Chocolate%') AND CostServing < 2.00)
FlavorID FlavorName         CostServing SinglePrice DoublePrice
-------- ------------------- ----------- ----------- -----------
       3 Chocolate Chug             1.08        2.35        3.25
      29 Watermelon Whale           1.17        2.35        3.25
```

What's this query doing, exactly? SQL Server 2005 Express interprets it, and applies the following logic:

1. Gets all the columns from the Flavors table.

2. As long as the flavor's name does not begin with Vanilla.

3. And it costs more than $1.00 to make per serving.

4. Or the flavor's name begins with Chocolate.

5. And it costs less than $2.00 to make per serving.

As this example shows, coming up with incorrect Boolean searches is very easy, especially if you misplace a parenthesis. Build and test your queries carefully before making any decisions based on a complex Boolean search.

Sorting your results

Getting data back in an unsorted blob is not very helpful. Fortunately, the designers of SQL took this into consideration, and offered some very beneficial sorting features. To begin, you can include a simple ORDER BY with your query to sort the result set in any way you like:

```
SELECT FlavorName, CostServing
FROM Flavors
ORDER BY CostServing
```

```
FlavorName                                    CostServing
--------------------------------------------- -----------
Apricot Ambush                                        .54
Vanilla Vertigo                                       .59
Banana Blizzard                                       .73
Chocolate Chug                                       1.08
Watermelon Whale                                     1.17
Vanilla Volcano                                      1.17
```

See how the CostServing column nicely sorts the rows? You can sort by multiple columns; just separate them with a comma:

```
SELECT FlavorName, CostServing
FROM Flavors
ORDER BY CostServing, FlavorName
```

In this example, SQL Server 2005 Express firsts sort the results by the CostServing column, and then uses the contents of the FlavorName column to sort any rows that have the same CostServing value.

Built-in functions

SQL Server 2005 Express includes many helpful built-in functions. These functions take large quantities of data and group them into a single result. Here are some of the more popular basic aggregation functions, along with how you can use them:

✔ **Summing up data:** You can use the SUM() function to add up the values in a particular numeric column. For example, here's how you would get the sum of all transactions in the Sales table:

```
SELECT SUM(Amount)
FROM Sales
```

SQL Server 2005 Express adds up the values of the `Amount` column for all the rows in the table. Of course, you're free to provide a filter if you only want the sum of values for a smaller set of data:

```
SELECT SUM(Amount)
FROM Sales
WHERE DateOfSale BETWEEN '1/1/2006' AND '12/31/2006'
```

These functions generally require numeric columns. If you try to run a function on a character column, SQL Server 2005 Express complains:

```
SELECT SUM(FlavorName)
FROM Flavors
```

```
Operand data type varchar is invalid for

sum aggregate operator.
```

✔ **Averaging data:** You can tell SQL Server 2005 Express to calculate the average value for a given numeric column. For example, if you want to find the average cost per serving of ice cream, you would use the `AVG()` function:

```
SELECT AVG(CostServing)
FROM Flavors
```

✔ **Counting data:** As you might expect, the `COUNT()` function tallies the number of rows that meet a certain criteria. If you just want to get a count of all the rows in a table, here's what you would enter:

```
SELECT COUNT(*)
FROM Sales
```

In this case, the wildcard means that you want to count up all the rows in the table.

✔ **Finding the maximum value for a column:** Some times you'll want to know the maximum value for a particular column. For example, you might want to know the largest sale you've ever made. You can use the `MAX()` function to get your answer:

```
SELECT MAX(Amount)
FROM Sales
```

✔ **Finding the minimum value for a column:** Just as the `MAX()` function tells you the largest value for a column, the `MIN()` function does the opposite: It reports on the smallest value from a column. If you need to filter the candidate rows, you can include a `WHERE` clause:

```
SELECT MIN(Amount)
FROM Sales
WHERE DateOfSale BETWEEN '12/1/2006' AND '12/31/2006'
```

Renaming output columns

Transact-SQL gives you great flexibility when formatting your output. Formatting is more than cosmetic: Easy-to-understand column headings make your results much easier to interpret.

Suppose that you run a query that includes a variety of aggregation functions. If you don't provide column names, your output is difficult to comprehend, as shown in Figure 9-6.

You can slightly alter your SQL to provide meaningful output column names, which Figure 9-7 shows.

Joining tables

You can build powerful queries with relatively simple SQL. So far in this chapter, though, I've showed you only single-table queries. Of course, the real world is rarely that black-and-white. It's now time to enter the colorful world of multi-table joins.

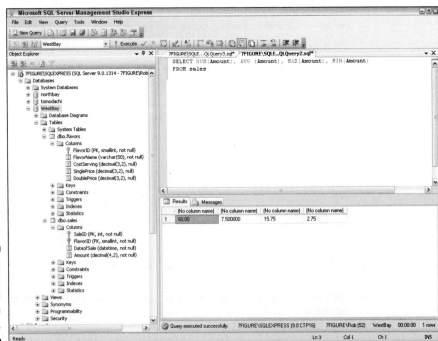

Figure 9-6:
Unaltered aggregation function output.

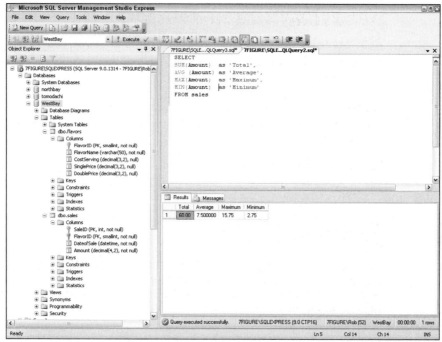

Figure 9-7:
Aggregation
function
output with
easier-to-
understand
column
names.

By design, relational databases break information into tables. To present a single picture of this data, you need to join these tables together as part of your query. To relate information from multiple tables is known as *joining* the tables.

Joins are possible only with common keys, so before you write a join, you need to figure out what the two tables have in common. You can then use that common key to construct your query. For example, suppose that you want to get a list of all the sales for a particular flavor of ice cream. Here's what that query would look like:

```
SELECT f.FlavorName, s.DateOfSale, s.Amount
FROM Flavors f JOIN Sales s ON (f.FlavorID = s.FlavorID)
WHERE f.FlavorName = 'Watermelon Whale'
ORDER BY s.DateofSale
```

Here's how SQL Server 2005 Express works with this query:

1. **Get the data from the `FlavorName`, `DateofSale`, and `Amount` columns.**

   The f and s prefixes instruct SQL Server 2005 Express what table these columns come from.

2. **Join the data from each table for any rows that have the `FlavorID` columns in common.**

3. **Apply a filter to make sure the flavor is `Watermelon Whale`.**

4. **Return the results sorted by the date of sale.**

The join takes place during Step 2. Note that SQL Server 2005 Express may first elect to filter for any rows that are Watermelon Whale, and then locate transactions for that flavor.

Here's another way to write this query:

```
SELECT f.FlavorName, s.DateOfSale
FROM Flavors f, Sales s
WHERE (f.FlavorID = s.FlavorID)
AND (f.FlavorName = 'Watermelon Whale')
ORDER BY s.DateofSale
```

Standard joins return only those rows that are present in both tables. What happens when only one table has a given row? For example, how would you get a list of those flavors that haven't seen any sales? You use outer joins in these situations to find the exact information you need. Here's an example of an outer join:

```
SELECT f.FlavorName, s.DateOfSale
FROM Flavors f LEFT OUTER JOIN Sales s
ON (f.FlavorID = s.FlavorID)
```

FlavorName	DateOfSale
Chocolate Chug	2006-12-30 18:35:01.000
...	
Walnut Wipeout	NULL
...	
Banana Boom	2006-12-30 21:14:23.000
Grape Gusher	NULL

What can you infer from this data? Unfortunately, the Walnut Wipeout and Grape Gusher flavors have not sold at all. The LEFT OUTER JOIN clause tells SQL Server 2005 Express to return flavors, even the ones with no sales. That's why the DateOfSale column has a value of NULL; the Sales table has no related rows. You use LEFT OUTER JOIN here because the Flavors table is on the left part of the statement; if it were on the other side you would use RIGHT OUTER JOIN instead:

```
SELECT f.FlavorName, s.DateOfSales
FROM Sales s RIGHT OUTER JOIN Flavors f ON
(s.FlavorID = f.FlavorID)
```

Subqueries

One way to greatly increase the power of your queries is to take advantage of subqueries. You can think of these as nested searches that all work together to give you the answers you seek from your SQL Server 2005 Express database. The alternative would be to write copious amounts of code that kept track of all the information necessary to answer your question.

For example, imagine that you want to get a list of the names for all the flavors that have had at least one sale between $10 and $15. You could write a program to retrieve all rows from the `Sales` table, and then keep internal counters, but a subquery does the job quickly:

```
SELECT FlavorName
FROM Flavors
WHERE FlavorID IN
    (SELECT FlavorID
     FROM Sales
     WHERE Amount BETWEEN 10.00 AND 15.00)
```

What's happening here? When you're faced with either building or analyzing a subquery, starting with the innermost query and then working your way out is always best. In this case, SQL Server 2005 Express processes the query as follows:

1. Get the values from the `FlavorID` column in the `Sales` table.

2. Apply a filter so that only those rows that have an `Amount` of between $10 and $15.

   This step likely finds thousands of candidates.

3. Return those `FlavorID` values to the outer query.

4. Using the returned `FlavorID` list, look up the values in the `FlavorName` column from within the `Flavor` table.

5. Only return a unique list of `FlavorName` column values to the user; there's no need to show the same value twice or more.

Subqueries are helpful for other types of operation, too. For example, a slight tweak to the SQL statement instructs it to delete all those flavors where any transaction was less than $2.99. This treatment is somewhat harsh for your less-than-popular flavors, but it works:

```
DELETE
FROM Flavors
WHERE FlavorID IN
(SELECT FlavorID
 FROM Sales
 WHERE Amount < 2.99)
```

Consider using subqueries whenever you need to perform one or more passes through your database and then feed those results to a higher-level operation.

Speeding up your queries

For small, infrequently accessed databases, performance isn't usually an issue. However, after you start storing serious amounts of information in your SQL Server 2005 Express database, you can expect to spend some time making sure that system response is acceptable. What's acceptable is largely dependent on your users' expectations. Some users are easygoing; others expect an answer before they've even asked the question!

The simplest thing you can do to increase your queries' speed is to provide proper indexing. Think of an index as a shortcut that SQL Server 2005 Express can use to find your data.

For example, suppose that you need to find your friend's entry in the phone book for a large city. The phone book for this city contains millions of entries. Furthermore, imagine that you have a poorly designed phone book: All the entries are in random order, rather than in the familiar last-name order of most sane phone books. Of course, in reality a normal phone book is indexed by last name. Without this index, you would have to open the book and start paging through all the names until you ran across your friend's name. Chances are that after five or ten pages, your eyes would glaze over and you'd probably miss it. SQL Server 2005 Express doesn't get tired, but it can take a long time to find information when no index is available.

Contrast this fatiguing experience with what happens when the phone book is indexed: You immediately open the book to the vicinity of your friend's name, and then review a much smaller set of information to find the right entry. For SQL Server 2005 Express, things are even better: Rather than churning through the entire table, it is able to find the right record in milliseconds.

SQL Server 2005 Express uses a sophisticated technology called an *optimizer* to pick the fastest index. The optimizer's job is to understand the database, including its structure, data distribution, and so on. Armed with that understanding, it's able to make informed recommendations to the database server when it comes time to retrieve or alter information.

Getting a list of indexes

Figuring out what indexes are in place for a given table is easy. Just follow these steps:

1. **Open SQL Server Management Studio Express.**

2. **Expand the Databases entry.**

3. **Open the entry for your database.**

4. **Pick a table that you want to explore.**

5. **Expand the table's entry.**

6. **Open the Indexes view.**

Figure 9-8 shows an example of two tables, their columns, and their primary key indexes. I've also opened a window showing properties for one of the indexes.

Deciding what to index

Because indexes are so important, your job as a database or query designer is to make sure that you create the right indexes. How can you know which columns to index? While performance optimization merits its own book, you can follow a few guidelines. Indexing these kinds of columns likely removes most index-driven performance impediments:

- **Primary keys:** This column, or group of columns, provides a unique definition for a given row. By definition, no two rows in the same table can have the same primary key value. Defining a primary key for each table is important. When you do this extra step, SQL Server 2005 Express automatically creates an index on the primary key. Chapter 8 has more about primary keys.

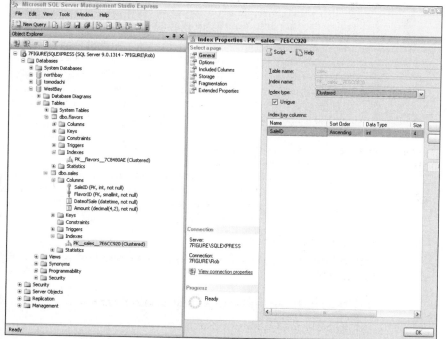

Figure 9-8:
Index information as reported by SQL Server Management Studio Express.

✔ **Foreign keys:** By enforcing relationships among your tables, foreign keys help protect your database's referential integrity. When faced with a database operation that could violate referential integrity, SQL Server 2005 Express checks to see if any foreign keys are in place, and blocks any potential problems. In fact, this is so important for performance that SQL Server blocks any new foreign key constraints if no candidate indexes are in place:

```
There are no primary or candidate keys in the
       referenced
table 'parent_table' that match the referencing
column list in the foreign key
 'FK__child_tabl__col1__03317E3D'.
```

You can get more details about foreign keys in Chapter 8.

✔ **Filter columns:** Filter columns help SQL Server 2005 Express narrow the range of results for your queries. Without a filter, a query returns all the rows from a table. You should plan on indexing your most frequently used filter columns, especially if the underlying table has many rows.

For example, using the Sales table from earlier in the chapter, imagine that you want to run frequent queries to identify rows based on the Amount column. A typical query might look like this:

```
SELECT DateOfSales, Amount
FROM Sales
WHERE Amount = 9.99
```

Can you see which column should be indexed here? Because you're filtering on Amount, giving SQL Server 2005 Express the option of using an index for this column often significantly improves performance.

✔ **Join columns:** Join columns are the mechanism that SQL Server 2005 Express uses to establish equivalency between two or more tables, which retrieves a unified view of your data. In most cases, you must make sure that both sides of the join are indexed. For example, look at this query:

```
SELECT f.FlavorName, s.DateOfSales, s.Amount
FROM Flavors f JOIN Sales s ON (f.FlavorID =
       s.FlavorID)
```

Placing an index on the FlavorID column in both the Flavors and Sales tables would help the SQL Server 2005 Express optimizer find candidate rows more quickly. As it turns out, because the FlavorID column is the primary key of the Flavors table, it's already been indexed.

✔ **Sort columns:** Users appreciate a logically sorted group of rows, rather than an undifferentiated blob of data. However, sorting takes time and costs system resources, so it is not free. One way to keep the costs as low as possible is to make sure that the sort column is indexed. Imagine that a large query looks like this:

```
SELECT *
FROM Sales
ORDER BY DateOfSale
```

If an index isn't on the `DateOfSale` column, it takes more effort for SQL Server 2005 Express to organize and return the rows to you.

Building multiple column indexes

So far, I've only demonstrated indexes on single columns. You can build much more comprehensive, multiple column indexes if need be. For example, suppose that you have a table of customer information like in Table 9-3.

Table 9-3	Customers	
CustomerID	**LastName**	**FirstName**
1	Olsen	Caroline
2	Jonnsan	Katlyn
...		
4175	Fischer	Bert

By speaking with your users, you know that they're searching for customers based on the combination of `LastName`, `FirstName`. Given this fact, you can create a composite index on these two columns. This composite index helps future queries and other database activities that need to filter or sort on these two columns.

When building a composite index, make sure that users are employing the index from left to right. That is, if a given composite index is built on columns A, B, and C (in that order), searches and sorts that successfully use this index can include any of the following combinations:

- ✔ Column A, B, C
- ✔ Column A, B
- ✔ Column A

Creating indexes

Indexes have many benefits to offer, so you're probably wondering how you can create one of these wonderful creatures. Fear not — they're very easy to generate. In fact, SQL Server 2005 Express often creates them for you by default. For example, when you define a primary key, SQL Server 2005 Express automatically generates a unique index for that column(s).

However, what if you want to build an index for another kind of column? Here's an example of putting an index on the `FlavorName` column from the `Flavors` table:

```
CREATE INDEX IDX1 ON Flavors(FlavorName)
```

The syntax is identical if you want to create a composite index; you just need to add the additional column name:

```
CREATE INDEX IDX2 ON Flavors(CostServing,SinglePrice)
```

SQL Server 2005 Express lets you define your indexes as unique or non-unique, as well as clustered or non-clustered. By choosing unique, you're telling SQL Server 2005 Express not to permit any duplicates in the index keys. For example, if you create an index on the `LastName` column, you can't insert or update any values if they would create two rows with the same data in that column.

When you elect to define an index as clustered, you're telling SQL Server 2005 Express that you want the table to be physically ordered by that index. Continuing with the example of placing an index on `LastName`, if you instructed SQL Server 2005 Express to make this index clustered, it lays the table out on disk in `LastName` order. Naturally, you can only have one clustered index per table.

If you decide to use clustered indexes, define them first before requesting non-clustered indexes.

Changing Data

Putting information into a database is not like chiseling it in stone: You can easily make changes any time you need. In this section, I show you how easy changing your data is.

Just like the INSERT statement places data into a SQL Server 2005 Express database and the SELECT statement retrieves information, the UPDATE statement is responsible for adjusting this data.

For the sake of simplicity, I'm continuing with the ice cream example that I lay out earlier in this chapter (in the "Storing Information in Your Database" section). Suppose that you decide to improve your products by purchasing higher-quality ingredients. Of course, you're running a business, not a charity, so you need to pass on some of these costs to your customers. You need to record these higher costs in your database, so you write a simple UPDATE statement to make the changes:

```
UPDATE Flavors
SET CostServing = CostServing * 1.10,
SinglePrice = SinglePrice * 1.05,
DoublePrice = DoublePrice * 1.05
```

What is this statement doing?

1. Only the Flavors table is being altered.

2. The values contained in the CostServing columns are being increased by 10 percent.

3. The values contained in the SinglePrice and DoublePrice columns are being increased by 5 percent.

Can you spot a potentially dangerous problem with this statement? It doesn't contain a filtering WHERE clause; all the rows in the table are updated.

Be careful when writing blanket UPDATE statements. Unless you want to change all the rows in a table, you probably need a WHERE clause.

In this case, given the terrible reception that the Walnut Wipeout and Grape Gusher flavors have received in the market, perhaps you shouldn't be raising prices on those two flavors. You can easily change the query so that all the rows except for those two problem children are updated:

```
UPDATE Flavors
SET CostServing = CostServing * 1.10,
SinglePrice = SinglePrice * 1.05,
DoublePrice = DoublePrice * 1.05
WHERE FlavorName NOT IN ('Grape Gusher','Walnut Wipeout')
```

This statement is a more selective UPDATE statement: The two poorly selling flavors still remain a bargain. Perhaps this pricing can improve sales of those two.

Naturally, you can write more complicated UPDATE statements. To do so, you often use the same advanced search syntax that you use in your SELECT statements.

Before running any blanket, potentially widespread UPDATE statements, why not try them out as a SELECT statement first? You have nothing to lose by doing so, and you can also spot errors before your data gets changed.

Deleting Data

Nothing lasts forever, including data. The time likely arises when you need to remove certain information from your SQL Server 2005 Express database. Several useful statements are at your disposal for removing this unneeded data.

To begin, the DELETE statement offers an easy way to get rid of redundant rows in a particular table. In this case, suppose that you're tired of seeing the lackluster sales for the Grape Gusher and Walnut Wipeout flavors. The time has come to remove them from your Flavors table:

```
DELETE FROM Flavors
Where FlavorName IN ('Grape Geyser','Walnut Wipeout')
```

A DELETE statement without a WHERE clause obliterates all the rows in a table. Be very mindful when you invoke this statement.

Because you have sales transactions in your Sales table, perhaps a better idea is to first remove the sales records, and then the flavor itself. Here's how you would do that:

```
DELETE FROM Sales
WHERE FlavorID =
(SELECT FlavorID
 FROM Flavors
 WHERE FlavorName = 'Grape Geyser')
```

```
DELETE FROM Flavors
WHERE FlavorName = 'Grape Geyser'
```

If you have foreign key constraints in place, you must process DELETE statements in this order (that is, children first, parents last). A little earlier in this chapter, I placed a foreign key on the Sales table (refer to Table 9-2). The reason for doing this is to prevent erroneous deletion of parent (that is, Flavor) rows while child (that is, Sales) rows still exist. In fact, if you try to delete the parent before the child — thereby violating the foreign key constraint — you receive a warning message like this one:

```
The DELETE statement conflicted with the REFERENCE
            constraint
 "FK__sales__FlavorID__412EB0B6".
The conflict occurred in database
 "WestBay", table "sales", column 'FlavorID'.
The statement has been terminated.
```

Removing all rows from a table

If you need to eliminate all the rows from a given table, using either the TRUNCATE TABLE or DROP TABLE statements is much faster; running the DELETE command takes much longer. Here's how you use both of these statements:

```
TRUNCATE TABLE Sales
```

This statement removes all the rows from the Sales table, leaving the table structure and all its constraints, indexes, and so on in place. However, it doesn't bypass any referential integrity constraints that you have specified. For example, what happens if you try to remove all the rows from the Flavors table?

```
TRUNCATE TABLE Flavors

Msg 4712, Level 16, State 1, Server DBSERVER\SQLEXPRESS,
Line 1
Cannot truncate table 'Flavors' because it is
being referenced by a FOREIGN KEY constraint.
```

After you truncate a table, you can continue using it: no application code has to change (but the data is gone, of course).

If you're sure that you won't ever need the table or its data again, you can simply use the DROP TABLE statement:

```
DROP TABLE Sales
```

Unlike the TRUNCATE TABLE statement, DROP TABLE obliterates all constraints, indexes, and other table structures, so be very careful when you use it.

Removing some of the rows from a table

What if you need to get rid of a significant number of rows in a table, but not all of them? Transact-SQL offers some handy features to make this possible.

Deleting rows by using a filter

You can use a WHERE clause to create a filter that SQL Server 2005 Express uses to determine candidate rows to be removed. For example, suppose that you want to remove all the rows from the Sales table where the amount of the sale is less than $5.00. All that you need to do is pair a simple WHERE clause with your DELETE statement:

```
DELETE FR  Sales
WHERE Amount < 5.00
```

In most cases in which you need to remove a subset of the table's data, just appending a filter to your DELETE statement is all you must do to identify and eliminate the right information.

Deleting a set quantity of rows

Sometimes, you may want to delete a set quantity of rows based on some criteria. This typically happens when you have a table that contains large numbers of rows that don't have much value after a certain period of time.

For example, suppose that you've been selling ice cream like crazy, and you want to delete a number of your older transactions. How can you isolate and delete the right candidate rows without affecting newer data? One option would be to write a program that looks at all the rows in the table, and deletes only those that meet a certain criteria. However, this action requires much more effort than is necessary.

In this case, how about using the TOP extension to Transact-SQL? You can instruct SQL Server 2005 Express to remove a percentage of sales data that is older than a given date:

```
DELETE TOP(10)
FROM sales
WHERE DateOfSale < '12/30/2006'
```

This operation tells SQL Server 2005 Express to remove ten rows from the Sales table, as long as those rows are from a date earlier than December 30, 2006.

Unfortunately, this statement has a problem: Eligible rows are removed at random. As long as the rows are old enough, SQL Server 2005 Express deletes them until ten rows are gone. After the dust settles, the ten oldest rows may not have been deleted. You can easily see why: What if more than ten rows with a DateOfSale are older than December 30, 2006?

To make matters worse, because the rows are removed at random, a good chance some very old rows may survive, while some younger rows are eradicated.

If you want to ensure a more orderly removal process, try this statement instead:

```
DELETE FROM Sales
WHERE SaleID IN
(SELECT TOP 10 SaleID
 FROM Sales
 WHERE DateOfSale < '12/30/2006'
 ORDER BY DateOfSale ASC
)
```

This statement removes the oldest ten rows from the Sales table, as long as the rows are older than the target date. You still may have rows that were created before December 30, 2006, but the ten oldest rows are gone.

Deleting a percentage of rows

If you're more focused on percentages, you can include a PERCENT directive with your DELETE statement. This statement tells SQL Server 2005 Express to remove a specific percentage of rows from a given table. To intelligently target rows, including a filter is a good idea:

```
DELETE FROM Sales
WHERE SaleID IN
(SELECT TOP 10 PERCENT SaleID
 FROM Sales
 WHERE DateOfSale < '12/30/2006'
 ORDER BY DateOfSale ASC
)
```

Can you see what's happening here? You've told SQL Server 2005 Express that you want to delete the top (that is, oldest) ten percent of those rows for transactions that happened prior to December 30, 2006. If this operation still leaves candidate rows, you can repeat the statement until all eligible rows are gone. You see a shrinking number of rows until all the relevant rows are history:

```
(92 row(s) affected)
(18 row(s) affected)
(0 row(s) affected)
```

In summary, the set quantity and percentage means of partial-delete operations are helpful when you want to remove a general subset of information. However, in most cases just including a WHERE clause with your DELETE statement gives you the results you want.

Chapter 10

Transact-SQL: Beyond the Basics

*I*f you have an appetite for some more advanced interaction with your SQL Server 2005 Express database, this chapter is for you. I begin by showing you how to define your data structures to increase the reliability of your information. You also find out how to speed up your database operations by creating and using indexes. Finally, I tell you all about some cutting edge capabilities for locating and organizing information in your database.

Advanced Data Definition

As the SQL standard and Microsoft's Transact-SQL version have grown and matured over time, database designers and administrators can use increasingly powerful and refined tools to help ensure the quality, security, and accessibility of their data. In this section, you see how to use constraints, views, and XML to extend the power of your database engine, while reducing the amount of work that you or your programmers need to do.

Constraints

When you build a database application, you're responsible for making sure that no bad data gets put into your database. If you fall down on the job, you may make a bad decision, because what's stored in your database doesn't accurately reflect reality. Constraints are a way for you to define, at the database level, rules that help protect your database from data anomalies. Your toolbox includes a number of constraints: primary and foreign keys and NOT NULL, UNIQUE, and CHECK constraints.

Primary key

By defining a primary key constraint, you're telling SQL Server 2005 Express that the values contained in one or more columns must be unique across all rows. As well as protecting your data's integrity, a primary key constraint is a great help to database performance: Using the primary key, SQL Server 2005 Express can find a row almost instantaneously.

In fact, the database server thinks so highly of primary keys that it even takes ownership of generating them for you automatically. All you need to do is specify IDENTITY when creating your table:

```
CREATE TABLE auto_manufacturers
(
    ManufacturerID SMALLINT PRIMARY KEY NOT NULL IDENTITY,
    ManufacturerName VARCHAR(30)
)
```

Now, all you need to do to insert rows into this table is to provide a value for the ManufacturerName column; SQL Server Express does the rest:

```
INSERT INTO auto_manufacturers (ManufacturerName) VALUES ('Aston Martin')
INSERT INTO auto_manufacturers (ManufacturerName) VALUES ('BMW')

SELECT * FROM auto_manufacturers

ManufacturerID ManufacturerName
-------------- ------------------------------
             1 Aston Martin
             2 BMW
```

The alternative to this approach requires you to write application code to determine the highest identifier, and then add 1 to the number to generate a new primary key value. This is time-consuming at best; at worst, you can generate erroneous primary keys. As an added benefit, you can instruct SQL Server 2005 Express to start your numbering sequence at a number other than 1, and you can request increments larger than 1. For example, I modified the previous table creation statement:

```
CREATE TABLE auto_manufacturers
(
    ManufacturerID INTEGER PRIMARY KEY NOT NULL IDENTITY(1000,250),
    ManufacturerName VARCHAR(30)
)
```

The first row in this table has a ManufacturerID value of 1000; the second row has 1250, and so on.

A Global Unique Identifier (GUID) is another choice for primary keys. These are system-generated values that are built using truly unique information: your network card's internal serial number. In addition to their unique properties (which can come in handy in networked applications), GUIDs can hold extremely large numbers. However, they can be confusing to people, and they consume extra storage and CPU resources.

To use GUIDs, all you must do is have your primary key column use the uniqueidentifier data type. With that task out of the way, your next step is to set the column's Is RowGuid property to Yes. After you do this, SQL Server 2005 Express automatically generates lovely values like the following for your primary key:

```
B3E1988C-38F2-411F-AC4C-BC3ED64D0ED3
EB7BA81A-DB19-4F9A-9011-37DACBABADF2
9011785F-B0C4-4306-99A5-7B637D71C4B5
```

These primary key values are for a 3-row table. As you can see, these values — at least to the human eye — have no rhyme or reason. However, GUIDs are great when you may need to merge values from the same table deployed in multiple locations.

Foreign key

Most relational database applications spread their knowledge among multiple tables. Each table ordinarily holds a specialized type of data. For example, suppose that you're building an application to track student grades. A common way of maintaining this information is to store demographic details about the students (name, address, and so on) in one table, and test-specific aspects of their grades (class, date of test, score, and so on) in a second table.

Here's where things can get tricky. If you're not careful, your application could delete a student's demographic data without deleting the associated test data. Alternatively, you could create a detailed test score record but omit creating a student demographic record. You've damaged your data's integrity in both of these cases. Foreign key constraints are specifically designed to prevent these unhappy situations from ever occurring.

When you place a foreign key constraint on two or more tables, you're telling SQL Server 2005 Express to intercept any attempts, deliberate or otherwise, where your data's integrity can be compromised.

NOT NULL

The NOT NULL constraint helps make sure that any database applications provide data for one or more of your columns. If you attempt to enter an empty (that is, NULL) value on a column that has a NOT NULL constraint, SQL Server 2005 Express intercepts the call:

```
Cannot insert the value NULL into column 'LastName',
table 'Westbay.dbo.Employees'; column does not allow
        nulls.
INSERT fails.
```

The database server is smart enough to trap an illegal update, too.

UNIQUE

The UNIQUE constraint is very similar to a primary key constraint, but unlike primary keys, UNIQUE constraints let you place a NULL value in the column. However, you generally define a UNIQUE constraint when you already have a primary key in place, but also want to enforce non-duplication on another column. For example, look at this table's syntax:

```
CREATE TABLE Employees
(
    EmployeeID INT PRIMARY KEY NOT NULL,
    LastName VARCHAR(30),
    FirstName VARCHAR(30),
    SocialSecurity CHAR(11) UNIQUE
)
```

For this table, you're using the EmployeeID column as the primary key, but you also want to prevent duplicates in the SocialSecurity column. This is a job for a UNIQUE constraint.

CHECK

Think of CHECK constraints as bits of application logic that you can place on your tables to guarantee that they reject any attempts to violate a business or other data rule that you want to enforce.

For example, imagine that you've extended the Employees table from the previous UNIQUE constraint example. You've now been asked to track the employee's work status. An employee can either be full or part-time; no other value is permitted in that column. This scenario is ideal for a CHECK constraint:

```
CREATE TABLE Employees
(
    EmployeeID INT PRIMARY KEY NOT NULL,
    LastName VARCHAR(30),
    FirstName VARCHAR(30),
    SocialSecurity CHAR(11) UNIQUE,
    WorkStatus VARCHAR(20) NOT NULL,
    CONSTRAINT Con_WorkStatus CHECK (WorkStatus =
            'FullTime'
    OR WorkStatus = 'PartTime')
)
```

With this constraint in place, you can rest assured that no one can sneak something by SQL Server 2005 Express:

```
INSERT INTO Employees VALUES (1798,'Von Zell','Harry',
'123-45-6789','Slacker')
```

```
The INSERT statement conflicted with the CHECK constraint
"Con_WorkStatus". The conflict occurred in
database "Westbay",table "Employees", column 'WorkStatus'.
```

Views

When you want to access or modify information that is spread among multiple tables, you must first build your Transact-SQL statement so that it joins these tables to produce a cohesive result set. This often isn't so simple, especially if any or all the following sets of circumstances are true for your organization:

- ✔ You have relatively unsophisticated users accessing your database directly via SQL or a graphical query tool.
- ✔ You have a complex database structure.
- ✔ You have security concerns: Not all users are allowed to see all columns.
- ✔ You have especially sensitive performance concerns.

Any of these situations can cause all kinds of problems as people attempt to navigate the complexities of your SQL Server 2005 Express installation. Fortunately, as a database designer or administrator, you have the power to present a much simpler — and more secure — picture of this information to these folks. To do this, you create what is known as a view.

Views are virtual representations of information from one or more tables. Their main purpose is to hide complexity from the database user, which allows them to easily locate and work with data. You can build a view on a single table, or on dozens of tables. The end result is the same: A more straightforward way to gain access to information.

In this next section, I describe some ways that you can use views to give your users a better experience with information you've entrusted to SQL Server 2005 Express.

Viewing your views

Getting a list of your views is no problem. Here's how to do so using SQL Server Management Studio Express, which is available from Microsoft:

1. **Launch SQL Server Management Studio Express.**

2. **Connect to the appropriate database engine.**

3. **On the Databases entry, expand the database entry for the database you're interested in.**

4. **Expand the Views folder.**

   With the Views folder expanded, you now see a System Views subfolder. If you're curious about the dozens of built-in views available, just open this folder.

   If, on the other hand, you're interested only in the database-specific views that have been created by users and database administrators, you see a list of them here as well. If you're curious about what makes up a particular view, go to the next step.

5. **Expand the view you're interested in examining.**

   Each user-defined view entry contains several columns of interest. These include

   - **Columns:** Expanding this folder gives you a list of all the columns that make up the view.

   - **Triggers:** A trigger is a set of activities that SQL Server 2005 Express performs when a certain event occurs. These events can be INSERT, UPDATE, or DELETE. By using an INSTEAD OF trigger, you can instruct SQL Server 2005 Express to take actions on the base tables when any of these events happen. This folder offers a list of any triggers driven by this view.

   - **Indexes:** Here's a list of all indexes that relate to this view. Note that while you can create indexes on views in SQL Server 2005 Express, they won't be of benefit to you unless you upgrade to the Enterprise edition.

   - **Statistics**: To help improve performance, SQL Server 2005 Express' Query Optimizer keeps track of a number of important facts about your data. Expanding this folder shows you what the optimizer currently knows; you can also create new statistical profiles.

If you're more of a Transact-SQL person, you can also get a list of views by consulting the sys.views table:

```
SELECT * FROM sys.views
```

A lot of information returns, especially if you're using a DOS command window; you may want to restrict your query to retrieve only the name of the view:

```
SELECT name FROM sys.views
```

When you have these details in hand, you can use the `sp_helptext` stored procedure to go to the next level and see the actual Transact-SQL syntax that created your view:

```
sp_helptext MyViewName
```

Creating a single table view

Although views really shine when they group information from multiple tables, they still can be very valuable for single tables. Look at the following SQL that creates a table of employee information:

```
CREATE TABLE Employees
(
    EmployeeID INT PRIMARY KEY NOT NULL,
    LastName VARCHAR(30),
    FirstName VARCHAR(30),
    SocialSecurity CHAR(11) UNIQUE,
    WorkStatus VARCHAR(20),
    Salary DECIMAL(6,2),
    EmployeeRank SMALLINT
)
```

This table holds some sensitive material, such as employee salaries, their Social Security numbers, and their rankings. You might want to restrict access to some of this intelligence, but people still need to view other parts of the data. One option is to set permissions for various users, but this can be cumbersome. In this case, a better choice is to create a view. You could then instruct users to work with the view; they would never know that the underlying table even existed.

To create a single table view, just follow these easy steps:

1. **Identify the candidate table for the view.**

2. **Choose the columns that you want to be present in the view.**

3. **Create the view, using standard SQL syntax.**

   Here's what it would look like for this table:

   ```
   CREATE VIEW V_Employees AS
   (SELECT EmployeeID, LastName, FirstName
   FROM Employees)
   ```

Users can now interact with this view. Figure 10-1 shows query results for both the base table as well as the view.

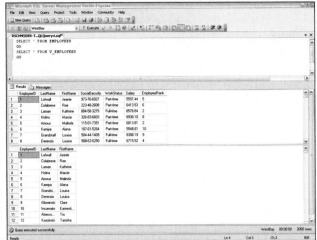

Figure 10-1:
Comparing
query
results from
a view
versus a
table.

From the users' perspective, this view walks and talks just like a regular table. In fact, because it's a single table-based view, you can even make data alterations via the INSERT, UPDATE, or DELETE statements:

```
INSERT INTO V_Employees VALUES (59229, 'Fields', 'Sidney')
```

This statement actually creates a new row in the Employees table; the view also shows this new row instantaneously.

Creating a multiple table view

In the previous section, I show you how to build and use a view on a single table. While a single table view is helpful, views really help out when you need to condense multiple tables into a single user experience.

Multiple table views are very helpful for retrieving information; however, unlike a single table view, you can't update a multiple table view.

Here's how you can create a multiple table view:

1. **Identify the candidate tables for the view.**

   Your goal should be to create a single window into these tables. The data should be related and meaningful.

2. **Choose the columns that you want present in the view.**

   You need to do this step for each table in question. Starting with a clean slate is a good idea: Don't assume that you need to include all columns from all the tables in your view.

3. **Determine how to join the tables.**

   Because your view's purpose in life is to combine data from multiple tables into a single user experience, it's really important that you get the right join syntax working among all the tables. Otherwise, the view itself possibly reflects an incorrect picture of reality, and you may find tracing the problem very hard after you put the view into production.

   Before creating your view, build some test queries that use the join syntax you plan to include in the view. Make sure that the data you're seeing matches your expectations before deploying the view.

4. **Build the view.**

   You can write standard SQL to do this, or you can use a tool to make it easier. Figure 10-2 shows what Visual Studio looks like when you're building a view.

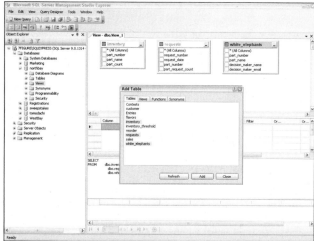

Figure 10-2: Creating a view from within SQL Server Management Studio Express.

Using XML

Since its introduction in the mid 1990s, the Extensible Markup Language (XML) has become an incredibly popular way of representing, manipulating, and transmitting information. It offers many advantages over older approaches, including

✔ **Standards-based:** Originally developed by the Worldwide Web Consortium (W3C), the XML is open, not owned by anyone, and based on well-documented standards. In fact, the XML standard has become the foundation of numerous other specifications.

✔ **Platform independence:** From the beginning, XML was designed to work with a huge range of operating systems, hardware platforms, computer languages, and so on. Its support of Unicode means that it is truly internationalized, as well.

✔ **Open, text-based file format:** You can use a simple text editor to read and write an XML document; there's no need to struggle with any proprietary, arcane file structures or cumbersome editors.

✔ **Well-defined, enforced syntax:** Rather than being simple amorphous blobs of data, XML documents are in fact subject to easily enforced structural rules. This helps maintain integrity of information stored and transmitted in XML.

Here's an example of a purchase order written in XML format:

```
<?xml version="1.0" encoding="UTF-8"?>

<PO Identifier="RR89291QQZ" date_generated="2005-25-Jun"
  application="Optimize v4.3">
  <customer>
      <name>Soze Imports</name>
      <identifier>21109332</identifier>
  </customer>
  <creator>Michael McManus</creator>
  <product quantity="1" price="9.99">GG2911</product>
  <product quantity="6" price="54.94">TK3020</product>
  <Delivery>
    <instruction>Call Mr. Hockney in
            receiving</instruction>
    <instruction>Fax bill to Mr. Kobayashi</instruction>
  </Delivery>
</PO>
```

Using XML with SQL Server 2005 Express

Recognizing the importance of XML, Microsoft has integrated it into the SQL Server product family. Here are some things to be aware of when it comes to SQL Server 2005 Express and XML storage:

✔ **The xml data type:** To store XML information in a particular column, simply create the column, using the xml data type. You can then decide whether to include a full XML document in the column, or to simply place a subset of this information, known as a *fragment*, into SQL Server 2005 Express.

You can store only as much as 2GB worth of XML information in your database.

Finally, you can elect to have SQL Server 2005 Express enforce the integrity of your XML data by relating an XML schema collection with the column(s) that store the XML information. If you go this route, you can consider your XML data to be typed: That is, SQL Server 2005 Express takes on the responsibility of making sure that no incorrectly structured XML data goes into your database.

✔ **XML-based indexes:** Internally, SQL Server 2005 Express stores XML information in binary large object (BLOB) format. While BLOB is an efficient way of storing data, querying or extracting information at runtime can be quite time-consuming.

Fortunately, administrators can place indexes on frequently queried XML columns. These indexes are defined as either primary or secondary. SQL Server 2005 Express uses a primary index to conduct a sequential search through your XML data. A secondary index provides an alternative mechanism to locate information, one that bypasses the potentially time-consuming sequential search of a primary index.

Now that you know how to store XML information in your database, in the next section, I show you how to derive value from these highly structured documents.

Working with XML

After you define one or more columns as storing XML, here are some ways that you can work with this information:

✔ **Transact-SQL:** You can use standard Transact-SQL statements to work with XML data. However, the fundamental structural differences between the XML and relational data models likely means that you also end up including one or both of the next two approaches to work with this information.

✔ **XML methods:** Five dedicated methods are available to work with XML information:

```
query()

value()

exist()

nodes()

modify()
```

✔ **XQuery:** Because XML represents a different way of storing information than that followed by traditional relational databases, it stands to reason that there would be specialized ways to work with this data. In fact, the XQuery query language was specifically developed for XML. You can use this language to perform sophisticated interaction with the XML data that you've elected to store in your database.

If you want to know a lot more about using XML in conjunction with SQL Server 2005 Express, check out Chapter 21.

Indexing

When improving query and other data access performance, database designers and administrators have to come up with a good indexing strategy. What makes things a little complicated is that each application has its own, unique performance needs that then translate to different indexing approaches.

In this section, you find out what must be indexed, and why. You also check out some additional SQL Server Express indexing features that you might want to use, depending on your application profile and performance needs.

Deciding what to index

At a minimum, you'll want to create indexes for the following types of columns:

✔ **Primary key columns:** A primary key serves to uniquely identify a row within a table; it preserves data integrity by preventing duplication. It also allows for very fast queries and other data access operations. You should define a primary key for every one of your tables. SQL Server 2005 Express thanks you by automatically creating an index on your primary key column(s).

If you can't come up with a primary key on your own, you can always create the table with an extra column that can be set to IDENTITY. SQL Server Express generates unique values for this column.

✔ **Foreign key columns:** Setting up foreign key relationships among tables helps safeguard your database's integrity by preventing erroneous information modifications. For example, if you're building a shipment system, you may want to enforce a rule that no order record (kept in the Order table) gets created without a corresponding customer record (stored in the Customer table). You can use a foreign key to help make sure that this rule doesn't get broken.

If you do go down this path, make sure that the column that serves as the foreign key (in this case, the customer identifier from Customer table) is indexed. In fact, SQL Server 2005 Express blocks you from even creating the foreign key if you haven't created the proper index.

✔ **Filter columns:** You use filter columns to narrow your data access results. For example, you might want to get a list of all customers who live in Costa Rica. When you write your query, you tell SQL Server 2005 Express what — if any — filters to apply. To help boost performance, creating indexes on commonly used filters is a good idea. In this case, this would translate to an index on the field that defines the customer's country.

✔ **Sort columns:** One nice feature of SQL is how easy you can request information in sorted order. However, if you want SQL Server 2005 Express to sort significant amounts of data, you would be wise to place an index on the columns that are most frequently designated as responsible for sorting. Doing so helps reduce the amount of overhead that the database server must undertake to process your request.

All of the SQL Server 2005 database products offer a specialized type of structure known as a *clustered index*. When a clustered index is in place on a table, that table is then physically stored in the order of the index. For example, suppose that you have a table that contains a column that stores people's last names. If you create a clustered index on that column, SQL Server 2005 Express physically sorts the table by last name, and rearrange its internal structures so that the table is in that order. Note that you can only have one clustered index per table. If you don't define any indexes as clustered, your primary key serves as the clustered index.

Creating an index

Building an index is very easy. Just follow these straightforward steps:

1. **Decide what you want to index.**

   Use the guidelines I describe in the preceding section to help you settle on those columns that need indexes. Don't be afraid of making a mistake — you can always drop any unnecessary indexes later.

2. **Decide what tool you'll use to build your index.**

   You have a wide variety of choices here. You can use SQL Server Management Studio Express (which is what I use in this example), the command-line interface, or a third-party tool. I also show you the SQL that you need to type it yourself.

3. **Expand the Data Connections entry.**

   If you don't see any valid data connections, just right-click the Data Connections entry and choose the Add Connection option.

4. **Expand the particular database where you want to create the index.**

5. **Open the Tables folder.**

6. **Right-click the table where you want to create an index and choose the Modify option.**

7. **Right-click anywhere in the list of table columns and choose the Indexes/Keys option.**

   The Indexes/Keys dialog box appears.

8. **Click the Add button.**

   This creates a new index prefixed by IX_. It's now time to pick the column(s) and set the properties for your new index.

9. **Click the `Columns` property, and then click the ellipses to get a list of candidate columns.**

10. **Choose as many columns as you like, and specify whether the index will be ascending or descending for each column.**

11. **Set other properties for the index and then click Close when you're finished; save the modified table by choosing File⇨Save.**

These can include properties like its name, and whether you want SQL Server 2005 Express to re-compute its internal statistics after creating the index.

Figure 10-3 shows the rich user interface that Visual Studio offers for constructing indexes.

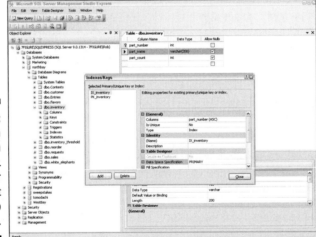

Figure 10-3: Creating an index from within SQL Server Management Studio Express.

Doing things graphically is fine, but what if you want to directly enter the SQL to create this index? That's easy enough — here it is for a scenario where you want to use the SQLCMD utility to generate an index on the `LastName` column in the `Employees` table:

```
CREATE INDEX IX_EMPLOYEES ON Employees(LastName)
```

Searching, Grouping, and Summarizing Data

Transact-SQL offers a number of useful query language expressions that help you make sense of your data. In this section, I list each of these tools, as well as provide illustrations of how you can use them. For the purposes of these examples, look at the structure and sample data in Table 10-1.

Table 10-1		Daily Sales		
TransactionID	*Item*	*Region*	*DateOfSale*	*Amount*
17090	Widget 1	East	10/17/2006	45.90
17091	Widget 4	UK	10/17/2006	17.23
..				
29040	Widget 6	Japan	12/30/2006	132.93

Note: For simplicity, I've included the item and region's name in this table. In reality, if you subscribed to good relational database design theory, this would likely be represented by a number that pointed to a table containing a master list of all items, as well as a number that referred to a list of regions.

GROUP BY

You can use GROUP BY to help aggregate information, which is very beneficial when you want to provide higher-level summarization of your data. For example, suppose that you need to break out and total your sales figures by region. It's easy to do with GROUP BY:

```
SELECT Region, SUM(Amount) as 'Total'
FROM DailySales
GROUP BY Region
```

SQL Server 2005 Express neatly sums up your information and returns the results:

```
Central                                    234252.75
Japan                                      242278.92
East                                       227365.08
Latin America                              235740.14
UK                                         306054.29
West                                       246750.58
China                                      248140.43
Germany                                    258725.60
```

Of course, you're free to add other requirements to your query, such as filtering, sorting, and so on:

```
SELECT Region, SUM(Amount) as 'Total'
FROM DailySales
WHERE Item = 'Square Wheel'
GROUP BY Region
ORDER BY 'Total' DESC
```

This query focuses on one item, and sorts the results in descending order of the total amount sold.

ROLLUP

Including ROLLUP with your query instructs SQL Server 2005 Express to take your query results and help create subtotals and totals. For example, suppose that you want to run a search that summarizes sales by region and item. Here's how you would use ROLLUP:

```
SELECT Region, Item, SUM(Amount) as 'Total'
FROM DailySales
GROUP BY Region, Item WITH ROLLUP
```

Here's a small subset of the output from this query:

```
Central      Widget 1                        36674.00
...
Central      Widget 8                        19915.89
Central      NULL                            34252.75
...
China        Widget 1                        38395.36
...
China        Widget 8                        36389.85
China        NULL                           248140.43
...
East         Widget 1                        32198.16
...
East         Widget 8                        28977.62
East         NULL                           227365.08
NULL         NULL                          1999307.79
```

SQL Server 2005 Express has considerately reported on how each item sold within each region. Total sales for the region are tabulated at the bottom of each region; their item name is NULL. The very last row reports on total sales for all items for all regions.

CUBE

Adding CUBE to your query produces very similar results as ROLLUP. The main exception is that CUBE also summarizes all combination of your output columns. For example, look at the slight modification to the previous query:

```
SELECT Region, Item, SUM(Amount) as 'Total'
FROM DailySales
GROUP BY Region, Item WITH CUBE
```

Here's the net new output from this query:

```
NULL        Widget 1                        322746.38
NULL        Widget 2                        225510.42
...
NULL        Widget 8                         35606.70
```

SQL Server 2005 Express would report on further combinations if you had requested added columns as part of your query.

HAVING

In a nutshell, including HAVING with your aggregation query tells SQL Server 2005 Express to further filter your results. This is very powerful, and really helps you isolate and focus on important data.

For example, suppose that you want to see only sales summaries from those regions that sold more than $250,000. You could write an application that walked through the data and then reported only relevant results. However, a better idea would be to use HAVING:

```
SELECT Region, SUM(Amount) as 'Total'
FROM DailySales
GROUP BY Region
HAVING SUM(Amount) > 250000
```

By adding HAVING, you ask SQL Server 2005 Express to avoid reporting on regions that didn't hit the revenue target. Your result set is quite small, but exactly what you wanted to see:

```
UK          306054.29
Germany     258725.60
```

TIMESTAMP

Keeping track of changes in your database can be tricky, especially when you're actively working with a row and want to make sure that nothing has changed before you update the database with your own alterations. In cases like this, try taking advantage of the TIMESTAMP data type to help you stay on top of the exact state of your information.

When you build a table that includes a TIMESTAMP column, SQL Server 2005 Express automatically inserts an internal identifier into the column anytime a given row is inserted or updated. You can then use this value to see if something has changed. Here's the exact set of steps to follow:

1. **Create your table, making sure to include one (and only one) column defined as TIMESTAMP:**

```
CREATE TABLE Accounts
(
    CustomerID INTEGER PRIMARY KEY NOT NULL,
    CurrentBalance DECIMAL(10,2) NOT NULL,
    TIMESTAMP
)
```

Notice that you don't need to give the TIMESTAMP column a name. Also, note that you can't insert a value into this column directly, so you need to specify your column names (and omit the timestamp) when adding data to your table.

2. **Use your table normally: Add, alter, and retrieve information with standard Transact-SQL.**

The timestamp value doesn't change unless you change a row.

3. **Check the timestamp value before you update a row.**

A good way to do this step is to first retrieve the timestamp, make your changes in your application, and then retrieve the timestamp one more time (but put it into a different variable). If the two timestamps match, the row has not changed from the time you first retrieved it. Otherwise, someone has updated the row while you were working with it.

To get the current database timestamp, run the following query:

```
SELECT @@DBTS

0x00000000A9C20FA0
```

This returns a hexadecimal value, which changes every time someone alters timestamped information in the database.

Don't confuse TIMESTAMP with the DATETIME data type: The former refers to the internal database identifier; the latter refers to a point in time.

Part IV

Keeping Your Data Safe from Harm

The 5th Wave   By Rich Tennant

In this part . . .

What's a harried database owner to do? Sometimes you'll feel like everyone's out to get you, or at least your data. Uneducated users, apathetic developers, malicious hackers, mutant viruses, and even cosmic rays all seem to conspire to deliberately or carelessly damage or even destroy your vital information. Luckily, you can do a lot to protect yourself.

To begin, you see how to take advantage of the rich security capabilities of SQL Server 2005 Express. After that, I show you how transactions can help keep your data in order. Finally, you get the hang of setting up and implementing a robust backup and recovery strategy.

Chapter 11

Securing Your Data

1 n a perfect world, you wouldn't need this chapter. You would also have no need for police or locks on doors, but, alas, that is not reality. As it turns out, you have good reason to be concerned about the safety of the information entrusted to your SQL Server 2005 Express database. Fortunately, Microsoft has done a very good job of creating a robust security infrastructure for the entire SQL Server database product family. However, the sheer volume of security-related capabilities can be somewhat daunting.

This chapter is all about quickly helping you make the most of the security features at your disposal. To begin, I list some questions that you can use to help determine the degree of emphasis you need to place on security. Because you likely require at least some security configuration, the next section talks about the broad range of database objects that you can lock down. Finally, with the overview complete, I show you how to perform some of the most commonplace security tasks.

This chapter is not a comprehensive guide to all the possible SQL Server 2005 Express security permutations; that would fill its own book!

Why Bother with Security?

As you see in this chapter, the SQL Server 2005 Express security system has a lot to it. You may wonder what all the fuss is about, and whether your time is well spent learning about securing your database. Both are valid questions, and after reading this section you might indeed decide that you don't need to implement a broad-based security strategy. But first, you should understand the risks of an unsecured database.

Insufficient security: When bad things happen to good data

Your data has two primary threats when your SQL Server 2005 Express database doesn't have the right security configuration. The first hazard is *unauthorized access to information*. For example, an unauthorized employee or outsider may figure out a way to view sensitive details, such as salary, trade secrets, and other intelligence that you don't want made public. The interloper doesn't change any data or damage things, but your sensitive information is now compromised.

Things get worse in the second type of security exposure: *unauthorized data modifications*. In this case, that rogue employee who was viewing salary data has decided to give himself a raise, while rolling back the wages of all his co-workers to 1970s levels. Of course, you may eventually figure out what has happened to your information, but obviously a tremendous amount of damage can happen before you can correct things. This example is actually fairly mild; a security gap can lead to much more serious information injuries.

Should you secure your database?

Now that I've filled your head with scary visions of damaged data, you can decide if you need to implement a security plan. If you answer Yes to any of the following questions, you need to take the time to set up a decent security plan:

- ✔ Will your database hold sensitive information?
- ✔ Will multiple people work with your data?
- ✔ Will other computers connect to your database?
- ✔ Will your database server be available over a local network or the Internet?

Chances are that at least one of the preceding questions applies to you. With that in mind, you can get started setting up the right security plan for your database.

What Can You Secure?

If you can store it or represent it in SQL Server 2005 Express, chances are that you can secure it. These security-ready structures are known as *securables*. One securable may in fact enclose additional securables, thereby producing a group of objects. These are known as *scopes*, and by setting security at the scope level, all securables contained within the scope receive the same security settings. As I show you in this section, many securables can make up each scope; however, for the purposes of this chapter, I focus on a few of the *object securables* within the schema scope.

To give you an idea of how many security options you have, take a look at the following list, which is categorized by the SQL Server 2005 Express three securable scopes, each containing its own securables:

Server:

| Endpoint | Login |
| Database | |

Database:

User	Role
Application role	Assembly
Message type	Route
Service	Remote service binding
Fulltext catalog	Certificate
Asymmetric key	Symmetric key
Contract	

Schema:

| Type | XML Schema Collection |
| Object | |

The Object securable is of most interest for this chapter. It contains the following components:

Aggregate	Statistic
Constraint	Synonym
Function	Table
Procedure	View
Queue	

If some of the items in these lists look a little unfamiliar to you, don't worry: The balance of the chapter focuses on securing the more recognizable objects, such as tables and views.

Who Can You Let Use Your Database?

In the preceding section, I show you all the items that you can secure. The next question to answer is what kind of users can work with your database. In fact, some of these users aren't people at all, but application programs and processes. Regardless of whether the entity accessing your database has a heartbeat or voltage, SQL Server 2005 Express uses the term *principal* to describe them. Principals have three major classifications, which in turn contain resources as follows:

Operating system-based principals:

Windows domain login   Windows local

SQL Server-based principals:

SQL Server login

Database-based principals:

Database user   Database role

Application role

SQL Server 2005 Express also supports the concept of prepackaged permissions. These are known as *roles*, but you can think of them as a one-stop shop that lets you grant permissions en masse. Table 11-1 lists all the fixed server-level roles along with their purposes. Table 11-2 does the same for fixed database-level roles.

Table 11-1	SQL Server Express Fixed Server Roles
Name	**Permission Available**
bulkadmin	Run the BULK INSERT command
dbcreator	Create, change, restore, or drop a database
diskadmin	Administer disk files
processadmin	End SQL Server processes
securityadmin	Set server and database-level permissions; set password
serveradmin	Shut down the server; modify server configuration values
setupadmin	Manage linked servers; run system stored procedures
sysadmin	Perform any administrative task on the server

Table 11-2	SQL Server Express Fixed Database Roles
Name	**Permission Available**
public	Default role for all database users
db_accessadmin	Maintain access permissions to the database
db_backupoperator	Archive the database
db_datareader	Read all data from any user table
db_datawriter	Make any modifications to any user's data
db_ddladmin	Execute any DDL command in any database
db_denydatareader	Blocked from reading data in a database
db_denydatawriter	Prevented from making any data modifications
db_owner	Perform all setup and database maintenance
db_securityadmin	Administer permissions and roles

Understanding that all new database users are associated with the public database role is important. If you don't explicitly set permissions for a given securable, these users automatically inherit the permissions that have been granted to the public database role for the securable in question. Later in this chapter, I show you how to define permissions, including for the public database role.

What Can You Let Users Do?

Previously in this chapter, I've shown the type of objects that you can secure, as well as the types of users and roles that you can support. The next step in realizing your security vision is to decide who you want to work with your database, and then grant them the appropriate permissions.

Who gets to use the database?

Knowing all the configurable security options at your fingertips, you may be tempted to rush out and start setting up profiles and granting access to your database server. However, because no two enterprises can have the same security profile, taking a little more time and getting a better handle on exactly what you need to do for your own organization is worth your time.

A great start is to simply figure out the types of users that you need to support. In this section, I list some of the typical SQL Server 2005 Express user profiles that you're likely to encounter, in increasing order of responsibility. Note that your site may not have all these functions; you may also have the same person handling multiple jobs, or you may be faced with additional roles and responsibilities. Nevertheless, use this handy list as a starting point:

- ✔ **Reporting user:** This kind of user typically connects to your database via a third-party reporting tool and runs reports or other data analysis. Generally, you can safely restrict these people's ability to make changes to the database, because they're primarily interested in reading data, not altering it.

- ✔ **Application user:** This type of SQL Server 2005 Express user often doesn't even know that a database server is part of the picture. Instead, they generally log in to an application and perform work that just happens to get registered in your database. By and large, you don't need to give tremendous power to this class of user; in fact, you can usually look to your application developer or vendor for guidance on the right security profile. Certain types of applications handle their own security, which usually translates into a smaller set of SQL Server 2005 Express-based logins.

- ✔ **Database user:** Akin to reporting users, these people are generally interested in the raw contents of your database, rather than information filtered by any third-party applications.

- ✔ **Application power user:** These sophisticated users often need to have higher levels of database privileges for tasks such as creating views and new tables or even granting access to additional users. Nevertheless, you would be wise to concede only as little additional privileges as possible. They can always request more control if it's really necessary.

- ✔ **Operator:** Normally, operators are concerned only with routine (but essential) database administration tasks, such as backup and restore operations. Unless they need to have higher authority, you can generally limit their access to your database to these purely administrative tasks.

- ✔ **Application developer:** These folks usually want broad security power, which can trigger an adversarial relationship with the database administrator. Developers themselves are often subject to the changing whims of their application users, whose requests often require changes to the database or underlying server.

  However, by setting up development and test servers, you can have your cake and eat it, too: The developers can have wide open security permissions on these non-production servers, and you can sleep better knowing that your production environment is safe.

✔ **System administrator:** It's quite understandable if a system administrator views database administration as a bit of a nuisance: After all, their primary job is ensuring the health of the server computer itself. However, you need to give these overseers sufficient permission to fill in or otherwise assist the person with the ultimate responsibility for the database's health: the database administrator.

✔ **Database administrator:** This profile represents the alpha and omega of SQL Server 2005 Express security. Typically, the database administrator can perform any task on a SQL Server 2005 Express server. However, all this power comes neatly packaged with a great deal of responsibility, so be careful about handing this role out lightly.

Choosing from the permissions menu

You use permissions to grant or remove privileges to a principal on one or more securables. For example, you might want to give a certain user full privileges for table 1, partial privileges for table 2, and no privileges for table 3. I show you how to set permissions as part of the next section.

Implementing Security

After you read through the previous sections and get up to speed on all the clever SQL Server 2005 Express security possibilities, you can put them to the test. To begin, I show you how to figure out who can already access your server and databases. When you know that, you then get the hang of granting access to your database server and databases, followed by how you can set specific permissions on particular objects.

Because the graphical SQL Server Management Studio Express (SSMSE) is the most straightforward way of getting administrative tasks done, I focus on this helpful tool. You could also use SQLCMD to manage security, but you have to wield a combination of stored procedures and Transact-SQL.

Getting a list of authorized users

Whether you've created 100 users or none, here's a quick, easy way to see who is authorized to connect to your system.

Getting a login list

Just as a login lets you access a computer, a SQL Server 2005 Express login lets people (or processes) connect to your database system. Here's what you need to do to get a full list of authorized logins:

1. **Start SQL Server Management Studio Express.**

2. **Connect to your database server.**

3. **Expand the Security folder.**

4. **Open the Logins folder.**

That's all there is to it. All the people or processes listed in the Logins folder (see Figure 11-1) can log in to your system.

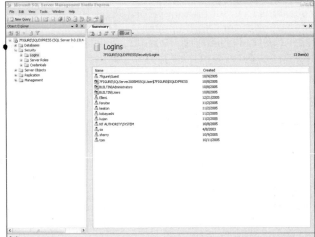

Figure 11-1:
Getting a list of server logins.

Of course, the next thing you need to know is who can actually work with your databases, which is what I show you next.

Getting a user list

Just logging in to a SQL Server Express system is not enough. You also need permission to connect and work with one or more databases. Here's how you can tell who is allowed to do this:

1. **Start SQL Server Management Studio Express.**

2. **Connect to your database server.**

3. **Expand the Databases folder.**

4. **Open the specific folder for the database that you want to check.**

5. **Open the Security folder for the database.**

6. **Expand the Users folder.**

Everyone listed in the Users folder is authorized to connect to this particular database. Figure 11-2 shows a fully expanded security view, from the logins to the database users.

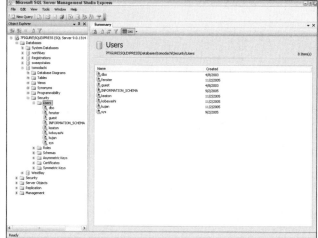

Figure 11-2:
A consolidated list of server logins and database users.

Granting access

Authorizing people and applications to work with your SQL Server 2005 Express system is the most common security-related administrative task that you're likely to face. In this section, I show you the sequence of events you need to follow to make that happen.

For this example, assume that a new employee named Hal has just joined your organization. His job is to analyze sales and marketing trends, so he needs direct access to a specific database named Marketing. Also assume that your Windows system administrator has already created an appropriate Windows login and profile for Hal.

Creating database server logins

To begin, anyone who wants to talk with your SQL Server 2005 Express database server must have a login. Here's how to create one, using SQL Server Management Studio Express:

1. **Start SQL Server Management Studio Express.**

2. **Connect to your database server.**

3. **Expand the Security folder.**

4. **Open the Logins folder.**

5. **Right-click the Logins folder, and choose New Login.**

   The New Login window appears.

6. **Decide if you want to use Windows or SQL Server authentication.**

   When you choose Windows authentication, you're instructing SQL Server 2005 Express to obtain its login information directly from the operating system. This integrated security approach makes a lot of sense, especially if you're using the same login architecture for other applications. You can search your computer or others on your network for login details.

   On the other hand, choosing SQL Server authentication means that you're creating a login that is meaningful only within the confines of your database server; it has no relationship with the operating system.

7. **Fill in additional general properties.**

   After you select your user, you now have several pages worth of security-related properties for the new login. Figure 11-3 shows the general properties page where you can set the default database and language for this login.

Figure 11-3:
The Login –
New
General
Properties
page.

8. **Switch to the Server Roles page, and authorize any server roles that you want this login to have.**

   I list the available server roles in the section "Who Can You Let Use Your Database?" (earlier in the chapter); be careful about giving new logins broad capabilities. In this example, because Hal is just a run-of-the-mill user, he doesn't need server-wide permissions.

9. **Switch to the User Mapping page, and enable connectivity to all relevant databases.**

   By enabling database connectivity here, SQL Server 2005 Express automatically creates a user with this name in each database, which saves you time later. In this case, simply checking the Map box next to the Marketing database and picking a database role is all that's necessary to grant Hal connectivity to the database.

10. **After you finish setting the properties for this login, click OK to save it.**

    This login is now ready to connect to your database server. If you associated the login with one or more databases, and those databases have `public` permissions set, this login can now work with those databases.

Creating database users

A database user is someone who not only has permission to connect to your SQL Server 2005 Express instance, but also has the ability to work with one or more databases. You can make this happen by simply associating a login with one or more databases, which I point out earlier in this chapter. On the other hand, if you want to do this manually, here's how to get the job done:

1. **Start SQL Server Management Studio Express.**

2. **Connect to your database server.**

3. **Expand the Databases folder.**

4. **Expand the folder for the specific database where you want to create the user.**

5. **Expand the Security folder.**

6. **Right-click the Users folder, and choose New User.**

   The Database User window opens with a series of different pages. Figure 11-4 shows the General Properties page.

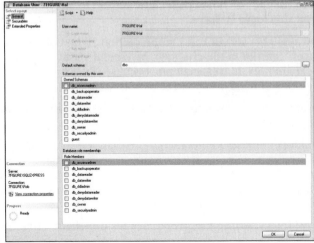

Figure 11-4:
The new
user
General
Properties
page.

7. **Associate the new user with any owned schemas.**

In this example, Hal's default schema is dbo.

8. **If applicable, assign the new user to any database roles.**

9. **Switch to the Securables page, and set up authorization for the new user.**

You can set security permissions by user, or you can set them for the public database role (which is faster and more convenient). If you want to set them by user, use the Permissions page. You can search for the specific types of securables from within this page, as shown in Figure 11-5.

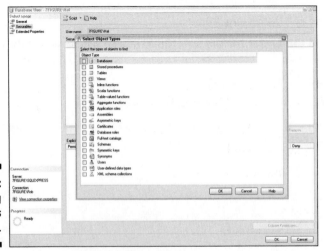

Figure 11-5:
Searching
for objects
to authorize.

After you pick one or more types of securables, SQL Server 2005 Express returns a list of the available objects to secure, as shown in Figure 11-6.

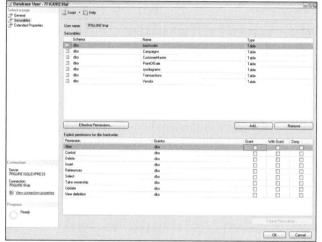

Figure 11-6:
Authorizing
access for
a given
object.

10. **After setting the right security profile for the new user, click OK to save the record.**

Your user is now ready to work with all authorized objects in this database.

Setting permissions by securable

So far, I've described security from the perspective of the user. However, you can implement your security architecture is a different (and often better) way. In this case, you set your security at the securable level, granting or revoking permissions for users, database roles, or application roles.

For example, suppose that you want to set permissions on a given table. Here's what you need to do to make this possible:

1. **Start SQL Server Management Studio Express.**

2. **Connect to your database server.**

3. **Expand the Databases folder.**

4. **Expand the folder for the specific database where you want to set the permissions.**

5. **Expand the Tables folder.**

6. **Right-click the table in question, and choose Properties.**

7. **On the Permissions page, click the Add button.**

   A dialog box appears in which you can locate users, application roles, and database roles.

8. **Click Browse to see a list of candidates.**

9. **Choose at least one candidate for permission granting, and click OK.**

10. **Set permissions for the candidate, and click OK.**

    With your candidates identified, you can now set their permissions according to your security policies, as show in Figure 11-7. In this case, I'm about to grant permissions on the PointOfSale table to the public database role, which in turn affects all registered users. Because Hal is a member of this role, he too has these permissions.

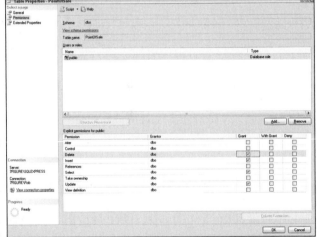

Figure 11-7: Authorizing access for a given object.

Modifying or revoking permissions

Altering or denying permissions is a relatively straightforward affair. In the case of SQL Server Management Studio Express, you generally use the same sequence of steps to make these changes as you do when adding permissions; the main difference is that you're removing them instead of adding permissions.

You may also elect to set user-specific permissions. In Figure 11-8, I've checked the Deny box to specifically prevent Hal from creating any new records in this particular table. For Hal, this overrides the Insert permission that I granted to the public group.

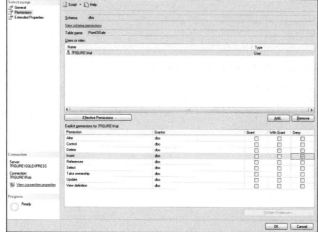

Figure 11-8:
Denying
permission
for a
specific
user to
insert
records in
the table.

Chapter 12

Keeping It Together: Using Transactions to Maintain Data Integrity

*U*nlike many other databases, SQL Server 2005 Express combines ease-of-use and low cost (actually, it's free) with very sophisticated database engine features. Transactions are one of the most important capabilities offered by any high-end database. In this chapter, you get a good idea of data integrity, and why transactions are important in keeping your data nice and clean. Because transactions are one of the main guardians of your data, you also see how you can use them to keep everything running smoothly.

What Is Data Integrity?

Simply put, *data integrity* means that you can trust your database server to accurately store and report on your information. Without integrity, you can easily make bad or inaccurate decisions because you're not really getting a true picture of reality. In this section, I describe several ways that your data can lose its integrity, along with the SQL Server 2005 Express transaction capabilities that help preserve integrity. Transactions play a big role in preventing loss of integrity, so I also describe what makes a transaction a transaction.

Shocking tales of lost integrity

Brace yourself: You're about to read several ways that your information can lose its integrity. Fortunately, you can avoid each of these unpleasant scenarios by simply employing a combination of referential integrity (primary and foreign keys) and transactions.

- ✔ **Parent and child differences:** Imagine that your database includes data stored in *parent* (header) and *child* (detail) tables. Furthermore, suppose that you keep a running total of information in the parent table about records in the child table. A good example is customer details (name, address, financial summary) in the parent table, and customer transactions (transaction date, amount, and so on) in the child table. If you're not careful, these two tables can get out of sync, which might lead to someone looking at data in the parent table to make an incorrect assumption.

- ✔ **Orphans:** Continuing with the preceding example, what happens if you intentionally delete a parent record but somehow overlook deleting its related children? You're left with the sad prospect of orphaned child records forever doomed to a lonely existence in your database.

- ✔ **Partial updates:** A partial update can happen when all the tables that are supposed to be updated at one time don't actually successfully complete their modifications. The classic example of this problem is a failure when transferring money between savings and checking tables. If the application only reduces the savings balance but does not increase the checking balance, the customer is quite unhappy, and the data's integrity (and possibly the bank manager's office) is damaged.

- ✔ **Business rule violations:** Although rules are generally meant to be broken from time to time, this is not true with information carefully entrusted to your SQL Server Express database. For example, you might be building an application to track credit ratings for your customers. Valid values for the credit score range between 0 and 100. If a rogue person or program places a value of –291 or 1,259 in this column, your data's integrity is no longer intact.

Passing the ACID test

SQL Server 2005 Express is a robust, industrial-strength database server. One hurdle that any database server must pass to belong to this club is known as the ACID test. It does not refer to the database's propensity to ingest psychedelic drugs, nor does it have anything to do with its ability to withstand corrosive liquids. Instead, passing this test means that the database server supports a minimum level of transaction integrity. ACID is an acronym that stands for Atomicity, Consistency, Integrity, and Durability. I describe each of these components in the following list:

- ✔ **Atomicity:** This doesn't refer to the radioactivity of your database. Instead, you can consider a transaction to be atomic if all its steps happen as a group, or none of them do. For example, a transaction may update four tables at one time. Atomicity means that either all four tables receive their updates correctly, or all of them are restored to their initial state. Without this trait, your database could easily become inconsistent.

- ✔ **Consistency:** Part of your job as a database designer or administrator is to set up referential integrity and other business rules. The database engine's job is to take these rules into consideration when processing a transaction. If the transaction attempts to violate even one rule, the database server must abort the transaction and roll the database back to its original state. For example, if you specify that a column can only contain a numeric value between 1 and 5, and a transaction attempts to place a 6 into that column, SQL Server 2005 Express rolls the whole transaction back, even for any other tables or columns that were not violated.

- ✔ **Integrity:** In the context of a SQL Server 2005 Express transaction, integrity has nothing to do with paying debts, obeying the speed limit, or helping old ladies across the street. Instead, it means that while a transaction is underway, no other processes other than the transaction itself can see the database in an intermediate state. For example, suppose that your transaction is processing an order, which involves decrementing inventory while updating a customer's shopping cart. The integrity trait means that any other process sees both the inventory and shopping cart data structures in their original states while the transaction is running. Of course, after you finish the transaction both these results are available at the same time.

- ✔ **Durability:** A durable database server transaction does not refer to its ability to withstand heat and cold, or resist thermal viscosity breakdown. Rather, it means that after you state that the transaction is finished, and the database reports this to be true, SQL Server 2005 Express doesn't suddenly develop amnesia and disregard your work. It's true that another user or process may come along and make changes to your data, but this is not the same as the database itself casually forgetting what you did.

Key Transaction Structures

To make transactions possible, SQL Server 2005 Express uses a sophisticated set of technologies all working together to help ensure that things go smoothly. At the beginning of a transaction, SQL Server 2005 Express uses the set of internal structures that I describe here to record the details about the transaction, as well as coordinate interaction between your transaction and other database users and processes. Some of these key components include

- ✔ **Log cache:** SQL Server 2005 Express uses this memory-based structure as a temporary storage buffer for details about a transaction. Because it's based in memory, and separate from the standard buffer cache used for data, it's very fast and efficient.

- ✔ **Transaction log:** This file, or group of files, is a journal that contains information about your transactions. It works in conjunction with the log cache. If you need to roll back your transaction, or restore from a backup, this journal is vital to setting things right with your database. It also serves as a source of guidance for database replication and standby servers. Administrators typically back up their transaction logs as part of normal maintenance.

- ✔ **Locks:** Because SQL Server 2005 Express supports multiple concurrent users and processes, a series of locking mechanisms must coordinate access to information. A lock's scope can be very granular — such as at the data page level — or very wide — such as at the table or even database level.

- ✔ **Checkpoints:** As you might guess from its name, a checkpoint is an intricate, internal SQL Server 2005 Express event that serves to synchronize all the other internal transaction structures so that everything is consistent.

Isolation Levels

Each SQL Server 2005 Express transaction has an *isolation level*. This term describes how the transaction interacts with other database users and processes.

To make transaction isolation levels work, SQL Server 2005 Express employs a variety of locks on data and indexes, as well as other internal controls. Locks may be at the row, page, or table level, and they may be *exclusive* (completely restricting access to data) or *shared* (which allows other transactions to access information).

SQL Server 2005 Express offers a series of increasingly stringent isolation levels:

- ✔ **READ UNCOMMITTED:** Also described as *dirty read*, this isolation level is the most permissive. It lets other users and processes see your transaction's work even if it hasn't yet been formally committed to the SQL Server 2005 Express database. For example, you may insert a row into a particular table. Other users see that row even before the transaction is finished. If you then roll back the transaction, the row never truly existed; yet other users saw it. This is known as *phantom data*, and can lead others to make scarily incorrect decisions.

- ✔ **READ COMMITTED:** As the default for SQL Server 2005 Express, this isolation level prevents other users or processes from seeing your transaction's work until it's finished. However, these outside parties can make alterations to any of the data that your transaction has read. For example, suppose that your transaction reads 100 rows from a given table and then takes action based on what it read. Another program can modify any of those 100 rows even while your transaction is active. This may be a problem if your transaction needs those rows to remain in their original condition. Fortunately, the next isolation level addresses that kind of potential issue.

- ✔ **REPEATABLE READ:** This level is just like the READ COMMITTED isolation level, except that REPEATABLE READ prevents other transactions from modifying any rows that were consulted by your transaction. To continue the READ COMMITTED example, this isolation level means that no other transactions could change any of the 100 rows that your transaction has read until your transaction has finished.

- ✔ **SNAPSHOT:** By requesting this isolation level, you can be assured that all the data that your transaction reads or modifies remains in that state until you complete your work. It uses versioning to achieve this high degree of interoperability, which comes at a much lower overhead cost than other isolation levels, such as REPEATABLE READ. Of course, others may come along after you finish your transaction and make their own changes, but this isolation level does at least keep things consistent until your work is done.

- ✔ **SERIALIZABLE:** This isolation level is by far the most restrictive. Not only does it block other transactions from seeing any changes that your active transaction has made, and changing any data that you've read, it also prevents outside transactions from inserting any new rows if the index values for those rows would fall in the range of data that you've read. For example, suppose that your transaction has read rows with an index value between 0 and 100. With this setting, no other transactions could insert a new row with an index value anywhere between 0 and 100.

Be careful when using the more restrictive isolation levels. Although they do a great job of preserving data integrity, the cost can be significantly reduced system speed and throughput.

Using Transactions

In the previous sections of this chapter, I tell you all about transactions. So now you're probably wondering how you can put these powerful features to work. Fortunately, despite their rich capabilities, transactions are quite simple to use. In a nutshell, just follow these steps:

1. **Determine the isolation level that you need to do your work.**

   In the preceding section of this chapter, I show you that SQL Server 2005 Express offers five different transaction isolation levels. Your job as a developer is to pick the right one.

   Pick the least restrictive transaction isolation level that your application can afford. In other words, don't use the more draconian isolation levels (such as SERIALIZABLE) unless your transaction demands the control and restrictions provided by this isolation level. As a matter of fact, in most cases, you'll probably find that the default isolation level will suffice.

2. **Set the isolation level.**

   Because SQL Server Express supports numerous development languages and technologies, I use straight SQL transaction invocations for the balance of this section.

   To specify your choice of isolation level, just use the SET TRANSACTION ISOLATION LEVEL statement:

   ```
   SET TRANSACTION ISOLATION LEVEL REPEATABLE READ
   ```

   Your chosen isolation level remains in effect until you explicitly change it, or your session closes.

3. **Start the transaction.**

   Use the BEGIN TRANSACTION statement to indicate that your transaction is now underway:

   ```
   BEGIN TRANSACTION
   ```

   You may also specify a name for your transaction, but a name is optional. In any case, after you invoke this statement, you are now in an active transaction.

4. **Make your data alterations.**

   You can use whatever SQL or other database access language you're accustomed to. The fact that you're in a transaction doesn't change your syntax at all.

5. **Check for any errors.**

   Carefully monitoring each statement to make sure that it works as you expected is important. These facts are very important when deciding whether you want to make your work permanent.

6. **Finalize the transaction.**

   By now you're ready to finish your work. Assuming that everything has gone well, you can tell SQL Server 2005 Express that you want your changes to be made permanent:

   ```
   COMMIT TRANSACTION
   ```

   If you have given your transaction a name as part of the BEGIN TRANSACTION statement, you need to include it here.

   If things didn't go well with your transaction, don't despair. You can tell SQL Server 2005 Express to forget the whole thing, and return your database to its pristine, original state:

   ```
   ROLLBACK TRANSACTION
   ```

   Remember that if you gave your transaction a name, you need to include it here:

   ```
   ROLLBACK TRANSACTION transaction name
   ```

Here, written in basic Transact-SQL, is a simple banking transaction that adds $5.00 into the balance of every customer who has been with the bank since before January 1, 2004:

```
DECLARE @ERROR_STATE INT;

SET TRANSACTION ISOLATION LEVEL REPEATABLE READ;

BEGIN TRANSACTION;

UPDATE Accounts SET Balance = Balance + 5
WHERE DateJoined < '1/1/2004';

SELECT @ERROR_STATE = @@ERROR;
IF (@ERROR_STATE <> 0)
   ROLLBACK TRANSACTION;
ELSE
   COMMIT TRANSACTION;
```

The @@ERROR function tells you if anything has gone wrong with your transaction, which gives you the chance to roll it back in time. To find out more about handling errors, take a look at Chapter 17.

Chapter 13

Preventing Data Loss

● ●

In This Chapter

▶ Using transactions to safeguard your data

▶ Keeping memory and disk in sync

▶ Backing up vital database information

▶ Restoring database archives

● ●

*W*aking up one morning to find some or all your precious data lost forever ranks with some of life's great moments — like root canals, tax audits, or endless flight delays. However, in this chapter, I show you that unlike death and taxes, you can avoid losing data.

To begin, I show you why using transactions can be one of the smartest things a software developer can do. Next, I expound on ways to keep your database server's memory consistent with the permanent information stored on disk. Finally, you see how to use the sophisticated backup and recovery features built into SQL Server 2005 Express to help safeguard your data.

Transactions: Your Data's Best Friend

Because relational database applications typically divide their information among multiple tables, things can go horribly wrong if one or more tables have a problem with a particular database operation.

For example, suppose that you write a program that updates rows in tables A, B, and C as part of the same unit of work. Furthermore, imagine that tables A and C happily accept your changes, but something is wrong with the modification that you want to apply to table B's data. If you're not careful, you could easily end up in a state where tables A and C think everything was fine, and table B does not. This translates into a corrupted and out-of-sync database. Months may go by before anyone notices, but rest assured: Your data has been damaged.

This situation is where *transactions* come in. By grouping all your data updates into one batch, you can definitely tell SQL Server 2005 Express to either keep or reject all your changes. In the preceding example, you could have put tables A, B, and C back to their original states if even one of them had a problem with your change. Your data remains in sync, and is safely preserved.

What are transactions?

In a nutshell, a transaction is a unit of work that you launch with a BEGIN TRANSACTION statement. You then proceed to issue one or more database operation requests, which SQL Server 2005 Express dutifully processes. Then, after all your work is finished, you complete the transaction with a COMMIT TRANSACTION statement. SQL Server 2005 Express then makes all your changes permanent: Everything that happened between BEGIN TRANS-ACTION and COMMIT TRANSACTION is now enshrined in your database for-ever (or at least until you change it later).

But wait a minute. What if something went wrong during all these operations? Fear not, because transactions let you change your mind. For example, sup-pose that you start a transaction, issue a bunch of statements, and then change your mind and want to go back to the way things were before? Luckily, you have the ROLLBACK TRANSACTION statement waiting in the wings. If you issue this statement instead of COMMIT TRANSACTION, SQL Server can rollback all your modifications, putting the database back into the state that it was just prior to the BEGIN TRANSACTION statement.

How do transactions work?

To make sure that your transactions work as advertised, SQL Server 2005 Express performs a sophisticated juggling act among a number of internal technologies.

When you start a transaction, the database server records this event in a memory structure known as the log cache. In addition, all your changes are also written into the log cache. This cache is then periodically written to the log cache's disk-based counterpart, which is known as the *transaction* log.

If the server were to crash in the middle of a transaction, SQL Server 2005 Express would use the transaction log as a guide to determine which transac-tions to rollback. On the other hand, if you simply change your mind, SQL Server 2005 Express can use the transaction log as a guide to reinstating your data to the way it was prior to the start of the transaction. If this rollback wasn't helpful enough, the transaction log is also useful when you need to restore from a backup. In any case, when the transaction completes, SQL Server 2005 Express also records this event in the log cache and transaction log.

Synchronizing Memory and Disk Storage

Most modern relational database systems are built to take advantage of the lightning speed of memory-based processing. SQL Server 2005 Express is no exception. To cut down on the number of performance-degrading disk accesses, it uses a sophisticated set of internal memory structures to buffer information. Because processing in memory is at least ten times faster than doing the same work on disk, these speed enhancements can really help your application hum along.

However, eventually all this fun has to come to an end, even if temporarily. Sooner or later, SQL Server 2005 Express must write the contents of its memory to disk, as part of an event known as a *checkpoint*. Otherwise, what would happen if the computer suddenly lost power? All your changes would be lost forever, vanishing into the ether before SQL Server 2005 Express could get the chance to commit them onto disk. Try explaining that to a user looking for last month's sales figures.

As you work with database information, SQL Server 2005 Express accumulates data on pages within a section of server memory known as the *buffer cache*. When you create, modify, or remove data, SQL Server 2005 Express records these alterations in the buffer cache on what are known as *dirty pages*. These pages are then synchronized to disk during a checkpoint.

In addition to keeping memory and disk in sync, checkpoints also serve to help SQL Server 2005 Express recover from an unanticipated shutdown or failure. A successful checkpoint acts as an anchor in time, letting SQL Server 2005 Express recover from that point forward. Checkpoints happen all the time, not just during transactions. Here are just a few events that trigger a checkpoint:

 ✔ Prior to backing up your database

 ✔ Stopping your database server

 ✔ The transaction log fills up to a preset threshold

Now that you know how checkpoints work, what do you have to do to make sure that your own checkpoints get run correctly? The good news here is that SQL Server 2005 Express handles all these chores automatically: You don't have to do anything.

However, you may want to tinker with the amount of resources that SQL Server 2005 Express dedicates to your checkpoint process. You can influence its behavior by running the CHECKPOINT command, passing in a value that states the maximum amount of time, expressed in seconds, that you want your checkpoints to take.

Normally, SQL Server 2005 Express uses its own internal algorithms to optimize how long a checkpoint takes. If you run this command with a low value (less than 60 seconds), the database server shuffles its resources to dedicate more to the job of getting your checkpoint done quickly. Conversely, a high value lets SQL Server 2005 Express make its own decisions about how to allocate resources to get checkpoints done as quickly as possible.

Unless you're really worried about squeezing the last bit of performance out of your SQL Server 2005 Express system, don't mess around with this setting. The database usually knows best!

Backing Up Your Data: Inexpensive Insurance You Can't Afford to Skip!

Predicting and preventing external threats to your data such as viruses, hackers, defective applications, and confused users is hard to do. However, by implementing a well-thought-out backup and restore strategy, you can protect your information and recover from just about any unfortunate event that befalls your SQL Server 2005 Express database. In this section, I describe the choices you have with this vital administrative task, as well as show you how to perform backup and recovery operations.

Choosing the right backup strategy

Choosing a backup strategy is not as simple as shopping for clothing. Safeguarding your information has no one-size-fits-all approach. In fact, no two enterprises are alike with regard to their data backup needs. However, to help you figure out the right information archiving plan for you, you can use a series of criteria that includes answering the following questions:

✔ How dynamic is your data?

✔ When does your information change most often? During business hours? At other times?

✔ What data can be recovered by means other than a database backup?

✔ What are the business and other implications of losing data?

✔ Do you have other computers standing by that can take over the load for a failed server?

✔ Do you take advantage of hardware-based high-availability technologies such as RAID?

Generally, an organization that has dynamic information coupled with intolerance for data loss or system outages is one that needs a robust backup strategy, perhaps even one that is not provided by a product such as SQL Server 2005 Express.

On the other hand, if you have relatively static data or have deployed alternative redundancy measures, you may not need a very strict data archiving regimen.

Recovery models

The full SQL Server 2005 product line offers three distinct classes of backup and recovery. Known as recovery models, these include

✔ **The full recovery model:** This recovery model is the most robust offered in the SQL Server product family. It provides maximal protection from just about any kind of data disaster you can think of, and lets you restore your information to a particular point in time.

However, this power and protection comes with more work and responsibilities for the database administrator. To begin, the transaction log has to be backed up on a regular basis, or data alterations can get lost.

If your transaction log fills up, you won't be able to make any changes until the log file is backed up.

If you're running a very dynamic database server, and want to have point-in-time recovery capabilities, you may need to use this model. You need to upgrade to the Enterprise edition of SQL Server.

✔ **The bulk-logged recovery model:** Using the full recovery model adds some performance overhead to your database server. This overhead can get very expensive when you perform bulk operations, such as loading a large data file into your database. One way to reduce these extra costs is to temporarily switch to the bulk-logged recovery model until the bulk operation finishes. The bulk recovery model saves on overhead costs by trimming bulk operation logging to the bare minimum. However, standard database interaction is still thoroughly logged, just like in the full recovery model.

✔ **The simple recovery model:** As you expect from its name, this recovery model is relatively straightforward to implement. It also offers two compelling operational features:

- You don't need to back up the transaction logs.
- You don't need to take the database offline.

Because there's no such thing as a free lunch, using this model means that you can't restore to a particular point in time, unless you happen to run a database backup at that moment. Any transactions that happened after your last backup are lost. You also can't restore individual pages. I spend the balance of this section reviewing this recovery model.

If all this info has your head spinning — not to worry: SQL Server lets you switch recovery models anytime you like.

To change your recovery model, simply use the ALTER DATABASE command. Here's an example of setting a database's recovery model to simple recovery:

```
ALTER DATABASE NorthBay SET RECOVERY SIMPLE
```

Best practices for protecting your data

Before I show you how to back up and restore information, using the simple recovery model, I want to give you a few ideas on how you can safeguard your information, regardless of which recovery model you follow:

✔ **Use redundant hardware.** Hardware prices keep falling. It's now possible to purchase and configure inexpensive, redundant components. For example, you can set up a Redundant Array of Inexpensive Disks (RAID) storage system for much less than you might think. These extra disks can greatly reduce the likelihood of a serious data loss should one of your disks encounter a problem.

✔ **Maintain a standby server.** Speaking of redundant hardware that can come to your rescue during difficult times, a standby server can be a great investment, especially if you keep it up to date by regularly restoring backups or replicating information onto it. Then, if something catastrophic happens to your production server, you can always switch over to the backup server.

✔ **Restore backups regularly.** You can devise the most brilliant backup strategy of all time, but if you can't restore a given backup, all your investment has been for naught. This is why you need to test your backup validity on a consistent basis. You can also combine two good ideas (restoring regular backups onto your standby server) to help ensure that you can gracefully recover from a database problem.

Types of backup available in the simple recovery model

SQL Server 2005 Express offers the administrator a choice of several different types of backup, using the simple recovery model. Here's a list of each of the major styles, along with the situations where you use them:

✔ **Full backup:** This data archiving is the most comprehensive type. It backs up all your data, including enough of the transaction log to restore the database to a consistent state. Think of this data archiving as a snapshot of your entire database at a given point in time.

In general, this backup is the easiest type to understand, but it also consumes the largest amount of storage.

Any open, uncommitted transactions that exist at the time of a backup are lost upon restore. The same holds true for any transactions that take place after starting the backup. Keep these potential losses in mind when you schedule your backups.

✔ **Full differential backup:** This style of backup is identical to a full backup, with one major difference: A full differential backup only archives information that has changed since the last full backup. This backup can be very handy if only small portions of your database change on a regular basis; by running differential backups you don't need to incur the time and media costs of full backups.

✔ **Partial backup:** As you can guess from its name, a partial backup archives a subset of your database, including

  • Data from the primary filegroup

  • Any requested read-only files

  • All read-write filegroups

✔ **Partial differential backup:** Just as a full differential backup is a subset of a full backup, a partial differential backup backs up only those portions of the last partial backup that have changed.

For the balance of this chapter, I focus on full and full differential backups because these make the most sense for the largest number of SQL Server 2005 Express installations. Although these backup types take longer and consume more media, they're also more straightforward to envision.

Using the simple recovery model to backup your data

Here's how to run a database backup:

1. **Choose which backup utility you want to use.**

   A perfectly good backup utility is built into SQL Server 2005 Express. Numerous third-party applications also handle database backups; you might want to use one of these tools instead. However, for this chapter, I assume that you're using built-in backup capabilities in SQL Server Management Studio Express, available via a free download from Microsoft.

2. **Connect to the right instance of your database server.**

3. **Expand the Databases folder, right-click the database you want to back up, and choose Back Up from the Tasks menu.**

   Figure 13-1 shows the backup settings at your disposal.

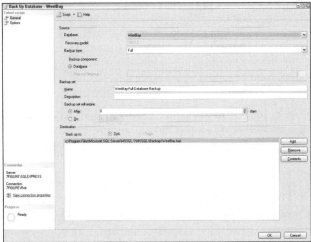

Figure 13-1: General backup settings.

Along with self-explanatory options such as the database you want to archive, the name of the backup set, and the expiration date (if any) for the backup, pay particular attention to the destination. If you have a tape device installed on your computer, you'll be given the option of selecting it as your backup destination. Otherwise, you'll need to back up to disk.

You should also select whether you want a full backup or a differential backup.

Using the same physical disk drive for your data and data backups is *not* a good idea. If something nasty happens to your disk drive, you lose both your data as well as your lifeline to restoring it: your backups. Separate these two key objects onto different disk drives.

4. **Fill in the required information on both the General page (shown in Figure 13-1) and the Options page (shown in Figure 13-2), and click OK to launch the backup.**

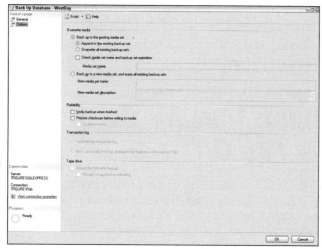

Figure 13-2:
Backup
option
settings.

On the Options page, you choose how you want your media managed, what should be done with the transaction log (if you chose the full recovery model), as well as if you want extra reliability checks performed.

Opting for backup verification and a media checksum operation adds a little extra time to your backup. However, these checks can identify a problem before you reach a crisis, and are generally worth the extra effort.

5. **Watch for any error messages.**

If everything went well, you should receive a message telling you that the backup completed successfully.

Why you should also export information

In the last few pages, I harangue you about how important backing up your data is. However, even if you have a bulletproof backup strategy in place, periodically exporting your information to text files, using either a third-party tool or the bcp utility is a good idea. If you're curious about bcp, check out Chapter 9.

Why is exporting important? In a nutshell, there is no limit to what can go wrong with a data backup, including the following:

✔ Lost or damaged media

✔ Corrupted data files

✔ Other data inconsistencies

By creating a text-based backup version of your data, you give yourself one more chance to recover from a catastrophic problem. Of course, you must take the same precautions with your text-based backup data as you do with your traditional data backups.

Restoring Data: Time for the Insurance to Pay Off

Just as you buy auto and fire insurance in case of a collision or conflagration, you back up your data in case one day you need to restore it. In this section, I walk you through the flip side of the backup process — that is, restoring data in case of disaster. After all, a backup is of no use if you can't later retrieve the information you backed up.

Restoring your database back to its original pristine state is pretty straightforward if you've done your backups correctly. Just follow these steps:

1. **Launch the backup utility you used to create the original data archive.**

   Throughout this chapter, I cite the built-in SQL Server 2005 Express utility, which you can access from within any SQL-ready tool. I continue to refer to this tool in this section, as well as assume that you're using SQL Server Management Studio Express.

2. **Connect to the right instance of your database server.**

3. **Expand the Databases folder, right-click the database you want to restore, and choose Restore from the Tasks menu.**

   Figure 13-3 shows the restore settings at your disposal.

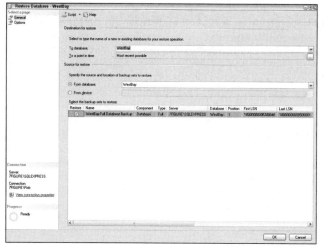

Figure 13-3:
General
restore
settings.

You can choose the database where you want the restore to be written, as well as whether you want to restore to a point in time. You may only restore to a point in time if you've chosen the full or bulk-logged recovery models.

You can also select whether you want the restore utility to locate the candidate backup set, using the database's internal record, or to use a backup set found on a device.

4. **Fill in the required information on both the General page (shown in Figure 13-3) and the Options page (shown in Figure 13-4), and click OK to launch the restore.**

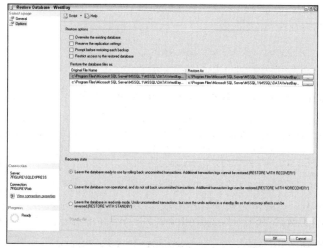

Figure 13-4:
Restore
option
settings.

The options page offers settings that help control the behavior of the restore operation, as well as the state of the database after the restore has been completed.

For the simple recovery model, choose the Restore With Recovery option in the Recovery state portion of the options page.

5. Watch for any error messages.

If everything went well, you should receive a message telling you that the restore completed successfully.

That's it. You're now ready to connect to your database and run some basic tests to see if everything restored correctly. After you're satisfied that things are in good shape, you can let users connect to the newly restored database to resume their work.

Part V

Putting the Tools to Work: Programming with SQL Server 2005 Express

The 5th Wave   By Rich Tennant

They're moving on to the JOIN syntax section. That should daze and confuse them enough for us to finish changing the tire and get the heck out of here.

ANSI Document Publishers

In this part . . .

You'll primarily use SQL Server 2005 Express as a data repository in conjunction with packaged, pre-built tools and applications. However, you may use it as the foundation of a new application. If you're building a new solution that relies on SQL Server 2005 Express, this part is for you.

Initially, I show you how to extend the power and flexibility of your database server by creating your own stored procedures and functions. Then I show you how to trigger these operations based on database activity. If you're inclined to write your software in a language other than Transact-SQL, Chapter 16 shows you how to leverage Microsoft's Common Language Runtime. Chapter 17 helps you gracefully deal with these anomalies. Chapter 18 shows you how to conduct full-text searching and reporting services.

Chapter 14

Using Stored Procedures and Functions

Designing, building, and maintaining a quality relational database-driven software solution is hard work. Users are understandably demanding, and expect accurate, prompt system response. Consolidating your application logic in stored procedures and functions is one of the best ways to improve both reliability and performance. In this chapter, you find out how to get the most out of these helpful features.

Introducing Stored Procedures and Functions

Simply put, *stored procedures* and *functions* are centralized, server-based software that are available for everyone (assuming that they have permission) to use. You can build your own stored procedures and functions, and you can also take advantage of the many built-in stored procedures and functions offered by SQL Server 2005 Express. If you write your own, you can use Transact-SQL or another Microsoft .NET programming language if you have enabled SQLCLR.

These helpful objects offer a number of marvelous benefits:

- ✔ **Better accuracy:** In any software project, one way to reduce complexity and increase accuracy is to reduce the number of moving parts. By centralizing your business logic into one place, and then making that logic available to anyone who needs it, you can go a long way toward eliminating those pesky and hard-to-trace errors that plague most applications.

  For example, suppose that you're building an application that performs a credit check in five key program modules. You could write separate credit-checking logic within each of these components, but that means you need to replicate the logic five times. To make matters worse, in the likely event that you encounter an error, you need to chase it down in five locations.

  In this case, writing and testing a centralized, credit checking stored procedure or function makes much more sense. Any module that needs to perform a credit check would simply invoke the procedure or function. If an error does rear its ugly head, you quickly know where to look.

- ✔ **Improved performance:** Generally, database servers are faster and more powerful than the clients that access them. One way to take advantage of the horsepower on a server is to let it handle as much processing as possible. Because stored procedures and functions run on the server, using them means that you lighten the load on your clients.

  You can think of this load as falling into three major buckets:

  - **CPU load:** The CPU must do this amount of work to satisfy a request. Running a stored procedure or function on the server transfers this work from the client to the server.

  - **Disk load:** Disk drives hold tons of information, but working with them can be costly from the point of view of performance. Anything you can do to reduce your disk usage on your clients usually translates to reduced load. Furthermore, servers generally (but not always) have faster disk drives, which makes them more efficient when they work with disks.

  - **Network load:** A database request from a client generates this amount of network traffic. Imagine that you have a client-side application that needs to review thousands of rows to arrive at an answer to a question. By moving that logic onto the server, you lighten the network load significantly: Those rows never need to travel across the network, but are instead handled on the server.

- ✔ **Language portability:** Programmers are a fickle lot; just when they get comfortable with one programming language, along comes a younger, better-looking replacement. Unfortunately, these infatuations come with a cost: extensive rewriting and redevelopment effort. By placing key portions of your business logic within stored procedures or functions, you insulate these parts of your software from the inevitable language alterations as computing technology advances.

Try to identify the purely business logic-oriented portions of your application. These candidates are good to be turned into stored procedures or functions.

✔ **Enhanced security:** Just because you're paranoid doesn't mean that people aren't out to get you — or, in this case, your proprietary application code. But you can protect yourself by using stored procedures and functions. For example, suppose that you develop some world-class algorithms, or other trade secrets that you don't want anyone else to see. In addition, suppose that you outsource large parts of your application development effort. In this case, you can encode your clandestine programming rules in a stored procedure or function, and let only your external developers make invocations to this centralized logic.

If this scenario weren't secure enough, Microsoft lets you encrypt your stored procedure, making it even harder for those pesky competitors to steal your trade secrets.

After you encrypt a stored procedure or function, you can't have SQL Server 2005 Express print out the original source code. For this reason, always store an unencrypted copy someplace safe for future reference.

Examples of stored procedures and functions

You can make stored procedures and functions do just about anything. Here's an example of a simple stored procedure that takes a customer identification number, checks the customer's purchase history, and returns a string describing the customer's relative standing:

```
CREATE PROCEDURE proc_CustomerLevel
@CustomerID INTEGER,
@CustomerLevel VARCHAR(20) OUT
AS
    DECLARE @PurchaseTotal DECIMAL(8,2)
    SET @PurchaseTotal =
    (SELECT SUM(amount)
    FROM transactions tr
    WHERE tr.CustomerID = @CustomerID)

    IF @PurchaseTotal > 1000
        BEGIN
            SET @CustomerLevel = 'Gold'
        END
    ELSE
        SET @CustomerLevel = 'Standard'
```

This example is very simple; SQL Server 2005 Express lets you build much more powerful stored procedures that run rich sets of business algorithms.

Now, here's an example of a function that performs the highly complex task of converting meters to inches:

```
CREATE FUNCTION dbo.MetersToInches (@Meters DECIMAL(10,3))
RETURNS DECIMAL(10,3)
AS
BEGIN
    DECLARE @Inches DECIMAL(10,3)
    SET @Inches = (@Meters * 3.281 ) * 12
    RETURN @Inches
END
```

While this function is very straightforward, imagine the sophisticated functions you could write that would add value to your own specific processing needs. You can then invoke these functions directly within SQL, adding new power and capabilities to your database interactions.

When not to use a stored procedure or function

After reading the preceding section, you would be forgiven for thinking that you should write your entire application in stored procedures and functions. However, these helpful tools are not the right choice in every situation. Here are some conditions when you should not use a stored procedure or function:

- ✔ **Overloaded database server:** Asking your database server to handle the extra processing load of stored procedures and functions is fine. However, if the server is already overloaded, you're asking for trouble. So, before you centralize your programming logic, take stock of how your server is performing. If it has plenty of extra capacity, go right ahead; otherwise, you should reconsider (or possibly get a more powerful server).

- ✔ **Advanced logic needs:** Transact-SQL is fine for most processing tasks. However, sometimes you need something more powerful for your computing requirements. You may find that using a more traditional, compiled computing language is a better choice in these circumstances.

  Here's some good news: The Microsoft .NET Framework Compiled Language Runtime (SQLCLR) lets you write stored procedures and functions in a variety of powerful procedural computer languages and then store these in your database, so you may be able to have your cake and eat it too. I discuss SQLCLR in more detail in the "Writing a Stored Procedure or Function" section, a little later in this chapter.

✔ **One-time operations:** Stored procedures and functions make the most sense when you need to create code that will be invoked over and over again by multiple users and programs. If, on the other hand, you're building software that will run infrequently, and by only one application, centralizing your logic may not be worth your effort.

Differences between stored procedures and functions

Stored procedures and functions are very similar in their design and purposes. The main difference between them is that a function must return a value; a value is optional for a stored procedure. Also, you can't use a stored procedure as part of an expression.

Generally, you include a function call directly within your SQL as part of a larger statement:

```
SELECT Weight, dbo.MetersToInches(Length), Cost, ...
FROM Products
WHERE ProductID = 199232
```

On the other hand, most applications that use stored procedures look to these objects to help outsource longer-lived, more involved processing, thereby passing control to them until the procedures finish their work. Of course, these rules have exceptions, but in most cases this is how things shake out.

System stored procedures and functions

Before you charge ahead and write your own collection of stored procedures and functions, here's some good news: Microsoft offers hundreds of really useful, built-in stored procedures and functions. You can use these to get a head start for your own applications or to configure and monitor important database indicators.

Microsoft prefixes system stored procedures with either an sp_ or xp_. Try not to use these prefixes when building your own procedures.

While this book doesn't have enough room to go through each of these built-in stored procedures and functions, in this section I show you how you can get a list of what's installed on your server, as well as go through some examples of some particularly appealing components.

Getting a list of stored procedures and functions

Using SQL Server Management Studio Express (which you can download free from Microsoft), you can figure out what you have available on your SQL Server 2005 Express system, whether you created them or Microsoft provided them. Just follow these simple steps:

1. **Launch SQL Server Management Studio Express.**

2. **Connect to the appropriate server.**

3. **Expand the Databases entry.**

4. **Expand the database entry for the database you're interested in.**

5. **Expand the Programmability folder.**

   Among the various objects listed here, you can choose between stored procedures and functions. For now, I focus on stored procedures. You can follow a similar path if you're interested in functions.

6. **Open the Stored Procedures folder.**

   You now see a list of any user-created stored procedures, along with a folder for system stored procedures.

7. **Expand the System Stored Procedures folder.**

   Be patient — you'll be surprised at how long the list of built-in stored procedures is.

8. **Open the folder for the stored procedure you want to research.**

9. **Open the Parameters folder.**

   You can now see all the input and output parameters for the stored procedure. This list helps you when using the procedure.

Figure 14-1 shows an example of a stored procedure hierarchy, all the way down to an individual procedure's parameters.

This listing is chock-full of important information that you can use to figure out how to work with the stored procedure. These details include

- The parameters the procedure expects
- Each parameter's data type
- If a parameter has a default value
- What the procedure returns (if anything)

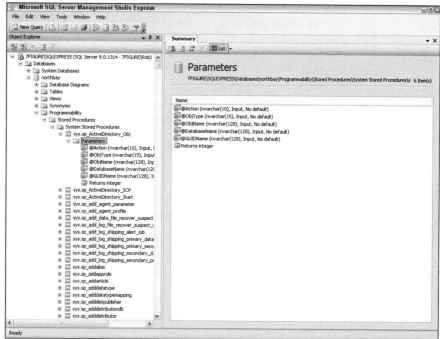

Figure 14-1:
A detailed view of the sp_Active Directory_ Obj stored procedure.

Some useful system stored procedures and functions

If I were to fully describe each of the built-in stored procedures and functions so generously provided by Microsoft, you would need a forklift to pick up this book. Nevertheless, to help give you an idea of how powerful these procedures are, I show you some selected examples, broken out by the general type of stored procedure.

Some of the current built-in stored procedures and functions (but none of the ones I name in the following list) are destined for that great CPU in the sky, so before relying on a particular procedure, consider consulting the documentation to check on its life expectancy.

To make things clearer, I divide this list of sample built-in stored procedures into three main categories, based on the primary role that the procedure plays. Note that there are many other ways to pigeonhole these objects:

✔ **Administrative:** These types of procedures enable SQL Server 2005 Express administrators to configure, manage, and monitor their own unique database server. Figure 14-2 shows the output of two procedures. The `sp_helpdb` procedure returns high-level information about your database, while the `sp_depends` procedure cites any dependencies around this database object.

✔ **Data access:** This class of procedure helps database designers and application developers understand details about their SQL Server 2005 Express databases. Figure 14-3 shows the output from the `sp_datatype_info` procedure, which describes all the potential data types at your command, as well as the detailed table structure cheerfully returned by the `sp_columns` procedure.

✔ **Security:** Numerous built-in stored procedures let administrators manage security for their database server. Two good examples are

• **sp_password:** This procedure lets you create or change a password for a SQL Server 2005 Express login.

• **sp_defaultdb:** You can use this procedure to change the default database for a given SQL Server 2005 Express login.

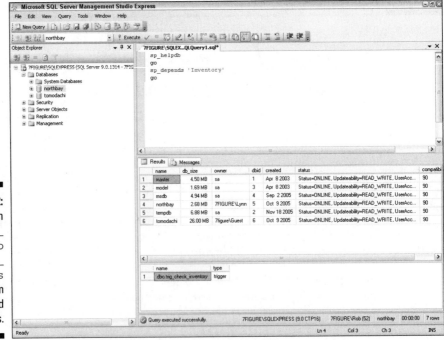

Figure 14-2:
Output from the `sp_helpdb` and `sp_depends` system stored procedures.

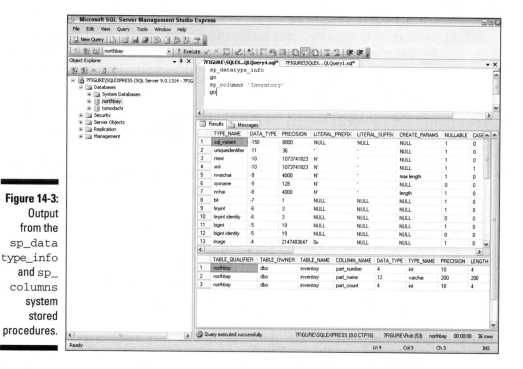

Figure 14-3:
Output
from the
`sp_data`
`type_info`
and `sp_`
`columns`
system
stored
procedures.

If you forget to include a parameter, don't worry: SQL Server 2005 Express is on the job. For example, if you don't tell `sp_defaultdb` what database you want it to use, it complains:

```
Procedure or Function 'sp_defaultdb' expects
parameter '@defdb', which was not supplied.
```

Writing a Stored Procedure or Function

After you understand all that you can do with stored procedures and functions, you're probably raring to go and develop your own. The first question you need to answer is whether you're writing your stored procedure or function in straight Transact-SQL, or if you're using SQLCLR (the Microsoft .NET Framework Common Language Runtime).

Using Transact-SQL

As it turns out, in most cases Transact-SQL can meet your processing needs. If you're unsure about whether to use Transact-SQL or SQLCLR, see the next section for more about when SQLCLR is the right choice.

To construct the stored procedure or function in Transact-SQL, use the CREATE PROCEDURE or CREATE FUNCTION statement, respectively. Keep these things in mind as you go about developing your own server-based logic:

✔ You can declare both input and output parameters.

✔ You can use default values for input parameters; if you're calling a function, you must include the DEFAULT keyword.

✔ A function must return at least one output value; a value is optional for a stored procedure.

✔ All parameters must be declared with a data type (such as VARCHAR, INT, and so on).

✔ You can declare variables within the procedure or function. You must also declare them with a data type.

✔ You can encrypt your stored procedure or function by including the ENCRYPTION directive.

✔ You can nest stored procedures and functions up to 32 levels deep.

✔ A function may also return information in the format of a table.

After you're ready to write your stored procedure or function, you can use any of the following tools offered by Microsoft:

✔ SQL Server Management Studio Express

✔ Visual Studio

✔ The SQLCMD utility

In fact, because you can write stored procedures and functions in Transact-SQL, you can use any third-party tool that gives you direct SQL capabilities. Assuming that you're using SQL Server Management Studio Express, here's all you need to do to create your logic, using stored procedures as a model:

1. **Launch SQL Server Management Studio Express.**

2. **Connect to the appropriate server.**

3. **Expand the database node where you want to create your procedure.**

4. **Right-click the Stored Procedures folder, and choose the New Stored Procedure option.**

   A template comes up that gives you a head start on the stored procedure authoring process, as you can see in Figure 14-4.

5. **Enter your customized stored procedure code.**

6. **Click the Execute button to generate your stored procedure.**

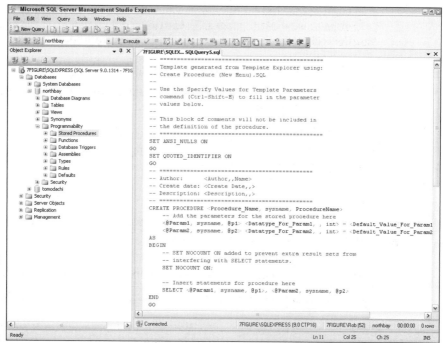

Figure 14-4:
New stored
procedure
template.

If everything goes according to plan, SQL Server 2005 Express reports that
your command executed successfully. You can then see your stored procedure or function by following the steps in the "Getting a list of stored procedures and functions" section, earlier in this chapter.

Using the SQL Common Language Runtime (SQLCLR)

Even though Transact-SQL is more than powerful and flexible enough for
most applications, you may have special needs that require the additional
computational clout offered .NET programming languages by using SQLCLR.
Here are some of the capabilities of SQLCLR that may be of interest to you:

✔ **Performance:** Given their compiled nature, CLR stored procedures and
functions are typically faster and more scalable than their Transact-SQL
counterparts.

✔ **Debugging:** Microsoft offers a very rich development and debugging
environment, which helps you solve any problems when building stored
procedures and functions.

✔ **Object orientation:** Microsoft Visual C# and Visual Basic .NET are object-oriented languages. These types of languages offer much higher flexibility and developer productivity than traditional procedural programming languages.

✔ **Extensibility:** Microsoft's .NET Framework Library contains copious software components that you can incorporate into your stored procedures and functions.

If any of these features seem particularly appealing, check out Chapter 16 for a detailed exposé on how to take advantage of SQLCLR to build stored procedures or functions.

Calling a Stored Procedure or Function

SQL Server Express 2005 allows you to easily call an existing stored procedure or function. Using the two examples from earlier in this chapter, here's a snippet of Transact-SQL that invokes the stored procedure, as well as prints its results:

```
DECLARE @CustomerLevel VARCHAR(20)
EXECUTE proc_CustomerLevel 12391, @CustomerLevel OUT
PRINT @CustomerLevel
```

In this example, you need to declare a variable to hold the results from the stored procedure; the PRINT statement simply displays what came back.

And here's how you call the function:

```
SELECT dbo.MetersToInches(123.45) AS 'Inches'

Inches
------------
    4860.473
```

Chapter 15

Understanding Triggers

*T*riggers are a great tool for centralizing and consolidating processing rules for your database, helping to improve your applications' accuracy and consistency. If that isn't enough of an incentive to find out what this feature does, triggers may also help boost application performance. In fact, triggers are so valuable that Microsoft offers two types: Data Definition Language (DDL) triggers, which handle changes to your data structure, and Data Manipulation Language (DML) triggers, which handle changes to your actual information.

This chapter introduces you to triggers. You begin by figuring out what they are, what they do, and how they work. After you pass that easy hurdle, your next step is to check out the differences between DML and DDL triggers.

As with any powerful feature, you need to understand when to use a trigger, as well as when it's not the right choice for the task at hand. For this reason, this chapter reviews several scenarios to help guide you toward the right decision.

Finally, after examining all these topics, you can easily create your own set of triggers.

Triggers: Actions Awaiting an Event

You can think of triggers as centrally stored sets of actions that take place only if something else happens. For example, if you write a letter to your friend and then drop it in a mailbox without putting enough postage on the envelope, you trigger the post office to return the letter to you along with a friendly reminder that you need to add postage. This reminder is triggered by the lack of a stamp; otherwise, the letter would have gone through the mail without any delays. Different post office triggers would be invoked if you provided enough postage but forgot to write your friend's address, wrote the address in Bulgarian, or tried to mail your cat.

From the post office's perspective, these triggers (or business rules) are vital. Without them, each letter carrier would make his or her own decisions about what constitutes a valid letter. Some overly zealous letter carriers would reject valid mail, while other, more easygoing civil servants would let invalid shipments gum up the works. By centralizing these rules, the post office enforces consistency, which makes the mail more predictable and easier to use for the customer.

Back in the database world, a *trigger* is actually a specialized stored procedure that gets launched when a certain event takes place. One of the things that makes triggers so attractive is that SQL Server 2005 Express does all the work — all you need to do is correctly define the trigger and the database engine patiently waits for the event to happen. When it happens, SQL Server 2005 Express launches the right trigger.

Trigger scope

You can define a trigger to be processed for a particular table or even a view that is made up of many tables. As I show you a little later in this chapter (in the "Writing new triggers" section), you can set up triggers to be invoked for a wide variety of statements that affect these tables or views. In fact, you can set up multiple triggers for the same object. After you decide on the type of statement that you want to invoke a trigger, you can nest your triggers: They can call other triggers or stored procedures as well.

 Because you don't want to have a potentially costly trigger processed in some situations (such as during large data loads or other batch operations), you can tell SQL Server 2005 Express to temporarily disable processing a particular trigger.

Trigger programming languages

You have great flexibility when developing your triggers. If Transact-SQL isn't your favorite, you can use any other .NET supported language via SQLCLR. For example, you may elect to write some of your simpler triggers in Transact-SQL, and use the power of C# to write your more complex triggers. In most situations, however, you can likely turn to Transact-SQL as your trigger programming language, so this chapter focuses on these types of triggers. See Chapters 9 and 10 for more about Transact-SQL.

How do triggers work?

Now that you know what triggers are, you may be wondering how they work. When you create a trigger, SQL Server 2005 Express makes an entry in the `sys.triggers` table. You can think of this entry as a header table, containing important information about the trigger:

- ✔ A unique identifier for the trigger
- ✔ The type of trigger (whether it's for a database or table/view)
- ✔ When the trigger was created
- ✔ Whether the trigger is disabled

For each trigger that you create, SQL Server 2005 Express also writes detail entries in the `sys.sql_modules` and `sys.trigger_events` tables. These tables hold additional information about the trigger:

- ✔ The actual SQL text for the trigger
- ✔ Which type of SQL statement invokes the trigger
- ✔ Other trigger properties

When the trigger is in place, the SQL Server 2005 Express engine consults these tables to find any relevant triggers for a given table or view. If it finds an appropriate candidate, it runs the trigger.

Types of Triggers

SQL Server 2005 Express divides its triggers into two categories: triggers that affect data definition tasks, and triggers that affect data manipulation tasks. I cover each category in this section.

Data Definition Language (DDL) triggers

You can invoke DDL triggers, newly available in the SQL Server 2005 family, whenever a statement executes that alters your database structure. These statements include

- ✔ CREATE
- ✔ ALTER
- ✔ GRANT

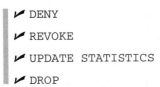

✔ DENY

✔ REVOKE

✔ UPDATE STATISTICS

✔ DROP

You typically use a DDL trigger to perform or regulate database management tasks. For example, you may want to thwart someone who is trying to create an index. By placing a DDL trigger for the CREATE INDEX statement, you can have SQL Server 2005 Express intercept this operation and warn the user that new index creation cannot take place without your approval. Alternatively, perhaps you want to be notified via e-mail if someone changes permissions for any database object. In this case, you can easily create a trigger for both the GRANT and REVOKE statements and have the trigger call a stored procedure to send you e-mail.

Data Manipulation Language (DML) triggers

Unlike DDL triggers, you can invoke DML triggers based on any statement that modifies data (rather than the database's structure). Candidate statements include

✔ INSERT

✔ UPDATE

✔ DELETE

DML triggers are incredibly useful for centralizing all kinds of important application processing. While you may never need or want to use a DDL trigger, you have a good chance of benefiting from a DML trigger. I show you a bunch of examples in the next section of this chapter.

To Trigger, or Not to Trigger?

If you've read the previous sections, in which I show you all that triggers can do, you're now probably wondering how to tell if they're the right tools for the job. In this section, I describe a number of scenarios where triggers make sense, as well as some when you should not bother with them.

Triggers to the rescue!

You use a trigger for many reasons. Some of the best include the following:

- ✓ **Enforcing business rules:** Suppose that you want to make sure that only your best customers get the VIP discount. You can rely on your programmers to make that determination, but a better, more consistent way is to use a trigger.

- ✓ **Protecting data integrity:** While SQL Server 2005 Express includes a host of referential integrity tools, you may at times need very specialized processing to protect and preserve data integrity. A trigger can be just the ticket to solve this kind of problem. In fact, this trigger is the most common.

- ✓ **Launching additional actions:** Because you can write very powerful and flexible triggers, using Transact-SQL and other languages, you can have these triggers launch follow-on actions. For example, suppose that you want to be notified if a particular part in your warehouse reaches a critically low inventory level. In this case, you can place a trigger on the part's table, and when the inventory fell below a set threshold, have it generate an e-mail alert. You can even automate the reordering process, all driven by triggers.

Don't be trigger happy

Triggers are so powerful, and so useful, that you can easily get carried away and use them when you shouldn't. Unfortunately, triggers do incur some overhead, so they can hurt performance. Here are some examples when you should not use a trigger:

- ✓ **One-time processing:** Triggers are very good at centralizing and enforcing business rules when a particular business rule needs to be enforced in multiple situations. On the other hand, if you have a specific rule that will be processed only one time or by one application, you won't gain much by creating a trigger.

- ✓ **Permission checking:** SQL Server 2005 Express provides a sophisticated security management system. Although you may be tempted to generate a slew of DDL triggers to enforce your own brand of permission management, you generally don't need to go to this effort: A better idea is to simply learn more about the built-in SQL Server 2005 Express security.

- ✓ **Default data validation:** SQL Server 2005 Express delivers a rich set of referential integrity capabilities designed to protect your information from deliberate or accidental damage. Unless you have cross-database data integrity issues to manage, writing your own referential integrity management triggers is not necessary.

Using Triggers

In the previous sections of this chapter, I show you what triggers are, how they operate, and when to use them. In this section, I welcome you to take the plunge and make triggers work for you.

Discovering already-existing triggers

Most Microsoft products offer a number of alternate ways of getting information. The same holds true for learning about existing triggers in SQL Server 2005 Express. You can find out about existing triggers in three ways. Of the three options, the first is by far the easiest to perform.

Via SQL Server Management Studio Express

You can quickly navigate to your triggers via this free database administration tool, available for download from Microsoft. Here's how to see all the triggers in place for a database.

1. **Launch SQL Server Management Studio Express.**

2. **Connect to the appropriate server.**

3. **Expand the Databases entry.**

4. **Expand the database folder for the database you're interested in.**

5. **Expand the Programmability folder.**

6. **Expand the Database Triggers folder.**

Via a stored procedure

The all-purpose `sp_helptext` procedure lists the statements that make up your trigger. Just pass it the name of the trigger you want to understand:

```
sp_helptext trig_check_inventory
```

It returns the exact statements that make up the trigger, including any embedded comments:

```
-- Now, create the trigger
CREATE TRIGGER trig_check_inventory ON requests
AFTER INSERT
AS
DECLARE @part_number INTEGER, @part_request_count INTEGER,
  @quantity_on_hand INTEGER, @minimum_number INTEGER,
         @bad_item
...
```

If you don't know the name of the trigger, you can always get a list of all the triggers for a table by running the `sp_helptrigger` procedure, and passing in the table's name.

Via the system catalogs

If you're intrepid and curious, you can consult the SQL Server 2005 Express system catalogs to get a handle on the number and types of triggers for your installation. Here's a simple query that neatly joins the three primary system catalogs to give you insight into your triggers:

```
SELECT tr.name, sm.definition, te.type_desc
FROM sys.triggers tr, sys.sql_modules sm,
          sys.trigger_events te
WHERE tr.object_id = sm.object_id
AND tr.object_id = te.object_id
```

Feel free to come up with your own queries against the SQL Server 2005 Express system catalogs — a tremendous amount of valuable information is stored there.

Writing new triggers

Creating a new trigger is easy — you simply enter your Transact-SQL, using SQL Server Management Studio Express (available via free download from Microsoft) or many other types of interactive query tools. After you successfully run your Transact-SQL, your trigger is ready to use.

Figure 15-1 shows an example of using SQL Server Management Studio Express to create a new trigger.

To build your triggers, just follow these steps:

1. **Determine what you want your new trigger to do.**

   What exactly does the DML trigger shown in Figure 15-1 do? It actually does quite a bit. For this example, suppose that you are maintaining an inventory management system. New requests arrive regularly, and you want to make sure that you never run out of stock. To prevent a shortage from happening, you want your trigger to automatically initiate reorder requests whenever a particular item runs low on inventory.

   Another job for this trigger is to alert buyers whenever an especially unpopular inventory item finally goes out the door. You could write another trigger to handle this work, but in this case you decide to combine all the code into one object.

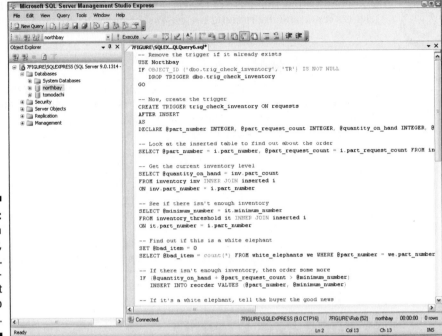

Figure 15-1:
Creating a
new trigger,
using SQL
Server Man-
agement
Studio
Express.

2. **Launch SQL Server Management Studio Express or the SQL tool of your choice.**

   SQL Server Management Studio Express is a great tool for entering Transact-SQL statements, including those that create triggers.

3. **Connect to the database where you want to create the trigger.**

4. **Write your trigger logic.**

   Using the inventory management example, I break down the code into manageable chunks to help illustrate how it works:

   ```
   -- Remove the trigger if it already exists
   USE NorthBay
   IF OBJECT_ID ('dbo.trig_check_inventory', 'TR')
   IS NOT NULL
       DROP TRIGGER dbo.trig_check_inventory
   GO
   ```

   If you try to create a trigger with the same name as one that already exists, SQL Server 2005 Express complains:

   ```
   .Net SqlClient Data Provider: Msg 2714, Level 16,
   State 2, Procedure trig_check_inventory, Line 34
   There is already an object named
           'trig_check_inventory'
   in the database.
   ```

Because this kind of error stops a script in its tracks, this first bit of code gets rid of the trigger if it already exists.

```
-- Now, create the trigger
CREATE TRIGGER trig_check_inventory ON requests
AFTER INSERT
```

By specifying AFTER INSERT, you tell SQL Server 2005 Express that you want this trigger to fire only if the SQL statement that invoked the trigger is correct, and only for those operations that put data into the table. You could also have this, or other, triggers fire for UPDATE or DELETE events.

```
AS
DECLARE @part_number INTEGER, @part_request_count
        INTEGER,
 @quantity_on_hand INTEGER, @minimum_number INTEGER,
 @bad_item TINYINT, @decision_maker_name VARCHAR(50),
 @decision_maker_email VARCHAR(50)
```

Here is where you declare all the variables that you want to use during your trigger. Remember that you can use all the power of Transact-SQL, so your triggers can be quite comprehensive.

Write the body of the trigger:

```
-- Look at the inserted table to find out about the
       order
SELECT @part_number = i.part_number,
@part_request_count = i.part_request_count FROM
        inserted i
```

```
-- Get the current inventory level
SELECT @quantity_on_hand = inv.part_count
FROM inventory inv INNER JOIN inserted i
ON inv.part_number = i.part_number
```

```
-- See if there isn't enough inventory
SELECT @minimum_number = it.minimum_number
FROM inventory_threshold it INNER JOIN inserted i
ON it.part_number = i.part_number
```

```
-- Find out if this is a white elephant
SET @bad_item = 0
SELECT @bad_item = COUNT(*) FROM white_elephants we
WHERE @part_number = we.part_number
```

This group of queries uses newly created information from the inserted table to help drive validity and other checks. You can think of the inserted table as a temporary repository of new information — a place where you can go to find out what the user has sent to SQL Server 2005 Express. The same holds true for the deleted table, except it holds data that has just been removed. You can use UPDATE() or COLUMNS_ UPDATED to determine the scope of an update.

Now that you have this information, you can take action if necessary:

```
-- If there isn't enough inventory, then order some
        more
IF (@quantity_on_hand + @part_request_count >
 @minimum_number)
    INSERT INTO reorder VALUES (@part_number,
@minimum_number)
```

```
-- If it's a white elephant, tell the buyer the good
        news
IF @bad_item > 0
    exec sqlexpress.msdb.dbo.sp_send_dbmail
        @recipients = @decision_maker_email,
        @subject = 'Just sold some of the white
        elephants!' ,
        @body = 'Check the sales activity report';
```

This trigger closes out by starting the reorder process when there is insufficient inventory. Finally, if a customer was foolish enough to buy one of the problem products, the trigger executes a system stored procedure to send a congratulatory e-mail to the person who made the decision to stock the troubled product.

5. **Run the Transact-SQL that creates the trigger.**

This trigger is fairly basic; you can write much more powerful code that encodes much more sophisticated business logic, invokes other triggers, and launches stored procedures.

Here's an example of a DDL trigger that's designed to block people from creating new indexes without first checking with you:

```
CREATE TRIGGER no_new_indexes
ON DATABASE
FOR CREATE_INDEX
AS
    PRINT 'Please call your friendly neighborhood DBA
    before creating a new index'
    ROLLBACK
```

Now, if users try to sneak a new index into the database, your new trigger stops them cold in their tracks:

```
Please call your friendly neighborhood DBA before creating
a new index
.Net SqlClient Data Provider: Msg 3609, Level 16, State 2,
        Line 1
The transaction ended in the trigger. The batch has been
        aborted.
```

You can use DDL triggers to safeguard your entire SQL Server 2005 Express installation.

Invoking triggers

Because the SQL Server 2005 Express database engine monitors and runs triggers, you do very little to make this process happen. In fact, all that needs to happen in most cases is for the triggering event to take place. For example, if you put an insert trigger on a particular table, SQL Server 2005 Express patiently waits until an insert happens on that table. After that insert happens, Express invokes the trigger and faithfully executes your instructions.

As I show you in the next section, you can disable a trigger. If you're concerned that a trigger isn't executing properly, you can easily check whether the trigger is in fact active. For example, here's how to tell if the `trig_check_inventory` trigger is disabled:

```
SELECT name, is_disabled FROM sys.triggers WHERE name = 'trig_check_inventory'
```

A value of `1` in the `is_disabled` column means that the trigger is disabled; a value of `0` means that it is active. Finally, if you're still not sure that your triggers are executing properly, you can always put debugging statements into them.

Disabling triggers

Sometimes, even the best of triggers can get in the way of what you're trying to accomplish. For example, suppose that you have a collection of rather complex triggers for a particular table. You wrote these triggers to perform a variety of data integrity and validation checks to protect your database from incorrect information. This strategy is a good one: Your database has very accurate data.

However, suppose that one day you're given a text file containing several million rows of already-cleaned data that need to be inserted into this table. These hard-working triggers will likely get in the way and cause the data load to take a very long time.

If you're using the `bcp` utility or the `BULK INSERT` command, SQL Server 2005 Express automatically disables triggers, which helps speed up these operations. However, for this example, assume that you're not using either of these options.

In this case, you don't want to drop and re-create the triggers, but you want this one-time job to finish as quickly as possible. Luckily, you can use the `DISABLE TRIGGER` statement to tell SQL Server 2005 Express to set one or more triggers aside:

```
DISABLE TRIGGER trig_validate_inventory, trig_validate_address ON requests
```

In this case, you tell SQL Server 2005 Express to disable two triggers for this table. If you want to disable all triggers for a table, you can do even less typing:

```
DISABLE TRIGGER ALL ON requests
```

But why stop there? A simple change disables the DDL triggers for the whole database:

```
DISABLE TRIGGER ALL ON DATABASE
```

Finally, if you have sufficient permission you can disable all the DDL triggers for the entire server:

```
DISABLE TRIGGER ALL ON ALL SERVER
```

Of course, invoking these kinds of statements exposes your database to the nasty, data-damaging events that you were concerned about when you first wrote the trigger. So remember to turn the triggers back on when you're ready. Doing so is very easy — just use the ENABLE TRIGGER statement. Here's an example of turning all the DDL triggers back on for your server:

```
ENABLE TRIGGER ALL ON ALL SERVER
```

Here's how to put your triggers back to work for a specific table:

```
ENABLE TRIGGER ALL ON requests
```

Modifying triggers

Mistakes happen to the best of us, so someday you'll probably need to change one of your existing triggers. If you need to make a modification to the trigger's logic, you can use the ALTER TRIGGER statement.

Unfortunately, altering a trigger often means that you must re-type the code for the entire trigger. But what if you forgot the code? Luckily, you can retrieve it by simply running the sp_helptext stored procedure:

```
sp_helptext trig_validate_address
```

On the other hand, if you want to rename the trigger, use the combination of DROP TRIGGER and CREATE TRIGGER statements.

Deleting triggers

One day, you and one or more of your triggers might have a falling out. Maybe it's just not working for you anymore, or one of you has grown and changed. In any case, if you can't patch things up with the trigger, you can pull the plug. SQL Server 2005 Express makes these awkward moments less difficult. The DROP TRIGGER statement instantly obliterates the trigger.

For a DML trigger, the DROP TRIGGER statement looks like this:

```
DROP TRIGGER trig_validate_address
```

To prevent global mistakes, SQL Server 2005 Express requires that you list each DML trigger that you want to delete. Getting rid of a DDL trigger for just one database looks like this:

```
DROP TRIGGER trig_no_new_index ON DATABASE
```

You can easily expand the DROP TRIGGER statement to remove a DDL trigger for all databases on your server:

```
DROP TRIGGER trig_no_new_index ON ALL SERVER
```

Another way to get rid of a DML trigger is to drop the entire table, but unless you truly don't care about the table, using the DROP TRIGGER statement instead is a better idea.

Chapter 16

Going Beyond Transact-SQL: Using the SQL Common Language Runtime (SQLCLR)

· ·

In This Chapter

▶ Introducing how SQLCLR works

▶ Discovering the benefits of deploying SQLCLR-based applications

▶ Integrating SQLCLR with SQL Server 2005 Express

▶ Developing SQLCLR stored procedures and functions

· ·

*L*ike all of us in the software industry, Microsoft is guilty of generating an occasional TLA. Oops — I just did it, too. TLA stands for *three-letter acronym*, and it's shorthand for one way that industry insiders and vendors express complex topics. CLR is yet another example of that; it stands for *Common Language Runtime*. As a cornerstone of Microsoft's approach to integration, it offers a wealth of interoperability and security features that extend far beyond just SQL Server 2005 Express. Microsoft has integrated the Common Language Runtime into SQL Server 2005 and has called this feature SQLCLR.

You can use any of the following programming languages as part of the SQLCLR environment:

✔ Microsoft Visual C++

✔ Microsoft Visual Basic .NET

✔ Microsoft Visual C# .NET

In this chapter, I describe how to take advantage of this technology to extend the power of your database applications. However, given the richness of this infrastructure along with the lack of space in a single chapter, please bear in mind that my immediate goal is to give you a basic overview of SQLCLR; I'm leaving many highly technical details out in the interest of clarity and brevity.

Finding Out How SQLCLR Works

A word of warning before I show you how this technology works: Just as using an electric light does not require understanding quantum physics, writing SQLCLR code for your database doesn't mandate deep knowledge of all the underlying software that makes this integration possible. Still, if you're curious about all the features that SQLCLR brings to the table, read on.

The .NET framework

Although we database-focused folks might like to believe otherwise, CLR plays a much bigger role in the Microsoft overall architecture than just in the context of SQL Server 2005 Express integration. It's actually part of the Microsoft .NET framework. Think of this framework as a unifying set of technologies that are designed to make the lives of programmers and other technical people easier.

Because the .NET framework handles so many of the tasks that were previously the responsibility of an individual developer, many applications have been built on top of this infrastructure. Known as *Managed Code*, and whether by design or not, these solutions leverage the following .NET framework services in the process:

- ✔ **Garbage collection:** Before you get your hopes up, no, CLR doesn't take the trash out for you or straighten up around your desk (although these tasks likely will be available by 2010). In this case, garbage collection refers to how CLR cleans up memory that is no longer needed. It helps make the most of an always-scarce resource; without it, your applications would consume more memory, and do so less efficiently.

- ✔ **Threading:** Threads are one way that modern computers and operating systems stretch performance. They are different strands of logic that your CPU juggles in near-real time. Threading boosts system throughput in a way that is completely transparent to your application. CLR employs sophisticated threading logic to increase your solution's responsiveness.

- ✔ **Security:** The power and flexibility of CLR-based applications can be a double-edged sword: It's easy to imagine a shady character trying to sneak some nefarious code into your database. However, the CLR has a number of built-in security restrictions designed to protect your database from unauthorized logic.

- ✔ **Assemblies:** After compiling your .NET-based application, Microsoft generates a composite object known as an assembly. In addition to your application code, these structures contain all sorts of information that the CLR uses when running this program. By using this intermediate arrangement, your application can easily interact with other programs that were built the same way.

Why use SQLCLR?

Transact-SQL is fine for many database-oriented tasks, but it has some significant shortcomings as a tool for more complex software development jobs. One of the reasons that SQLCLR exists is to help address these deficiencies. Here are some of its key advantages when building robust solutions:

- **Performance:** Transact-SQL is an interpreted language; the SQL Server 2005 Express engine generally validates every script each time it's run. However, the programming languages that you use to build a SQLCLR-based solution are all compiled. They greatly reduce the amount of work necessary at runtime, which helps increase throughput. On top of that, these languages are generally faster in their own right.

- **Security:** SQLCLR introduces numerous safeguards to prevent unauthorized access to, and operations on, your database. While Transact-SQL is no security slouch, SQLCLR adds yet another layer of defense for your information by leveraging the underlying SQL Server 2005 Express security system.

  In addition, because these languages are compiled, no one can have a peek at your code; the compilation process encrypts your application logic.

- **Proven programming model:** Given SQLCLR's tight coupling with the .NET framework, choosing one of these programming languages as your development infrastructure lets you take advantage of Microsoft's solid architectural foundation.

- **User-defined types and functions:** You can build your own types and functions in Transact-SQL; they just run more quickly and efficiently when coupled with the SQLCLR environment.

- **Productivity:** You can use the highly capable Visual Studio 2005 environment for any programming language supported by SQLCLR. This software development platform offers tremendous productivity enhancements when compared to the way that most developers construct Transact-SQL software.

What can you build with SQLCLR?

You can use SQLCLR-based programs to create any of the following SQL Server 2005 Express objects:

- Stored procedures
- Functions
- Aggregates

✔ User-defined types

✔ Triggers

If you're curious about what these objects do, check out Chapter 14 for details about the value of stored procedures and functions, and Chapter 15 for how triggers can add value to your applications.

Determining Whether You Should Use SQLCLR

How can you tell whether you need to switch from building database software with Transact-SQL to one of the SQLCLR-ready languages? Chances are you should if any of the following conditions apply in your environment:

✔ **Trade-secret algorithms:** Your application may contain one or more confidential, proprietary algorithms. For example, perhaps you're building a solution that determines credit risk, using some hard-won, closely guarded formulas. The last thing you'd want is for someone outside your organization to see how these formulas were constructed. The compiled nature of the SQLCLR languages — along with the added security provided by the framework — means that your trade secrets remain just that: secret.

✔ **High performance requirements:** You may be creating an application that needs extremely high rates of speed. On the other hand, you may just have extremely high maintenance users. Regardless of the reason, consider switching to SQLCLR if your goal is to wring every last drop of throughput from your solution.

✔ **Powerful clients:** With hardware costs continually dropping, many environments now feature client computers that a few years ago would have been acting as servers in their own right. While a Transact-SQL-based application needs its code to run on the server, a SQLCLR-based application's logic can be run on the server, the client, or a combination of the two.

✔ **Advanced language needs:** Transact-SQL is missing a number of key features and constructs that software developers have come to rely upon. All these are present in any of the SQLCLR-based languages:

- Arrays
- FOR/EACH loops
- Object orientation
- Classes

Using SQLCLR

Leveraging SQLCLR to extend your database applications is not as complicated as you may think (or fear!). First, I show you the basic steps needed to
employ SQLCLR in your database. Then, I use these steps to build two
sample SQLCLR-based objects.

1. **Launch Visual Studio 2005.**

2. **Create a new project, choosing your preferred language at the
   same time.**

3. **Choose a SQL Server template.**

4. **Choose the database connection you want to use.**

   If one doesn't exist, here's where you create it.

5. **Generate the foundation of your software.**

   You can choose among stored procedures, functions, triggers, aggregates, and user-defined types.

6. **Write your application logic, using the Visual Studio-generated foundation as a starting point.**

7. **Build and deploy your program.**

   To take advantage of SQLCLR-based logic, you must first enable
   CLR capabilities in your database server. To do so, execute the sp_
   configure stored procedure as follows:

   ```
   exec sp_configure 'clr enabled', 1
   ```

   You may also need to tinker with the security settings of your SQLCLR
   application, especially if it needs to make calls back into the database,
   access the user interface, or manipulate the file system.

   If administrative stored procedures aren't your cup of tea, you can use
   the SQL Server Surface Area configuration tool to set these parameters.
   Chapter 3 has all you need to know about this helpful utility.

8. **Test your solution.**

The preceding steps lay out the basic workflow for embedding SQLCLR logic;
with that in mind, check out the two different examples of how to embed
SQLCLR-based logic in your SQL Server 2005 Express database. Before beginning, here are a few assumptions and ground rules about these examples:

✔ **Visual Studio 2005 is the development platform.** Although there are
  other potential routes, if you plan to make frequent use of SQLCLR-
  based logic, Visual Studio is the way to go. Take the time to become
  familiar with the product.

✓ **I build a stored procedure in one example, and a function in the other.** You can also build objects such as triggers, aggregates, and user-defined types by using SQLCLR.

✓ **I use Visual Basic in one example, and Visual C# in the other.** SQLCLR includes support for other programming languages, but these two are the most popular.

✓ **You have some familiarity with Visual C# and/or Visual Basic.** Even some knowledge of any procedural language is of help here.

✓ **For clarity's sake, the examples are as simple as possible.** I don't subject you to deciphering 2,000 lines of intricate C# or Visual Basic code; instead, I show the bare minimum necessary for you to understand how to hook everything together and get productive.

Example 1: Customer classification stored procedure

This Visual Basic-based customer classification stored procedure expects a customer number, total quantity and value of transactions, average days to pay invoice, and a classification code. Using this information, it then executes a search in the database to find the minimum revenue target for that classification code. If the customer has generated more than the baseline revenue, the procedure writes a record into the database. Here's how the initial generated procedure looks:

```
Imports System
Imports System.Data
Imports System.Data.Sql
Imports System.Data.SqlTypes
Imports Microsoft.SqlServer.Server


Partial Public Class StoredProcedures
    <Microsoft.SqlServer.Server.SqlProcedure()> _
    Public Shared Sub  ClassifyCustomer ()
        ' Add your code here
    End Sub
End Class
```

Figure 16-1 shows how Visual Studio appears for this project. Notice how the database and project are closely integrated within the development user interface.

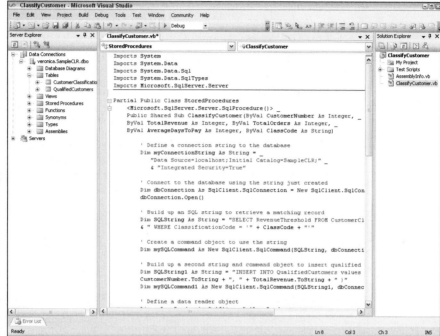

Figure 16-1:
Building a
SQLCLR
application
in the Visual
Studio
develop-
ment
environment.

Just a few lines of Visual Basic code complete the stored procedure. Here's what the finished product looks like:

```
Imports System
Imports System.Data
Imports System.Data.Sql
Imports System.Data.SqlTypes
Imports Microsoft.SqlServer.Server

Partial Public Class StoredProcedures
    <Microsoft.SqlServer.Server.SqlProcedure()> _
    Public Shared Sub ClassifyCustomer(ByVal CustomerNumber As Integer, _
     ByVal TotalRevenue As Integer, ByVal TotalOrders As Integer, _
     ByVal AverageDaysToPay As Integer, ByVal ClassCode As String)

        ' Define a connection string to the database
        Dim myConnectionString As String = _
            "Data Source=localhost;Initial Catalog=SampleCLR;" _
            & "Integrated Security=True"

        ' Connect to the database using the string just created
        Dim dbConnection As SqlClient.SqlConnection = _
            New SqlClient.SqlConnection(myConnectionString)
        dbConnection.Open()
```

```
' Build up an SQL string to retrieve a matching record
Dim SQLString As String = _
    "SELECT RevenueThreshold FROM CustomerClassification" _
    & " WHERE ClassificationCode = '" + ClassCode + "'"

' Create a command object to use the string
Dim mySQLCommand As New SqlClient.SqlCommand(SQLString, dbConnection)

' Build up a second string and command
' object to insert qualified records
Dim SQLString1 As String = "INSERT INTO QualifiedCustomers values (" + _
CustomerNumber.ToString + ", " + TotalRevenue.ToString + " )"
Dim mySQLCommand1 As New SqlClient.SqlCommand(SQLString1, dbConnection)

' Define a data reader object
Dim myDataReader As SqlClient.SqlDataReader
myDataReader = mySQLCommand.ExecuteReader()

' Set up a local variable to hold the retrieved threshold
' value from the database
Dim MinRevenue As Integer

' Walk through each retrieved record
Do While myDataReader.Read
    MinRevenue = myDataReader.GetInt32(0)
    If (TotalRevenue >= MinRevenue) Then
        mySQLCommand1.ExecuteNonQuery ()
    End If
Loop

' Shut down the connection to the database
dbConnection.Close()

    End Sub
End Class
```

Before spending lots of time filling in the blanks on an automatically generated SQLCLR object, try building and deploying it first. Discovering any product installation or problems early is for the best, before you invest too much time.

Example 2: Insurance risk function

In this example, I use C# to build a function that takes a series of parameters about a driver, including number of tickets, accidents, and late payments. It then uses an internal algorithm to determine if the driver is a good insurance risk, and then returns its answer to the person or process that invoked the function.

Here's how the initially generated code appears:

```
using System;
using System.Data;
using System.Data.Sql;
using System.Data.SqlTypes;
using Microsoft.SqlServer.Server;

public partial class UserDefinedFunctions
{
    [Microsoft.SqlServer.Server.SqlFunction]
    public static SqlString RiskProfile()
    {
                // Put your code here
                return new SqlString("Hello");
            }
};
```

Here's what the RiskProfile() function looks like after adding the risk validation logic:

```
[Microsoft.SqlServer.Server.SqlFunction]
public static SqlString RiskProfile(int numTickets,
    int numAccidents, int numLatePayments)
{
    // Driver starts out with no faults
    int Faults = 0;

    // This will be the variable used
    // to hold the driver's rating
    SqlString Rating = new SqlString();

    if (numTickets > 3)
        Faults++;
    if (numAccidents > 1)
        Faults++;
    if (numLatePayments > 3)
        Faults++;

    switch (Faults)
    {
        case 0:
            Rating = "Positive";
            break;
        case 1:
            Rating = "Neutral";
            break;
        case 2:
            Rating = "Negative";
            break;
```

```
        case 3:
            Rating = "Catastrophe";
            break;        default:
            Rating = "Neutral";
            break;
    }
    return Rating;
}
```

You can now invoke this function from within Transact-SQL, of course making sure to replace the database name and owner with the proper values for your site:

```
SELECT [DatabaseName].[Owner].[RiskProfile] (1,1,3)
```

Chapter 17

Sorry, I'll Try That Again: Adding Error Handling to Your Code

- -

In This Chapter

▶ Understanding the importance of handling errors

▶ Discovering the error management process

▶ Trapping errors in the database and application

▶ Defining your own types of errors

- -

*W*e all strive for perfection. Alas, errors, anomalies, and other unanticipated surprises are a fact of life. Nowhere is this fact more apparent than in computer-driven applications, and solutions built on top of SQL Server 2005 Express are no exception to this rule.

In this chapter, I show you why planning for, and handling, errors is so important. You see how to take advantage of the significant amount of error handling infrastructure offered by SQL Server 2005 Express, as well as the various application development technologies that work with this database server. Finally, I point out a number of common error scenarios, along with techniques that you can use to deal with them.

Don't Just Ignore It: Why You Should Care About Errors

Making your applications fully error-proof is hard work. Sometimes you might even be tempted to skip handling certain types of errors, and just hope for the best. After all, you put a lot of effort into building and debugging your application, and it's built on top of a solid database platform to boot. What could go wrong? Unfortunately, errors happen even in the most bulletproof applications, often through no fault of the software developer. Here are just a few benefits you accrue simply by monitoring and handling errors.

✔ **Transactional consistency:** In Chapter 12, I point out why transactions are such an integral part of keeping your data logically consistent. If you've followed my advice and added transactions to your applications: Good for you. However, you're not done yet. To correctly use transactions, you need to know when to *commit* (that is, save) or *rollback* (that is, cancel) an operation. If you don't check for errors, you can't instruct SQL Server 2005 Express to take the right action at the end of a transaction.

✔ **Application stability:** Even if a particular database error doesn't have any impact on any transactions, you still run the risk of a logically unstable application if you don't monitor and deal with any errors. For example, suppose that part of your application involves creating a temporary table and then inserting short-lived information into this new transitory table. Your software solution then uses this temporary table to help make decisions. If an error happens when you create the table or insert rows, and you don't catch or monitor this problem, you have a good chance that the downstream decision-making process will be inaccurate. Tracing and fixing this problem is very hard if no one knows about the initial issue.

✔ **Enhanced data integrity:** Implementing a solid error-handling strategy adds value — especially when safeguarding the integrity of your information even if you haven't used transactions when building your application. By intercepting and handling an error, you may prevent your application from introducing erroneous information into your database.

How to Handle Errors

I hope that I've convinced you that planning for and dealing with errors is important. In this section, I point out the useful and descriptive details that SQL Server 2005 Express provides whenever your application encounters an error, along with methods you can use to handle them.

Information about errors

To help you decipher and resolve any errors that your database server encounters, SQL Server 2005 Express provides the following error properties:

✔ **Error message:** Here's where you can find the exact wording of the error message.

✔ **Error number:** Each SQL Server 2005 Express error is associated with a predefined number; this property gives you that number.

✔ **Error procedure:** If your error happened in the middle of a stored procedure or trigger, here is where you can learn the name of the culprit. On the other hand, if it happened outside the context of either of these objects, this property is set to NULL.

✔ **Error line:** This property reports on where SQL Server 2005 Express found the error in your program or script.

✔ **Error severity:** Errors can range in severity, from 0 to 24. All these errors are not created equal. Some are cause for great concern, while you can practically laugh off others. Table 17-1 shows a summary of each major error severity group.

✔ **Error state:** Depending on where the error occurred, the same error number can have different error state values. So a given error number may indicate different problems.

Table 17-1	SQL Server Express Error Severity Groups
Severity	*Meaning*
0-9	Minor errors, or informational messages.
10	A synonym for error severity level zero.
11	Attempt to access a non-existent object.
12	Non-locking read queries return this error in certain situations.
13	A transaction deadlock has occurred.
14	A security violation was attempted.
15	SQL Server intercepted a syntax error in the Transact-SQL.
16	A catchall for user-correctable errors.
17	SQL Server ran out of a resource such as memory, locks, and so on.
18	An internal error happened in the database server.
19	A more severe internal database server error has occurred.
20	A specific statement has caused a problem.
21	A system-wide error has happened.
22	A database software or disk hardware problem has occurred.
23	The database's integrity has been compromised.
24	The underlying disk drive has been damaged.

Built-in system functions

In the preceding section, I inventory all the properties that you can discover about an error. If you're writing Transact-SQL and using TRY...CATCH logic (which I describe in a moment), you can invoke the following functions to obtain error properties programmatically:

- ✔ ERROR_NUMBER()
- ✔ ERROR_MESSAGE()
- ✔ ERROR_LINE()
- ✔ ERROR_PROCEDURE()

    If the error happened outside the context of a stored procedure or trigger, calling this function returns a NULL.

- ✔ ERROR_SEVERITY()
- ✔ ERROR_STATE()

These functions are relevant only in a TRY...CATCH block. Otherwise, they return NULL. Also, be sure to check your errors frequently. If you omit error checking in a given place, you may inadvertently pick up the error conditions from another section of code.

Handling errors in the database

Think of managing any issues within the database itself as a good first line defense against problems. This concept is especially true if your application takes advantage of stored procedures, triggers, or functions. You can embed error-handling logic in these server-side objects to intercept and deal with problems before your application fails.

TRY...CATCH

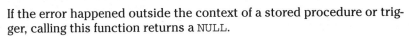

Unplanned-for problems often caused a total failure of the program in earlier generations of software applications. These errors frequently made the program so unstable that it was unable to continue, an event I'm sure you've seen. In an effort to help stabilize what are increasingly complex programs, many modern programming languages contain exception handlers that can catch and handle problems.

Transact-SQL now also provides this ability, via a construct known as TRY...CATCH. This feature contains two blocks. The first, which wraps its database access code between the BEGIN TRY and END TRY statements, is known as the TRY block. Immediately following this block is the error-handling logic, wrapped between BEGIN CATCH and END CATCH. This CATCH block is where you can write logic to take any or all the following actions:

✔ Report the error to the user or invoking application; ask them to correct the mistake if possible.

✔ Attempt to programmatically correct the error; the user may not even know there was a problem.

✔ Invoke a standardized error handler to manage the problem.

✔ Rollback any open transactions.

You can nest TRY...CATCH blocks, but note that errors with a severity level of less than 10 (that is, minor errors, simple informational, and other advisory messages) won't trigger the CATCH block. Refer to Table 18-1 for a listing of error severity groups.

Here's an example of a simple TRY...CATCH that launches a transaction, inserts a row, and then rollbacks the transaction in case a problem occurs. In this case, the value 'one oh one' should actually be 101 because the field expects a numeric value:

```
BEGIN TRY
    BEGIN TRANSACTION;
        INSERT INTO products VALUES
        ('one oh one','Paisley leisure suit',
         'Everything old is new again! Be the talk of
          your town with this cutting edge leisure suit'
         );
    COMMIT TRANSACTION;
END TRY
BEGIN CATCH
    IF (XACT_STATE()) = -1
        BEGIN
            PRINT N'The transaction contains errors, so
                it is being rolled back.';
            ROLLBACK TRANSACTION;
        END;
END CATCH;
```

You may be wondering what purpose the XACT_STATE() function serves in this example. You can use this built-in function to determine the current state of your transaction. It returns three possible values:

✔ **-1:** An active transaction can't be committed due to errors or other problems. You need to issue a ROLLBACK TRANSACTION statement as soon as possible.

- ✔ **0:** This session has no active transactions.

- ✔ **1:** This session has an active transaction, and everything is working normally. You are free to commit or rollback the transaction as you see fit.

As you see in a moment when I discuss handling errors in the application, database-centric error handling can go only so far: The TRY . . . CATCH construct won't easily catch a significant number of error situations.

@@ERROR

Unlike the TRY . . . CATCH block, which requires a more structured approach to your Transact-SQL application code, you can simply consult the @@ERROR operation to check the error number for the most recent statement. Successful invocations return 0 (a zero); errors return a non-zero value.

Because every SQL statement resets this value, make sure to check it immediately after an operation. Otherwise, you may not have a true picture of any error conditions.

After you save the value contained in @@ERROR, you can take action depending on what you've learned. Your Transact-SQL logic, however, is probably more effective using the TRY . . . CATCH block rather than the more informal @@ERROR construct.

Handling errors in the application

Despite your best efforts to intercept errors at their source in the database, I can guarantee that some will sneak by and make it all the way back into your application. Fortunately, all modern programming languages and technologies incorporate mechanisms to gracefully cope with all sorts of issues — database problems included.

A highly detailed review of each software development technology's error management structure would fill its own book. In the following list, I simply describe how each major application infrastructure handles errors:

- ✔ **Open Database Connectivity (ODBC):** When your ODBC-based application encounters a database error, three bits of diagnostic information are at your disposal:

  - **The native error number.** This is a SQL Server 2005 Express-specific error code.

  - **A message that describes the error condition.**

  - **A database-independent error code, known as SQLSTATE.** By building your solutions to handle this generic, cross-database error code, you can more easily switch your application logic between different database engines.

After you determine that an error has occurred (which you know if anything other than SQL_SUCCESS is returned from an ODBC function call), you can invoke the ODBC SQLGetDiagRec operation to retrieve the three diagnostic indicators.

- ✔ **Active Data Objects (ADO):** This database API offers the same diagnostic information as I describe for ODBC in the preceding bullet.

- ✔ **Object Linking and Embedding for Databases (OLE DB):** This API also provides the same error result information as ODBC. You can use the IErrorInfo interface to fetch these details. If you're interested in SQL Server 2005 Express-specific aspects, check out the ISQLServerError Info interface.

- ✔ **SqlClient:** If you're using this API, make sure to catch SqlException exceptions. Once caught, you can then retrieve details about what caused the issue to occur.

- ✔ **Microsoft Foundation Classes (MFC):** Just as with ADO and OLE DB, this popular programming technology also offers the error detail information available via the ODBC interface.

Error Examples

By now you're probably wondering what some real-world errors look like. Never fear: I'm about to show you a wide variety of what you may encounter as you build and maintain your SQL Server 2005 Express-based application.

No two development environments are exactly alike, so I use straight Transact-SQL to illustrate these examples. Also, recall that the TRY...CATCH block can't handle any errors that are caused by bad syntax, or object names issues that aren't discovered until runtime.

For these examples, I work with two tables from a product rating application, as defined here:

```
CREATE TABLE PRODUCTS
(
    product_id INTEGER NOT NULL PRIMARY KEY,
    product_name VARCHAR(255) NOT NULL,
    product_description TEXT NOT NULL
)
CREATE TABLE ratings
(
    rating_id INTEGER NOT NULL PRIMARY KEY,
    rating_date DATETIME NOT NULL,
    product_id INTEGER NOT NULL REFERENCES products,
    rating_code SMALLINT NOT NULL,
    product_rating TEXT NOT NULL
)
```

Syntax error

Sometimes even the simplest problem can drive you nuts. Mistyping SQL syntax ranks with some of the most common, yet hard-to-debug obstacles. Unfortunately, unless you embed the TRY...CATCH block within a stored procedure, even a simple syntax error isn't caught. For example, look at this block of code, its simple typo, and its output:

```
BEGIN TRY
    SLEECT * FROM Products;
END TRY
BEGIN CATCH
    SELECT
        ERROR_LINE() as 'Error Location',
        ERROR_NUMBER() as 'SQL Server Error Number',
        ERROR_MESSAGE() as 'Error Description'
END CATCH
Msg 102, Level 15, State 1, Line 2
Incorrect syntax near 'SLEECT'.
```

Why didn't the CATCH block intercept this message and give a formatted error result? Syntax errors and recompilation mistakes aren't caught, unless they happen to be embedded in a stored procedure or other lower-level TRY...CATCH block.

Database schema issue

One reason why database administrators typically keep tight control over their SQL Server 2005 Express servers is to prevent inadvertent schema alterations. What makes these changes so dangerous is that they can easily damage previously working applications. For example, suppose that someone decides to rename the rating_number column in the ratings table to rating_code. Look at what happens to the following section of well-tested, and already-successful code.

```
BEGIN TRY
    SELECT rating_id, rating_code FROM ratings;
END TRY
BEGIN CATCH
    SELECT
        ERROR_LINE() as 'Error Location',
        ERROR_NUMBER() as 'SQL Server Error Number',
        ERROR_MESSAGE() as 'Error Description'
END CATCH

Msg 207, Level 16, State 1, Line 2
Invalid column name 'rating_code'.
```

Just as in the preceding syntax error example, here is another example where the TRY...CATCH block is unable to intercept and deal with a problem. Alternatively, you could use a Data Definition Language (DDL) trigger to thwart any attempts to modify your database's schema.

Data conversion problems

Many an application has fallen over when attempting an incorrect data conversion. Fortunately, proper error handling can head off an embarrassing failure in this area. Take a look at the following Transact-SQL snippet and results, where I'm trying to insert a string into a column that's expecting an integer:

```
BEGIN TRY
    INSERT INTO products VALUES ('Oh no','Widget 6',
    'High quality widget - available in lime green');
END TRY
BEGIN CATCH
    SELECT
        ERROR_LINE() as 'Error Location',
        ERROR_NUMBER() as 'SQL Server Error Number',
        ERROR_MESSAGE() as 'Error Description'
END CATCH

2   245   Conversion failed when converting the
varchar value 'Oh no' to data type int.
```

Referential integrity violation

As I describe in Chapter 8, referential integrity helps preserve the logical consistency of your SQL Server 2005 Express database. When you put this data safeguard in place, the database server enforces its rules. You can then manage any errors that arise at runtime, as I show in the following code block. In this example, I'm trying to insert a row into the ratings table that doesn't have a corresponding entry in the products table.

```
BEGIN TRY
    INSERT INTO ratings VALUES (1822,'12/30/2006',
    100, 15,'Product met my needs');
END TRY
BEGIN CATCH
    SELECT
        ERROR_LINE() as 'Error Location',
        ERROR_NUMBER() as 'SQL Server Error Number',
        ERROR_MESSAGE() as 'Error Description'
END CATCH
```

```
2   547  The INSERT statement conflicted with the
FOREIGN KEY constraint "FK__ratings__product__09DE7BCC".
The conflict occurred in database "Northbay", table
"dbo.PRODUCTS", column 'product_id'.
```

In this case, the TRY...CATCH block works as advertised, catching the error message and displaying it in the chosen format.

You typically encode some sort of error-handling flow control logic in a TRY...CATCH block. For these examples, I simply display the error message.

Trigger interception

In Chapter 15, I show you how to take advantage of triggers to use SQL Server 2005 Express as your agent in enforcing business and other rules. Of course, all rules are made to be broken, but the database server is rather strict in its interpretation of these guidelines. So you certainly receive an error if you attempt to violate a rule encoded in a trigger. Have a look at the following code snippet to see what I mean. Before beginning, note that a trigger is in place to prevent users from entering a very high rating if a sufficient number of reviews aren't already in place.

```
BEGIN TRY
    INSERT INTO ratings VALUES
    (11,'6/10/2007',1,100,'Best ever!');
END TRY
BEGIN CATCH
    SELECT
        ERROR_LINE() as 'Error Location',
        ERROR_NUMBER() as 'SQL Server Error Number',
        ERROR_MESSAGE() as 'Error Description'
END CATCH

9 50000  Not enough ratings to give this product
such a high score
```

The TRY...CATCH block works in tandem with the trigger, protecting the integrity of the database and allowing the application developer to handle the exception.

Defining Your Own Errors with RAISERROR

Even though SQL Server 2005 Express comes with a plethora of built-in error messages, you may want to create your own set of site-specific error diagnostics. Why would you go to the trouble? Here are just a few good reasons:

✔ **Application-specific messages:** As I describe in Chapters 14 and 15, you can customize SQL Server 2005 Express with your own set of stored procedures, functions, and triggers. These can make up the foundation of an application, and you may wish to define and report on your own set of errors that relate only to your solution.

✔ **Debugging:** Software developers frequently spend more time debugging software than developing new applications. You can use RAISERROR (which I describe in a minute) as a convenient shortcut to determining the state of your database-based application logic.

✔ **Informative messages:** Sometimes an error isn't an error. For example, perhaps you want to report advisory results back to a user. You could hardcode this message into your application, or you could just take advantage of RAISERROR.

When using the RAISERROR statement, you can choose between building a message at runtime or picking a predefined error message from the sys.messages system catalog. Here's how to store a user-defined error message in the database server:

1. **Open a command prompt.**

   Choose Start⇨Run and enter **cmd**. Or choose Programs⇨Accessories⇨ Command Prompt. After you see the friendly command prompt, you can launch SQLCMD.

2. **Run SQLCMD, connecting to the correct database server.**

3. **Run the sp_addmessage stored procedure.**

   Here's an example of creating an application-specific error message:

   ```
   exec sp_addmessage @msgnum = 75000, @severity=17,
   @msgtext = 'VIP status available only if annual purchases
   exceed $25,000 for customer %s'
   GO
   ```

   You can also use SQL Server Management Studio Express to create these user-defined error messages.

With the message safely stored in the database, here are some examples of using it in conjunction with RAISERROR. For the following examples, I show both runtime-generated messages as well as the message I stored in the database.

In this first case, here's an example of the RAISERROR command for a user-defined error message, using a similar message style to the one I describe in the preceding steps. You typically invoke this error via a stored procedure, function, or trigger:

```
RAISERROR(75000,17,1,'3D House of Beef')
```

Here's what the user sees:

```
Msg 75000, Level 17, State 1, Server DBSERVER, Line 1
VIP status available only if annual purchases exceed
$25,000 for customer 3D House of Beef.
```

Next, here's an example of a runtime-generated message, also typically constructed within a stored procedure, trigger, or function:

```
RAISERROR ('Customer credit is insufficient for
          order',16,1)
```

And here's what the user sees:

```
Msg 50000, Level 16, State 1, Line 1
Customer credit is insufficient for order
```

Note that 50000 is the default user-defined error code.

Chapter 18

Full-Text Searching and Reporting Services

*B*ecause no two data-processing environments are alike, the SQL Server 2005 product family offers specialized editions that you can use to construct database-driven solutions that are just right for your needs. These editions range from the freely downloadable SQL Server 2005 Express all the way up to the pricier Enterprise edition. What's great about this arrangement is that you can very easily move between editions: Database architecture and application logic that work with one version are compatible with other versions.

For entry-level users and developers, SQL Server 2005 Express offers tremendous functionality and power in a free package. However, certain key capabilities are not present in this edition. Thus, after taking feedback from early users into consideration, Microsoft took the baseline functionality from SQL Server 2005 Express and added some very helpful new capabilities, and created a new edition named SQL Server 2005 Express with Advanced Services. This product represents a middle way for those organizations that want the ease of use and low (actually, free) price point of the baseline SQL Server 2005 Express edition as well as higher-end features, such as full-text search and enhanced reporting capabilities. Prior to this new edition, the only way to gain access to this type of functionality was to purchase a more expensive version of SQL Server 2005.

In this chapter, I point out how you can make the most of this edition. To begin, I help you determine whether this is the right edition of SQL Server 2005 Express for you. Next, I show you how to correctly install the product. With that vital step out of the way, the next order of business is to see how to leverage the power of full-text searching. Finally, you see how to quickly create and deploy reports.

Deciding to Use the Advanced Services Edition

Given all the different SQL Server editions, you would be forgiven for wondering how Advanced Services version fits in and when you should choose it for your data storage project. It's actually quite simple: Choose this edition when the basic functionality provided by SQL Server Express *almost* meets your needs, but you require some additional capabilities. If any of the following features interests you, check out Advanced Services:

- ✔ **Full-text searching:** Quickly and efficiently search through mountains of text-based information.

- ✔ **Reporting services:** Present your valuable data in many different formats through a variety of interfaces.

- ✔ **Graphical management:** Perform database administration and information operations through an easy-to-use management tool.

I show you how to use the first two helpful features throughout the rest of this chapter.

Although the SQL Server Management Studio Express tool is highlighted as being part of this edition, you can use it with the baseline SQL Server 2005 Express product. As a matter of fact, I reference it throughout the rest of the book.

Installation Considerations

When installing this edition of SQL Server 2005 Express, be mindful to specifically request important product features. Otherwise, you may be unpleasantly surprised to find that they were skipped. For example, look at Figure 18-1 to see how the installation utility looks when selecting features.

Make sure that you enable any capabilities that you think are important in your environment: It's usually better to have them installed and simply not use them than not have them when you need them.

In terms of installing the report server, it's generally wise to choose the default configuration rather than skipping this step. Figure 18-2 shows you how to control the report server's configuration.

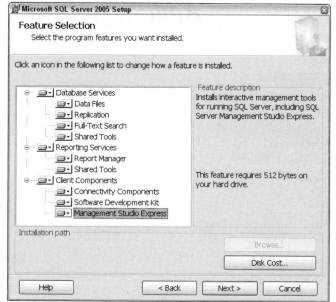

Figure 18-1:
Installation
feature
selection
dialog box.

Figure 18-2:
Report
server
installation
options.

To get a better idea of the exact configuration for your report server, just click the Details button. The window shown in Figure 18-3 appears, which provides more insight into how SQL Server 2005 Express adjusts your settings.

Figure 18-3:
Report
server
installation
details.

Speaking of reporting, to gain the full benefit of all that SQL Server 2005 Express with Advanced Services offers, make sure to download and install the SQL Express Toolkit. It includes these key technologies (see Figure 18-4):

- ✔ **Connectivity Components:** These technologies make it possible for database clients and servers to talk.

- ✔ **Business Intelligence Development Studio:** This is the foundation upon which you build reports.

- ✔ **Software Development Kit:** These tools help application developers build solutions to interact with SQL Server.

- ✔ **Management Studio Express:** This graphical environment is ideal for managing and interacting with your database.

Finally, you should bear in mind that if you want to share your reports with users logging in from other computers, you need to make sure that a web server such as Microsoft's Internet Information Services (IIS) is installed and configured. If it's not already set up on your computer, you can request it as follows:

1. **Launch Control Panel from the Start menu.**

2. **Double-click the Add or Remove Programs icon.**

3. **Click the Add/Remove Windows Components icon.**

   The Windows Components Wizard launches.

4. **Select the IIS check box and click Next to complete the wizard.**

   After the wizard finishes, IIS is installed on your computer.

With these details out of the way, it's now time to see how full-text searching can add measurable value to your database-driven solutions.

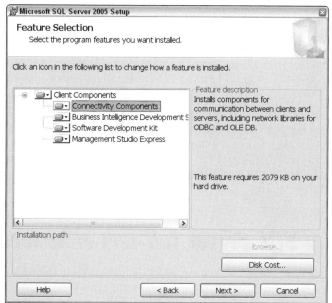

Figure 18-4: SQL Express Toolkit installation.

Full-Text Searching

Many modern database-driven applications need to store and process large volumes of text-based information. To help address these requirements, database vendors continually improve the capabilities of their product offerings. Microsoft is no exception. However, advanced text interrogation features have generally only been found in the pricier versions of its database products. By including these capabilities in this free version, SQL Server 2005 Express with Advanced Services represents a break from this tradition. In this section, I show you how this technology works and also how you can take advantage of its power to build richer, more sophisticated applications.

If you're unfamiliar with the challenges of processing large amounts of text-based data, you're probably wondering what all the fuss is about. Here are just a few of the benefits that you'll accrue simply by using full-text searches to locate information:

- ✔ **Speed:** When you need to search for the proverbial needle in a haystack — where your haystack is made up of reams of text-based data — you'll appreciate the dramatic performance gains that full-text searches offer versus traditional searches that use the `LIKE` SQL keyword.

- ✔ **Ease-of-use:** As I show you in the "Using full-text searching" section a little later in this chapter, you don't need a PhD in computer science from MIT to be productive with full-text searching. In fact, you can quickly and simply construct your own queries in minutes.

- ✔ **Broad document support:** Even a modern, sophisticated relational database management system such as SQL Server is only one source of information in most enterprises. Tons of additional data reside in all sorts of locations, from text files to documents such as PDF, Word, and Excel. Full-text searching lets you include these venues when constructing a query.

- ✔ **Localization:** Modern relational database management systems such as SQL Server 2005 Express can cope with information in any language, from Afrikaans to Zulu. When you use full-text searching (rather than the `LIKE` keyword), SQL Server 2005 Express applies sophisticated linguistic rules based on the data's language rather than a brute force character-matching exercise.

Special SQL Server full-text enhancements

To make possible the important capabilities I describe in the preceding bullets, this edition of SQL Server 2005 Express includes three highly specialized engine technologies, all of which interact with the standard SQL Server process and its ancillary capabilities:

- ✔ **Full-text engine:** This component is a dedicated indexing and search structure that is fully integrated with the main SQL Server database engine. It has three main tasks to perform:

    - Construct full-text indexes.

    - Maintain full-text indexes.

    - Enable searching on full-text data.

    To get the job done for these three tasks, the full-text engine includes a number of objects, ranging from a collection of language-specific thesaurus to a list of "noise" words that should be discarded when analyzing data. If you're curious, you can see this process running from the Windows Task Manager; it's called `MFTESQL`.

✔ **Full-text engine filter daemon:** Full-text searching wouldn't get very far without this technology. The full-text engine launches the daemon and makes it possible to sort through full-text information. It's made up of three specialized components:

- **Protocol handler:** This actually performs the job of interacting with a table to work with data.

- **Filter:** One of the best features of full-text searching is its ability to handle data from a variety of file formats. The filtering technology makes it possible for SQL Server to work with these specialized types of data.

- **Word breaker and stemmer:** This is how SQL Server 2005 Express parses and analyzes text-based data to find answers to your question. This component includes some very sophisticated language analysis. You can even instruct the database engine to use different language rules for different full-text columns.

This process is called MSFTEFD.

✔ **Full-text catalog:** This is where the actual index contents are stored. Interestingly, it's kept on the file system rather than within the database.

How full-text search works

Before you dive in and start going wild with full-text searching, I want to take you through a brief, educational journey into the nuts and bolts of how Microsoft implemented this important and powerful feature.

At its heart, full-text searching relies on special indexes that SQL Server 2005 Express rapidly creates in response to an administrator's request. Each index tracks details about words and phrases, including their specific row as well as location within a column. These indexes are stored on the file system rather than in the database.

You can create full-text indexes on columns that you define as any of the following:

✔ CHAR

✔ VARCHAR

✔ NVARCHAR

✔ VARBINARY

✔ IMAGE

In case you were wondering, the full-text indexing process skips over commonly used words, such as a, the, an, and so on. These are *noise words*.

Before you can create a full-text index, you need to make sure that your table already has a unique index in place on one or more columns that cannot be null. You should also know that you can create only one full-text index on a table.

The process by which SQL Server 2005 Express generates a full-text index is *population*. Three different mechanisms are available when undertaking this effort:

- ✓ **Full population:** As you may suspect from its name, this mechanism evaluates every row in the table and constructs the appropriate index entries based on what is learned during this process. Unless you specify otherwise, this is the default behavior when you create a new index.

- ✓ **Change-tracking population:** In this scenario, SQL Server keeps an eye on changes to the full-text–indexed data over time. Armed with this intelligence, it then updates the full-text index to reflect these alterations. As an administrator, you have control over how these updates occur. Although this edition doesn't include SQL Agent (which means that you can't schedule the update), you can have them run automatically or perform them manually.

- ✓ **Incremental-timestamp population:** If your table has a column with a type of TIMESTAMP, SQL Server can automatically update the full-text index as data changes.

Using full-text searching

Full-text searching comes in many flavors and varieties. In this section, I show you how to set up full-text searching on your database. After this is out of the way, you see examples of several different types of full-text search. To keep things consistent across all the examples, suppose that you're building an application that handles special shipping requests for your organization's products. Here are three of the more important tables for your solution:

```
CREATE TABLE Shipments
(
    ShipmentID INTEGER PRIMARY KEY NOT NULL,
    ShipmentDate DATETIME,
    ShippedParts XML,
    ShipmentWeight DECIMAL(5,2)
)

CREATE TABLE PackingInstructions
(
    PackingInstructionID INT PRIMARY KEY NOT NULL,
    ShipmentID INT REFERENCES Shipments,
    PackingDetails VARBINARY(MAX),
    PackingFileName VARCHAR(30),
```

```
      PackingFileType VARCHAR(30)
)

CREATE TABLE ShipRequests
(
    ShipmentRequestID INTEGER PRIMARY KEY NOT NULL,
    ShipmentID INTEGER NOT NULL REFERENCES Shipments,
    DeliveryInstructions TEXT
)
```

With your tables in place, here are the steps you follow to make full-text searching a reality. Before setting off down this path, you first need to make sure your database is configured to allow full-text searching. Here's how to make that happen when you create a new database:

1. **Launch SQL Server Management Studio Express.**

2. **Right-click the Databases folder and choose the New Database option.**

   The New Database dialog box opens, as shown in Figure 18-5.

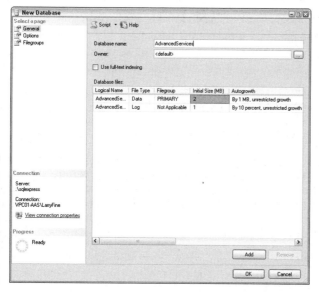

Figure 18-5:
Creating a
database
that
supports
full-text
searches.

3. **Select the Use Full-Text Indexing check box and continue entering the properties of this new database. When you're done, click OK to save your changes.**

That's all there is to it: Your database is now ready to support full-text searching. For an existing database, all you need to do is open its properties and switch to the Files property page; you'll see the same check box there. Check it, and you're ready to go. But before you break out the champagne, you still have a little more work to do; you now need to create the appropriate full-text indexes, after all. Here's how to do just that:

1. **Connect to your database using the tool of your choice.**

   For this example, I use SQL Server Management Studio Express, but any SQL-capable tool works.

2. **If one doesn't already exist, generate a default full-text catalog.**

   SQL Server 2005 Express uses these structures to support full-text indexes. When you create a full-text catalog, SQL Server 2005 Express places the catalog on the local disk drive of the server where the database engine is running. You need to create only one full-text catalog; multiple indexes can coexist within its confines. If necessary, you can also set up multiple full-text catalogs.

   To construct a new full-text catalog, use the logically named CREATE FULLTEXT CATALOG command. Here's the statement that generates the catalog that supports the examples you're about to see:

   ```
   CREATE FULLTEXT CATALOG Demo AS DEFAULT
   ```

3. **Run the CREATE FULLTEXT INDEX command.**

   Using the sample tables I show previously in this section, here's how to set up a full-text index on the DeliveryInstructions column:

   ```
   CREATE FULLTEXT INDEX ON ShipRequests
   KEY INDEX PK__ShipRequests__7E6CC920
   ```

   As you can see from the rather arcane syntax for this statement, you need to know the name of the single column-based index that provides a primary, unique key for your table. If you don't have such an index in place, you need to create one.

   When you want to index binary information, you must include some additional directives to help SQL Server choose the right filter at query time. For example, in this scenario, the PackingInstructions table's job is to store information found in external document files. Here's the syntax for creating a full-text index on the PackingDetails column:

   ```
   CREATE FULLTEXT INDEX ON PackingInstructions(PackingDetails
   TYPE COLUMN PackingFileType)
   KEY INDEX PK__PackingInstructi__164452B1
   ```

   When it's time to run a query, SQL Server looks at the PackingFileType column to decide what filter to use to retrieve information. I discuss this more in the upcoming "Examples" section.

   You can create only one full-text index on a given table.

Full-text predicates versus full-text functions

When you set out on the full-text road, one important decision you need to make is whether to use full-text predicates or full-text functions. Actually, they're not mutually exclusive, but you'll probably find that you prefer one or the other. Here's a brief overview of these two full-text search capabilities:

- ✔ **Full-text predicates:** This consists of the CONTAINS and FREETEXT keywords. You use CONTAINS when you want to perform an exact match, and you employ FREETEXT when you want to find words or phrases with similar meanings.

  You include these predicates in the WHERE or HAVING clause of your query. If your full-text query successfully locates a match, these predicates return TRUE; otherwise, they return FALSE.

- ✔ **Full-text functions:** The two full-text functions at your disposal are CONTAINSTABLE and FREETEXTTABLE. As you may suspect from their names, the first function is used for exact matches, and the second is used for a meaning match.

  The primary difference between predicates and functions is that the latter return *pseudo-tables* of information, which may be empty or have many rows (depending on whether data was located). Consequently, you use these functions in the FROM clause and must then join the results to the original tables. These functions return tables that include a column named RANK, which helps identify the relevance of your search results.

When you're getting started, I recommend working with the simpler full-text predicates. After you're up to speed, you can start to leverage the full-text functions.

For the balance of this section, I focus on full-text predicates.

Examples

With the full-text catalog and index in place (refer to the earlier section, "Using full-text searching"), you can finally start deriving some value from your text-based information. In this section, I show you several different classes of search, from the fairly commonplace to the more infrequent.

Simple text search using exact match

This is the most common type of full-text search (which is why I'm leading off with it!). In this scenario, you simply want to look for a phrase that matches a particular string. To make this happen, just use the CONTAINS predicate as follows:

```
SELECT DeliveryInstructions
FROM ShipRequests
WHERE CONTAINS (DeliveryInstructions, ' "no signature required" ')
```

In this example, you've asked SQL Server 2005 Express to locate any rows in the `ShipRequests` table that exactly match the string in the query.

You're free to use Boolean logic in your full-text queries. For example, you could modify the previous query to look for rows that match one of two phrases as follows:

```
SELECT DeliveryInstructions
FROM ShipRequests
WHERE CONTAINS (DeliveryInstructions, ' "no signature required" OR
"do not sign" ')
```

Of course, you can also combine full-text search conditions with other SQL conditional query logic in the WHERE clause.

Although these first examples that require exact matches are very helpful, sometimes you're likely to want to find all records that mean the same thing, even if they aren't worded the same. That brings me to the next type of search.

Simple text search using meanings

Although it's not psychic or omnipotent, SQL Server 2005 Express does its best to locate rows that mean the same thing as your query. To make this happen, use the FREETEXT keyword. When you make this request, the database engine performs some rather sophisticated text parsing and analysis, and even consults a thesaurus on your behalf. For example, suppose you want to find all rows that reference potential damage to shipments, even if the exact wording is different. Here's how you'd write this query.

```
SELECT DeliveryInstructions
FROM ShipRequests
WHERE FREETEXT (DeliveryInstructions, 'damage broke crush')
```

As written, this query finds rows containing damaged, damaging, broken, crushed, and so on.

Although very helpful, this feature may not always catch all appropriate matches. For example, searching for crush may not necessarily find an entry that contains crushable. Likewise, using broke as a search term may not correctly snag breakable. Keep these types of semantic challenges in mind as you construct your database applications.

Proximity search

As you may suspect from its name, a *proximity search* enables you to look for phrases or words that are located in the neighborhood of other phrases or words. For example, suppose that you want to look for the words *signature* and *required* but only when they appear in the same vicinity. You don't want to find rows that tell you that special packaging is required or that the customer's signature is on file. You want only those rows that provide some guidance on whether a signature is needed for delivery. You make this search happen by specifying NEAR in your query:

```
SELECT DeliveryInstructions
FROM ShipRequests
WHERE CONTAINS (DeliveryInstructions, '(signature NEAR required)')
```

Searching within other data formats

Data comes in all shapes, sizes, and formats. One nifty feature of full-text searching is its ability to interrogate multiple types of data formats. For example, suppose that you want to examine the contents of a Microsoft Word document to locate a particular phrase. In this case, you want to find data from an attached document of directions. Here's what to do.

1. **Make sure your table contains a column of with a type of VARBINARY(MAX).**

   This column serves as the destination for the contents of your file. In order to search it, you first need to load it into your database.

2. **Import your information via the OPENROWSET command.**

   You use this versatile command for all sorts of data interactions, typically involving setting up remote data connections. However, it also lets you load data from external files into columns that have been designated VARBINARY(MAX). Here's the command I used to load a Word document into the PackingInstructions table:

   ```
   INSERT INTO PackingInstructions(PackingInstructionID, ShipmentID,
   PackingFileName, PackingFileType, PackingDetails)
     SELECT 123 as 'PackingInstructionID', 17221 as 'ShipmentID',
     'Demo.doc' as PackingFileName, '.doc' as PackingFileType, * FROM
     OPENROWSET(BULK N'C:\Demo.doc', SINGLE_BLOB) AS ShipmentPackaging
   ```

   That's a lot of SQL, but it's all necessary. For SQL Server to apply the right query filter at runtime, you need to tell it what kind of data is being placed into the table. That's why you provide instructions in the PackingFileType column.

3. **Run your search.**

   With your data safely ensconced in its new home and SQL Server given instructions on what kind of filter to use, locating matching words and phrases is a cinch. Here's a search that attempts to locate all shipments that include packing instructions to use bubble wrap:

```
SELECT ShipmentID
FROM PackingInstructions
WHERE CONTAINS (PackingDetails, ' "bubble wrap" ')
```

Performance tips

As with most powerful tools, along with great capabilities come great responsibilities. Here are a few suggestions to help you keep your full-text searches
running as quickly and smoothly as possible:

✔ **Provide large tables with their own catalog.**

✔ **Associate similar processing profiles with a single catalog.**

✔ **Update full-text indexes in real time.**

Reporting Services

What good is having a database that's chock-full of great information if you
can't easily access your valuable data? Although Transact-SQL lets you build
very powerful queries, expecting the average user to master the intricacies of
this data access method is not realistic.

SQL Server 2005 Express with Advanced Services offers a collection of very
powerful reporting capabilities that are designed to securely distribute
important data to everyone that needs it. In this section, I take you on a tour
of all the components that make up SQL Server's reporting infrastructure. As
part of the tour, you'll get the hang of designing, publishing, and maintaining
your own reports.

The first thing to understand about SQL Server's reporting architecture is
that it's *modular.* This means that you can use the infrastructure as is or
make heavy customizations. I focus on using the reporting technology out of
the box; however, you should note that the amount of customizing that you
can do has no limit.

Take a look at the components that make up the reporting infrastructure:

✔ **Report Server:** This is the foundation of SQL Server's Reporting
   Services. It runs as a Windows service and is responsible for coordinat-
   ing all aspects of your reporting environment. It uses its own dedicated
   database to hold details about what reports have been created and
   deployed.

✔ **Reporting Services Configuration Tool:** This graphical interface lets
   you set up and maintain a broad range of reporting settings.

✔ **Report Designer:** Typically accessed via Visual Studio, this module offers a broad set of report development functionality that is aimed at the more sophisticated user. I focus on Report Designer for the balance of this section.

✔ **Report Builder:** This component was designed to meet the needs of the vast majority of database users who want to quickly and easily generate reports from their data. Unfortunately, it's not present in this edition, but you should be aware that it exists in the pricier versions.

✔ **SQL Server Management Studio Express:** This graphical management and information access tool is available by a free download from Microsoft. Although you don't create reports in this environment, you're likely to use it to create and maintain your database and its related information.

✔ **Report Manager:** In addition to viewing report content, you use this browser-based interface to perform a wide variety of reporting access and administration tasks.

Using these elements, you can construct a wide variety of reports:

✔ **Tabular:** Similar to a database table, this type of report is made up of rows and columns. The data selection criteria determine the exact number of rows displayed at runtime.

✔ **Matrix:** Akin to a spreadsheet's pivot tables, this class of report arranges its data into rows and columns, both of which are determined at runtime.

✔ **Graphical:** You use this type of report to spice up your data with charts, graphs, and so on.

✔ **Free-form:** Typically used with less-structured data, this report presents information in a more linear fashion.

With your report set up, you have a number of output options:

✔ HTML

✔ Excel

✔ Comma-separated value (CSV)

✔ Portable Document Format (PDF)

You can assemble and deliver your reports via several useful avenues:

✔ E-mail

✔ Portal

✔ Browser

✔ Extensible options

Creating your report

Now that you're an expert on all of the moving parts found in SQL Server's reporting architecture, it's time to start putting them to work for you. To begin, I call out those important but somewhat tedious tasks that you need to take care of before you can get to the fun stuff:

1. **Make sure that your computer has the complete reporting support infrastructure.**

   This runs the gamut from enough processor horsepower, memory, and bandwidth to software components. For example, if you grant remote users access to report content via a browser, you need to ensure that your computer has a working Web server.

2. **Make sure you download and install all the correct database components.**

   Simply downloading SQL Server 2005 Express with Advanced Services isn't enough; you also should obtain a copy of SQL Express Toolkit, available for free from Microsoft. Found among its technologies are SQL Server Management Studio Express as well as SQL Server Business Intelligence Development Studio, which contains the Report Designer. You can get the toolkit from the Microsoft Web site.

3. **Configure your report server.**

   You need to perform or verify a number of administrative tasks before you're ready to start building reports. You can address all these from Reporting Services Configuration Manager. For example, to successfully publish reports, you must set up at least one virtual directory on the server. As you can see in Figure 18-6, I created a virtual directory to serve as a destination for my reports.

4. **Make sure your database is created and populated.**

   For the example reports that I show you, the following two tables are all that's needed:

   ```
   CREATE TABLE Clients
   (
       ClientID INT PRIMARY KEY NOT NULL,
       CompanyName VARCHAR(50) NOT NULL,
       RegionCode CHAR(1) NOT NULL
   )

   CREATE TABLE Transactions
   (
       TransactionID INT PRIMARY KEY NOT NULL,
       ClientID INT NOT NULL REFERENCES Clients,
       TransactionDate DATETIME NOT NULL,
       TransactionAmount DECIMAL(5,2) NOT NULL
   )
   ```

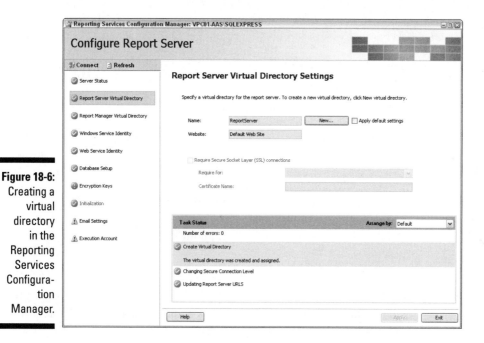

Figure 18-6:
Creating a
virtual
directory
in the
Reporting
Services
Configura-
tion
Manager.

With these introductory administrative tasks out of the way, now you're ready to create some reports. Just follow these steps:

1. **Launch Report Designer.**

   Report Designer is found within SQL Server Business Intelligence Studio. It starts up Visual Studio, which is Microsoft's flagship software development platform.

2. **Create a new project by choosing File➪New Project.**

   The New Project dialog box opens, as shown in Figure 18-7. In this example, I'm using the Report Server Project Wizard, which is a very handy tool for quickly designing, developing, and deploying a report.

3. **Create a new data source or use an existing one.**

   You can click the Edit button on the Report Wizard dialog box to enter the details of your database connection. After completing this task, you can then test things out, which is what's happening in Figure 18-8.

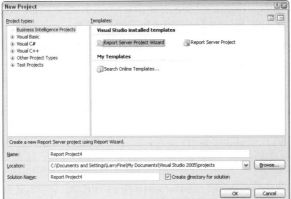

Figure 18-7:
The New
Project
dialog box.

4. Develop your query.

This logic is the foundation of your report. Luckily, the Report Server Project Wizard includes a tool to help quickly generate your query. You launch this tool by clicking the Query Builder button, which you now see in the Report Wizard dialog box.

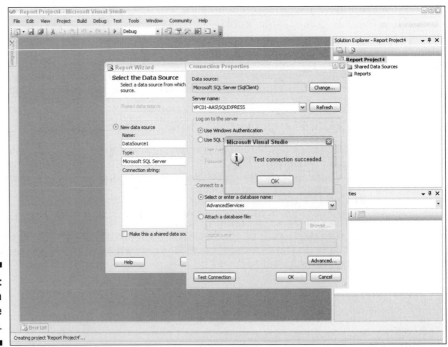

Figure 18-8:
Testing a
database
connection.

5. **With the Query Builder launched, either directly write your query or use the Generic Query Designer tool for help.**

   Click the upper leftmost button to launch this tool. You can use this tool to graphically develop your query, which is what's happening in Figure 18-9.

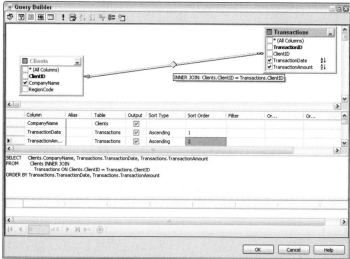

Figure 18-9:
The report's query, as generated by the Generic Query Designer.

6. **Pick the report type you want to generate.**

   Your choices are tabular or matrix.

7. **Choose the layout for your report.**

   Figure 18-10 shows how this example report appears.

8. **Continue customizing the look and feel of your report.**

   The wizard includes several dialog boxes specifically designed for this purpose.

9. **Decide how (and where) you want your report published.**

   Your options here are directly determined by what you did during Step 3 of the previous steps. Figure 18-11 shows that I'm deploying this report to the virtual directory I created earlier.

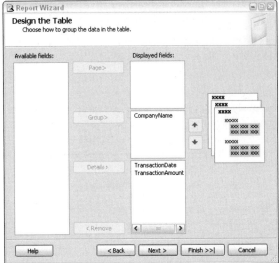

Figure 18-10:
The layout
for the new
report.

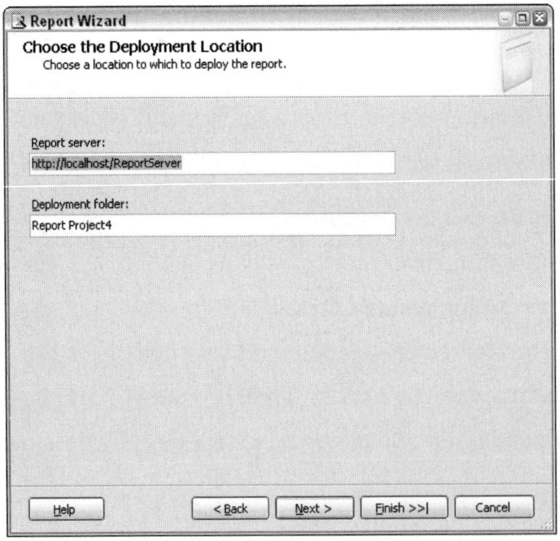

Figure 18-11:
Choose
where you
want to
publish your
report.

10. Verify your selections and click Finish to generate your new report.

Figure 18-12 shows where you verify your settings, and 18-13 shows the final output.

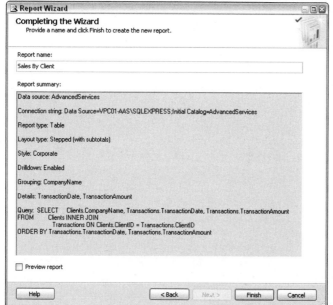

Figure 18-12:
The settings
for the new
report.

Figure 18-12:
The settings
for the new
report.

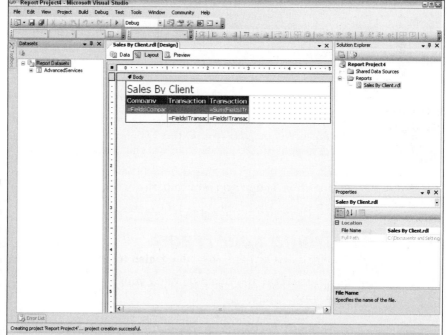

Figure 18-13:
The new
report as
seen from
within SQL
Server
Business
Intelligence
Studio.

You can customize, preview, and even debug your report from within SQL Server Business Intelligence Studio. In fact, you can even edit the XML-based report definition language (RDL) file that's generated as part of this process. Here's a small snippet from the file, which shows portions of both the data connection and formatting logic:

```
<?xml version="1.0" encoding="utf-8"?>
<Report
          xmlns="http://schemas.microsoft.com/sqlserver/reporting/2005/01/
          reportdefinition"
          xmlns:rd="http://schemas.microsoft.com/SQLServer/reporting/repor
          tdesigner">
  <DataSources>
    <DataSource Name="AdvancedServices">
      <rd:DataSourceID>e2e8470e-a912-4386-9f75-47b5bf26038b</
          rd:DataSourceID>
      <ConnectionProperties>
        <DataProvider>SQL</DataProvider>
        <ConnectString>Data Source=VPC01-AAS\SQLEXPRESS;Initial
          Catalog=AdvancedServices</ConnectString>
        <IntegratedSecurity>true</IntegratedSecurity>
      </ConnectionProperties>
    </DataSource>
  </DataSources>
  <rd:ReportID>1e9ca36c-9c3f-4fe1-945d-cc3a9d23490c</rd:ReportID>
  <Width>5in</Width>
  <Body>
    <Height>0.97in</Height>
    <ColumnSpacing>0.5in</ColumnSpacing>
    <ReportItems>
      <Textbox Name="textbox1">
        <Style>
          <FontFamily>Tahoma</FontFamily>
```

Unless you're a glutton for punishment, you'll want to do your report editing and debugging from within SQL Server Business Intelligence Development Studio rather than working with source code.

When you're done, you have a report that's ready to be published. In the next section, I show you how to perform this final step.

Publishing your report

After all the work you've put in designing, building, and testing your report, it's only logical that you make it available for others. You're almost home; here's what you need to do:

1. **Launch SQL Server Business Intelligence Development Studio.**

   If you left it running from the earlier sequence of steps, you can skip this step.

2. **Open the report project you created earlier.**

3. **Choose Build➪Deploy Report.**

   If everything goes well, you see output similar to the following:

```
Build complete -- 0 errors, 0 warnings
----- Deploy started: Project: Report Project4, Configuration: Debug -----
Deploying to http://localhost/ReportServer
Deploying report '/Report Project4/Sales By Client'.
Deploy complete -- 0 errors, 0 warnings
======== Build: 1 succeeded or up-to-date, 0 failed, 0 skipped ========
======== Deploy: 1 succeeded, 0 failed, 0 skipped ========
```

If your reporting plans include browser-based access to information, you need to install and configure Web server software on your database server.

With your report deployed, gaining access to it is quite easy. Assuming that you've set up the correct virtual directories and your Web server is running, all you need to do is instruct your users to point their browsers at the right report server. The users then can view the reports from within their Web browsers. Figures 18-14 and 18-15 show the sample report from the users' perspective.

You can print your report only on the client; server-side printing is not supported.

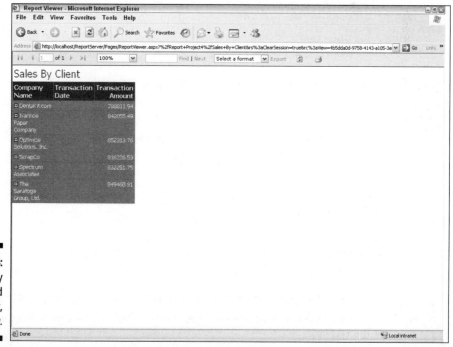

Figure 18-14:
The newly created report, header view.

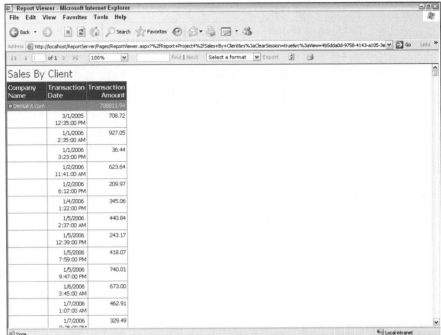

Figure 18-15:
The newly
created
report, detail
view.

Maintaining your report

After you build and deploy your report, performing standard maintenance is easy work. Here's what to do:

1. **Launch SQL Server Business Intelligence Development Studio.**

   If you left it running from the earlier sequence of steps, you can skip this step.

2. **Open the report project you created earlier.**

3. **Make changes as necessary and then save your work.**

   You may elect to change the look and feel of your report, or you may be inclined to embark on more substantial alterations to your query logic. In either case, you can choose File➪Save or click the Save button to commit your changes.

4. **Choose Build➪Deploy Report.**

   That's all there is to it: You just need to follow the same set of steps that you did during the original design cycle.

If you're considering making radical changes to a report, consider first creating a backup copy. With your original, working report backed up, you can safely proceed to make changes to your heart's content.

Part VI

Creating SQL Server 2005 Express Applications

The 5th Wave   By Rich Tennant

"You the guy having trouble staying connected to the network?"

In this part . . .

Many of you have chosen and deployed SQL Server 2005 Express as a low-cost, entry-level database product that just happens to be built on the feature-rich line of SQL Server database servers. And you may not be building new applications, but are using this database as an information store for packaged software solutions and tools. However, you could be interested in using SQL Server 2005 Express as the data storage foundation for new software applications. If that describes your goals, you'll find this part to be of interest.

To help make entry-level developers, hobbyists, and students aware of its complete line of software development technologies, Microsoft has introduced a group of powerful, yet low-priced tools collectively known as Visual Studio 2005 Express. In fact, SQL Server 2005 Express is just one of these offerings. In the first two chapters of this part, you see how to effectively couple this database server with two of the more popular application development choices: Visual Basic Express and Visual Web Developer Express.

Regardless of the application software language *du jour*, XML has become an extremely popular way of representing and storing information. The final chapter of this part explains how to most advantageously meld XML, SQL Server 2005 Express, and your chosen development technology.

Chapter 19

Building a Simple Desktop Application with Visual Basic Express

*O*ne of the most widely adopted software technologies from Microsoft is Visual Studio, along with languages such as Visual Basic, Visual C++, and Visual C#. Hundreds of thousands of application developers use this rich, full-featured platform and associated programming languages to construct software solutions. However, mastering all this functionality can be overwhelming, especially to students, entry-level, or hobbyist software developers.

In an effort to expand its influence with these more casual application developers, Microsoft has created a line of products that have a shallower learning curve: You'll find them easier and faster to get productive with. They also sport much lower price points. Collectively known as the *Express Editions*, these include the following software development technologies:

- ✔ Visual Basic 2005 Express

- ✔ Visual Web Developer 2005 Express

- ✔ Visual C# 2005 Express

- ✔ Visual C++ 2005 Express

- ✔ Visual J# 2005 Express

Although each of these programming language environments is somewhat less functional than the higher-end editions found in Visual Studio, you can still create very rich applications that you can then easily migrate to the more full-featured versions later.

Because this chapter's focus is Visual Basic 2005 Express, the remainder delves into how to team this programming language with SQL Server 2005 Express to rapidly build software solutions. Visual Basic 2005 Express offers a tremendous amount of features and capabilities; this chapter covers a relatively small percentage of this functionality, primarily as it pertains to database interaction. To find out more, check out a copy of *Visual Basic 2005 Express Edition For Dummies*, by Richard Mansfield (Wiley).

Just as Visual Basic 2005 Express represents a more easily understood implementation of Visual Basic, SQL Server 2005 Express offers a simpler set of features than those found in the more robust editions of the database server. Anticipating that people building applications with Visual Basic 2005 Express need an easily understood data repository, Microsoft bundles SQL Server 2005 Express with the software development environment. The Visual Basic 2005 Express download package includes the database server. Many developers find that this database is right for their applications' storage requirements.

Because they're designed to work together, the software development platform and database storage engine integrate very nicely. Stay tuned, because a little later in this chapter, I show you just how seamlessly they interoperate. I build a grid that lets you enter and search for customer information. To begin, you see how everything revolves around the concept of a project. Next, I associate either a new or existing database to the project, and then place information on a form. After that, you find out how to customize your application's behavior, and then easily deploy your finished product.

Laying the Groundwork for an Application

In this sequence of steps, your job is to prepare a workspace (also known as a project) that contains all your software logic, as well as linkages to your SQL Server 2005 Express database.

Creating a project

To begin, you need to set up a project in Visual Basic 2005 Express. Here's how to make that happen.

1. **Launch Visual Basic 2005 Express.**

2. **Choose File⇨New⇨Project.**

   The New Project dialog box opens where you can select the type of project you want to create, as shown in Figure 19-1.

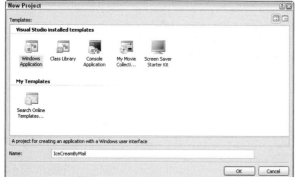

Figure 19-1:
Choosing
the type of
new project.

3. **Choose the Windows Application option from the New Project dialog box and click OK.**

   If you want to build another type of application, just choose the appropriate template. For this example, though, I stick to a Windows Application.

4. **In the Name box, enter a name for what you want to call your project, and then click OK.**

   Visual Basic 2005 Express then performs some initial housekeeping and setup. Eventually, a blank form appears on-screen. Your next task is to associate a database with this project, which you can do now or later.

Creating a new database

With your project now begun, the next step is to either generate a new database from scratch, or associate the project with an existing database. I begin by showing you how to create a database from scratch; in the next section, I show you how to connect to an existing database. If you have Visual Basic 2005 Express running, you can skip Steps 1 and 2.

1. **Launch Visual Basic 2005 Express.**

2. **Choose File⇨Open⇨Project, and then choose the project you've already created.**

3. **Choose Project➪Add New Item.**

   You're presented with a choice of pre-installed templates as shown in Figure 19-2.

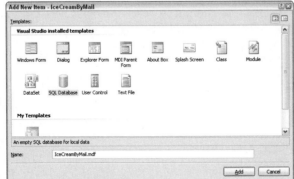

Figure 19-2:
Adding a
database to
the project.

4. **Select the SQL Database template, provide a name for your database, and click OK.**

   A new database is created, and then the Data Source Configuration Wizard launches. In the section coming up, I show you how to create tables, using this wizard.

Connecting to an existing database

If you already designed and built your database, using another tool, such as SQL Server Management Studio Express or the SQLCMD utility, then you need to associate this existing database to your new project. Here's how to do that. If you left your project open and Visual Basic 2005 Express running, you can skip Steps 1 and 2.

1. **Launch Visual Basic 2005 Express.**

2. **Choose File➪Open➪Project, and choose the project you've already created.**

3. **Choose Data➪Add New Data Source.**

   The Data Source Configuration Wizard starts.

4. **Choose Database from the list, and click Next.**

5. Click the New Connection button.

The Add Connection dialog box appears, where you can browse for an existing database or create a new one. Because I'm assuming that the database already exists, click the Browse button and locate the database.

6. If necessary, click the Advanced button to configure even more settings for this connection. Click OK when done.

Figure 19-3 shows just how many settings you can configure for a database connection.

Figure 19-3:
Setting
advanced
database
connection
properties.

Although I wish I could give you some hard-and-fast rules about what settings to use in this dialog box, each environment is different. Trial-and-error may be your best friends for this job. One area for particular attention is the User instance property. If you already have a running SQL Server 2005 Express instance, you want to set this property to False.

7. **To make sure everything is configured correctly, click the Test Connection button.**

   This step is one last sanity check. If you've designated your connection accurately, the test connection happens almost instantaneously. If not, you need to continue tuning your settings.

8. **Choose the database objects that you want to include in your dataset, and click Finish.**

   You're presented with a list showing all potential tables, views, stored procedures, and functions, as shown in Figure 19-4.

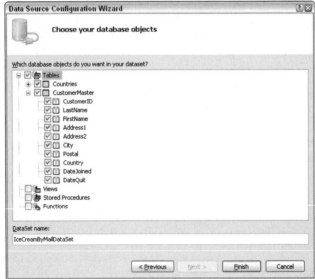

Figure 19-4:
Choosing objects for inclusion into dataset.

You have quite a bit of control here: You can even choose individual columns within a table for inclusion.

Unless you're sure that you won't want a given object in your application, include it in your dataset at this time.

After you finish, you see the new connection added to the Data Connections root node.

Creating new tables

Assuming that you just initialized a new database, you likely want to create some tables to hold your information. Fortunately, because Visual Basic 2005 Express tightly integrates with SQL Server 2005 Express means that you can create these tables directly from within Visual Basic. You can skip Steps 1 and 2 if you already have the development environment running.

1. **Launch Visual Basic 2005 Express.**

2. **Choose File⇨Open⇨Project, and choose the project you've already created.**

3. **Choose View⇨Database Explorer.**

4. **Expand the database you chose or created earlier, right-click the Tables node, and then choose Add New Table.**

   A table designer window opens.

5. **Create as many columns as you need, setting their properties as well.**

   You can set a variety of properties for each column, including

   - Data type

   - Size

   - Whether to allow nulls

   - Primary key status

   - Default values

   For each table you create, designate a column or group of columns as a primary key. A primary key preserves data integrity while speeding access to information as well.

   Take a look at Figure 19-5 to see the table I use in this example.

6. **When you finish adding your columns, click the Save icon to preserve your new table.**

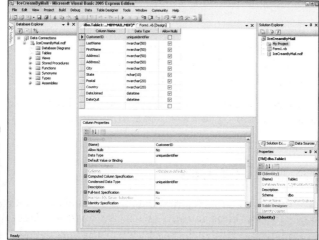

Figure 19-5:
Creating a table within Visual Basic 2005 Express.

You can test your new table very quickly from Visual Basic 2005 Express. Here's what to do. You can skip Steps 1 and 2 if you have the development environment running.

1. **Launch Visual Basic 2005 Express.**

2. **Choose File➪Open➪Project, and choose the project you've already created.**

3. **Choose View➪Database Explorer.**

4. **Expand the database you chose or created earlier, and then expand the Tables node.**

5. **Highlight the table where you want to view data.**

6. **Choose Data➪Show Table Data.**

   A fully functional, interactive window opens that lets you view, create, modify, and delete information in this table. Figure 19-6 shows how the sample table I create a little earlier in this section appears.

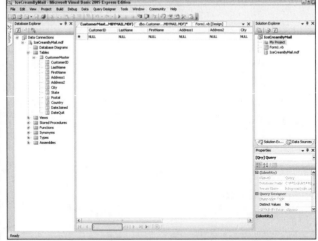

Figure 19-6:
Viewing
table data
within
Visual Basic
2005
Express.

Building the User Interface

Generally, you design and create your database before starting work on the user interface. After the database is in place, engineering a user interface takes very little time and effort, as I show you in this section.

As I mention at the start of this chapter, this sample program is a simple data entry grid that lets users interact with customer information. The first step on the road to this application is to build a form that houses the data entry grid. You can skip the first two steps if Visual Basic 2005 Express is already running.

1. **Launch Visual Basic 2005 Express.**

2. **Choose File⇨Open⇨Project, and choose the project you've already created.**

3. **Choose Project⇨Add Windows Form.**

   The Add New Item dialog box opens with a collection of forms templates.

4. **Choose the Windows Form option.**

   A new, blank form is created.

5. **Choose Data⇨Show Data Sources.**

   An explorer displays all the available data objects that you can include on your form.

6. **Highlight the objects you want to appear, and then drag them onto the form.**

   Assuming that everything is running smoothly, you can now run a quick test to see if all the components are hooked up correctly. You may want to tinker with the look-and-feel of the form now, or just wait until later.

7. **Choose Debug⇨Start Debugging.**

   This step quickly compiles all the components and runs the form. Congratulations! You have a working, albeit rudimentary, Visual Basic 2005 Express form, running in debug mode with full create, read, update, and delete capabilities for the SQL Server 2005 Express database. Figure 19-7 shows what this form looks like.

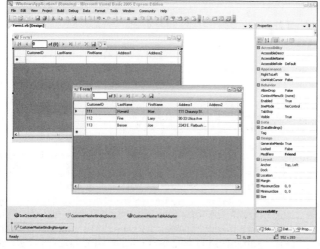

Figure 19-7:
A simple, yet powerful, database-aware form in Visual Basic 2005 Express.

8. **Stop debugging by closing the running form, and then save your new form by clicking the Save icon.**

With your table and form now in place, you have tremendous control over the look-and-feel and behavior of their information. Much of this power doesn't even require you to write any code. Continuing with the grid example I just created, here's all you need to do to gain access to these properties:

1. **Click the object you want to configure.**

   In this example, try selecting the grid of customer details.

2. **On the Properties tab, configure the properties to your liking.**

   As you can see, there are dozens of tunable parameters.

    Try changing only one property at a time; if you change too many at once, and don't like the outcome, figuring out what you did wrong may be difficult.

3. **Save your changes.**

Making Your Program Functional

By now, things are starting to come together. You've built a solid foundation, and probably even have a basic working application. The next step is to customize both the look-and-feel of your software solution, along with providing any specialized business logic. Finally, after you're ready to unleash your new program on the world, Visual Basic 2005 Express offers a robust packaging and shipping utility to make distribution a snap.

Adding application logic

In most cases, you probably want to customize the behavior of your Visual Basic 2005 Express application to reflect business rules or other site-specific behavior. To add customized processing code into your application, follow these simple steps. If you left your project open and Visual Basic 2005 Express running, you can skip Steps 1 and 2.

1. **Launch Visual Basic 2005 Express.**

2. **Choose File➪Open➪Project, and choose the project you've already created.**

3. **Switch to Code view of your program by choosing View➪Code.**

4. Click in the area in the code listing where you want to add the new application logic.

In this example, I'm adding some code to write information to a file once the grid is loaded.

5. Insert your code.

You can write your own logic, or you can take advantage of some very useful features to give you a head start. I describe these in a moment.

6. Click the Save button to record your changes.

Visual Basic 2005 Express offers some great programming productivity tools that you can use to shorten your development cycle. One of the most interesting of these technologies is known as *IntelliSense snippets* (blocks of pre-built code, tailored and customized for specific tasks). If you want to take advantage of pre-built code snippets, do the following:

1. Make sure you're viewing the code portion of your application.

2. Click into the area in the code listing where you want to insert the code.

3. From the main menu, choose Edit➪IntelliSense➪Insert Snippet, or right-click in the code listing and choose Insert Snippet.

Figure 19-8 shows the first level of IntelliSense snippet categories. I'm choosing the Processing Drives, Folders, and Files option, which brings up a listing of specific examples (see Figure 19-9).

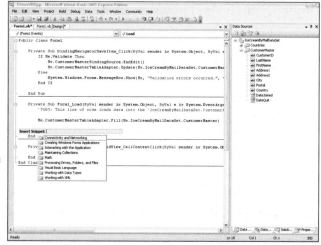

Figure 19-8:
High-level
IntelliSense
categories.

Figure 19-9:
IntelliSense
code
snippets.

After you include the IntelliSense code, your application code looks something like Figure 19-10.

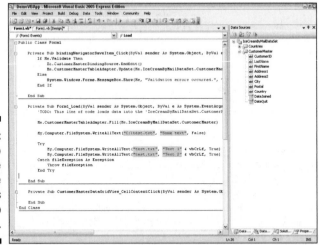

Figure 19-10:
Two
IntelliSense
code
snippets
inserted into
a file.

4. Make your site-specific changes to the generalized code snippet.

Use the IntelliSense-provided code as a template, overlaying your own code.

5. When finished, click the Save button to store your changes.

Debugging

Unless you are the as-yet-undiscovered perfect programmer, chances are you need at least one or two testing sessions with your application to make sure that it performs as expected. To help improve developer productivity, Microsoft offers an integrated debugger with Visual Basic 2005 Express. You can use this tool to quickly isolate and then correct any anomalies. All that's necessary is to choose the Debug menu for a full selection of program flow control and monitoring capabilities. Take a look at Figure 19-11 for a sample debugging session. In this example, I've deliberately turned off the SQL Server 2005 Express service, causing the application to fail when it tries to connect to the database.

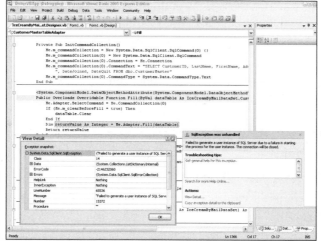

Figure 19-11:
A sample debugging session.

Take the time to learn how to use the debugger. Even if your first few programs are very simple, you'll eventually need to fix problems, and the debugger helps shave valuable time off of what is often a very tedious set of tasks.

Packaging and shipping

Traditionally, preparing a software solution for distribution is one of the more tedious and error-prone tasks. Things have improved significantly with Visual Basic 2005 Express. When you're ready to deliver your application, you can take advantage of the Publish Wizard to automate all the necessary steps. Here's all you need to do to take advantage of this technology. If your project is already open, you can skip the first two steps.

If you're distributing an application that makes local calls to a SQL Server 2005 Express database, you need to install the product on each of these computers. If, on the other hand, the application makes remote calls to a centralized database, you don't need to install SQL Server 2005 Express.

1. **Launch Visual Basic 2005 Express.**

2. **Choose File⇨Open⇨Project, and choose the project you've already created.**

3. **Make sure you're done with all development and debugging tasks.**

4. **Choose Build⇨Build, and provide your application name.**

   This step constructs your application, pulling in all necessary components.

5. **When there are no errors from the previous step, choose Build⇨ Publish, making sure to provide your application name.**

6. **Decide where to publish the application, and click Next.**

   You can choose among

   - Disk path

   - File share

   - FTP server

   - Web site

7. **Pick the installation option and click Next.**

   You can choose from

   - Web site

   - NC path or file share

   - CD or DVD ROM

8. **Decide whether the application is available both online and offline, or just online and click Next.**

9. **Review the build plan, and click Finish.**

   The wizard now packages your application, making it ready for installation on remote computers or access by remote users.

Chapter 20

Building a Simple Web Application with Visual Web Developer Express

*V*isual Studio, in conjunction with languages such as Visual Basic, Visual C++, and Visual C#, is the development platform of choice for hundreds of thousands of application developers. They leverage this rich, highly capable software development technology and associated programming languages to construct robust software solutions. However, for students, entry-level, or hobbyist software developers, Visual Studio can be too much of a good thing.

To help boost its presence with this community, Microsoft has created a line of products that are simply easier to use. Known as the *Express Editions*, they include the following languages and application development products:

- ✔ Visual Web Developer 2005 Express
- ✔ Visual Basic 2005 Express
- ✔ Visual C# 2005 Express
- ✔ Visual C++ 2005 Express
- ✔ Visual J# 2005 Express

Despite their relative simplicity, you can still construct industrial-strength applications, using the Express Editions as your foundation. This chapter's goal is to help you leverage Visual Web Developer 2005 Express, so I focus on this software development technology. Unfortunately, because it offers so much capability, and space is limited, I'm able to cover only a small percentage of its database-relevant functionality. If you need more info, check out *Visual Web Developer 2005 Express Edition For Dummies*, written by Alan Simpson (Wiley Publishing).

Visual Web Developer 2005 Express integrates nicely with SQL Server 2005 Express. That's a theme of this chapter, where I give you repeated examples of how closely the two products interoperate. In fact, to encourage this coupling, when you download the development platform, Microsoft thoughtfully bundles the database server. For most developers, SQL Server 2005 Express does a fine job of meeting their data storage needs. On the other hand, if you're inclined to use another database, you'll find that Visual Web Developer 2005 Express presents no obstacles.

Constructing a new, database-aware application is a cinch with Visual Web Developer 2005 Express. For the balance of the chapter, I walk you through the steps necessary to make this a reality. The application that I build is designed to help an adult education administrator manage student enrollments.

Laying the Groundwork for an Application

As you may expect from a product named Visual Web Developer 2005 Express, everything revolves around the concept of a Web site. After you set up a Web site, you can then proceed to designing your database. Keep in mind that if you want users from computers to have access to your Web site, you must make sure that you install a Web server, such as Internet Information Services (IIS) from Microsoft. This is a component included in most modern versions of its operating systems.

Creating a Web site

To begin, you need to create a Web site in Visual Web Developer 2005 Express. Here's what to do:

1. **Launch Visual Web Developer 2005 Express.**
2. **Choose File⇨New⇨Web Site.**

   The New Web Site dialog box appears.

3. **Choose the ASP.NET Web Site option.**

4. **Choose the language you want to use to build your Web site.**

   You can choose between Visual Basic, Visual C#, and Visual J#. For this example, I use Visual Basic.

5. **Choose where you want to store the Web site.**

   Your options are the file system, FTP, or HTTP. In this case, I use the file system.

6. **Provide a valid destination for the Web site.**

7. **Click OK to generate the new Web site.**

   Figure 20-1 shows what the completed New Web Site dialog box looks like.

   Visual Web Developer 2005 Express then performs some initial house-keeping and setup. Eventually, a new Web site appears on-screen, as shown in Figure 20-2. Your next task is to associate a database with this project, which you can do now or later.

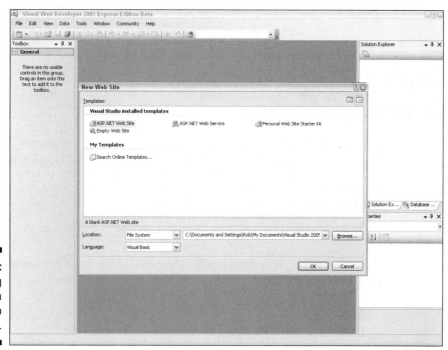

Figure 20-1: Providing details for a new Web site.

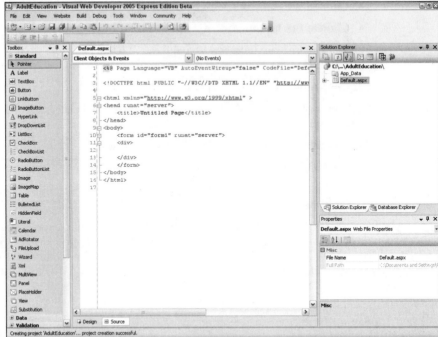

Figure 20-2:
The
beginnings
of a new
Web site.

Creating a new database

With your Web site a reality, the next step is to either create a new database from scratch, or associate an existing database. I begin by showing you how to create a database from scratch; in the next section, I show you how to connect to an existing database. If you have Visual Web Developer 2005 Express running, you can skip Steps 1 and 2.

1. **Launch Visual Web Developer 2005 Express.**

2. **Choose File➪Open➪Web Site, and choose the Web site you've already created.**

3. **Right-click at the top of the Solution Explorer, and choose the Add New Item option.**

   You're presented with a choice of pre-installed templates, as shown in Figure 20-3.

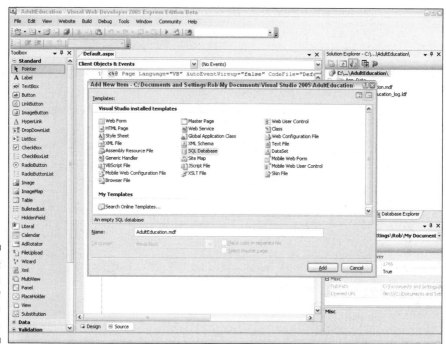

Figure 20-3:
Choosing
a new
database
template.

4. **Select the SQL Database template, provide a name for your database, and click Add.**

   You may be asked if you want to place the database in the App_Data folder. Click Yes to this question. The database creation may take some time to complete.

   Step 4 may create an error. If this happens in your environment, just follow the instructions in the next section.

Connecting to an existing database

If you already designed and built your database, using another tool, such as SQL Server Management Studio Express or the SQLCMD utility, then you need to associate this existing database to your new project. Here's how to do that. If you left Visual Web Developer 2005 Express running, you can skip Steps 1 and 2.

1. **Launch Visual Web Developer 2005 Express.**

2. **Choose File➪Open➪Web Site, and choose the Web site you've already created.**

3. **In the Database Explorer, right-click Data Connections, and then choose Add Connection.**

   If you had a problem with the preceding set of steps, choose the Create New SQL Server Database option instead.

4. **Fill in the name of the database and other details.**

   If necessary, you can also click the Advanced button to configure even more settings for this connection.

   If you're creating a new database, Visual Web Developer builds the empty database for you, as shown in Figure 20-4.

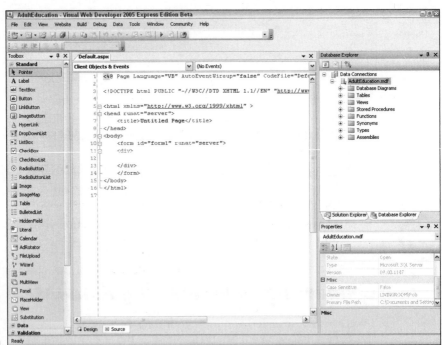

Figure 20-4:
Creating a
new empty
database.

Although I wish I could give you some hard-and-fast rules about what settings to use in this dialog box, each environment is different. Trial-and-error may be your best friends for this job. One area for particular attention is the User instance property. If you already have a running SQL Server 2005 Express instance, you want to set this property to False.

5. **To make sure everything is configured correctly, click the Test Connection button.**

   This is one last sanity check. If you've designated your connection accurately, the test connection happens almost instantaneously. If not, you need to continue tuning your settings.

6. **Click OK to complete creating the new connection.**

Creating new tables

Assuming that you've just initialized a new database, you'll likely want to create some tables to hold your information. Fortunately, the tight integration of Visual Web Developer 2005 Express with SQL Server 2005 Express means that you can do so directly from within the product. You can skip Steps 1 and 2 if you already have the development environment running.

1. **Launch Visual Web Developer 2005 Express.**

2. **Choose File⇨Open⇨Web Site, and choose the Web site you've already created.**

3. **Expand the Data Connections entry, and then expand the database's folder.**

4. **Right-click the Tables entry and choose Add New Table.**

5. **Add columns as needed.**

   You see something like what's shown in Figure 20-5.

6. **When you finish adding columns, make sure to click the Save icon.**

7. **Enter a name for the table, and click OK.**

   After saving the table, you can view it as shown in Figure 20-6.

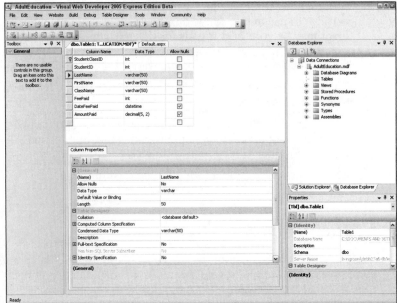

Figure 20-5:
Creating a
new table.

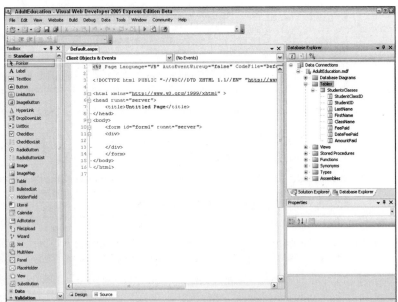

Figure 20-6:
Viewing a
new table.

Building the User Interface

Generally, designing and creating your database before starting work on the user interface is a good idea. After the database and its tables are in place, the process of incorporating these structures into your Web application is actually quite simple. In this section, I show you how to take the adult education sample database that I show you how to create in the previous section of the chapter, and turn it into a powerful Web application.

Before beginning, remember that Visual Web Developer 2005 Express is a functionally rich product, with tons of features that let you build slick Web sites. Fully exploring all its nooks and crannies would fill up the entire book, so for brevity's sake, I keep the example application as straightforward as possible.

To start, the first step is to construct a user interface that lets the administrator pick a class to view. Here's how to make that happen. If you have the product running, you can skip Steps 1 and 2.

1. **Launch Visual Web Developer 2005 Express.**

2. **Choose File⇨Open⇨Web Site, and choose the Web site you've already created.**

3. **On the Default.aspx page, switch to Design view by clicking the Design button at the bottom of the window.**

4. **Provide some descriptive text to help guide the user.**

    In this case, I'm adding `Select class to view student roster`. With this text in place, adding the first database-aware control to the form is the next step.

5. **Drag a DropDownList control onto the form.**

    The DropDownList control is just one control that can talk to databases. In many cases, you can extract a tremendous amount of functionality from these controls without the need to write any code. But first, you need to handle some housekeeping chores, and then associate the control with data.

6. **From the DropDownList Tasks menu (accessible by clicking the right-arrow icon), choose the Enable AutoPostBack option.**

    Your drop-down selection is automatically sent back to the server, rather than forcing the user to click a button to initiate the request. With this step out of the way, the next step is to connect to a data source.

7. **Select the Choose Data Source option from the DropDownList Tasks menu.**

    The Data Source Configuration Wizard launches, where you can configure this database connection.

8. **Choose the New Data Source option from the Select a Data Source drop-down list.**

9. **Click the Database icon.**

10. **Provide a meaningful name for the data source, or just choose the default.**

11. **Select the data connection you just configured, and click Next.**

12. **Save the connection string to the application configuration file.**

    With your connection now defined, the next task is to hook up the drop-down box you just added to the form with the database.

13. **Configure the SELECT statement according to your application's needs.**

    In this case, I'm asking Visual Web Developer 2005 Express to retrieve the ClassName from the Classes table.

14. **Save the Web page, and then test it by choosing Debug⇨Start Without Debugging, or pressing Ctrl+F5.**

    If everything went according to plan, you see a very basic, yet database-aware form, as shown in Figure 20-7.

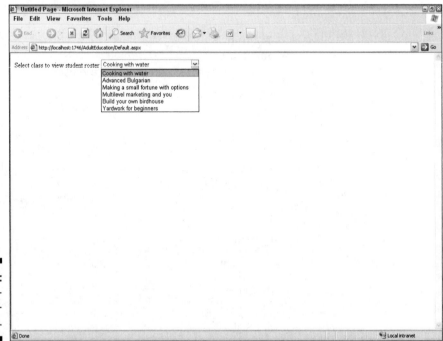

Figure 20-7:
A database-aware drop-down list.

If you did everything correctly, your drop-down list is now filled in with a list of classes. With that out of the way, you can move to listing the students that are in each class. The goal is to let the user view details about each student in the class, as well as make changes to each entry. Just follow these steps:

1. **Open (or reopen) the Web site, and its Default.aspx page.**

2. **Make sure you're in Design view.**

3. **Drag a GridView control onto the page.**

   You find this control under the Data portion of the Toolbox.

4. **On the GridView Tasks menu, choose New Data Source from the Choose Data Source drop-down list.**

   Using Steps 9 through 12 in the preceding step list as a guide, fill in the wizard. You're prompted, as before, to configure the data source.

5. **Select the table(s) and column(s) that you want to display.**

   In this case, I want to display relevant details about each student in the class that was selected in the drop-down list, so I pick those columns from the StudentsClasses table.

    To allow editing/inserting/deleting of information, make sure that a primary key is defined on the table and selected during this part of the workflow.

6. **Click the WHERE button to link the selected value from the drop-down list to your database query (see Figure 20-8).**

   The Add WHERE Clause dialog box opens. Fill in these fields:

   • **Column:** This is the table's column that will be filtered by the WHERE clause that you're currently creating.

   • **Operator:** This is the operator (=, >=, <>, and so on) that will be built into the SQL expression that makes up this WHERE clause.

   • **Source:** This is the location where your application will obtain the filtering criteria necessary to generate the WHERE clause. You can choose to retrieve a value from a control, cookie, form, profile, query string, and session.

   • **Parameter properties:** Depending on which source you chose, this portion of the dialog box contains additional details about how to construct the WHERE clause.

7. **After you finish assembling your WHERE clause parameters, click Add to see what you've built.**

   You see the exact SQL expression that your application will use.

8. **Click OK when you finish creating your WHERE clause.**

   In this example, my goal is to have what the user chooses from the drop-down list serve as input for the query against the data you plan to display and/or edit.

9. **Click the Advanced button, and enable the Generate INSERT, UPDATE, and DELETE Statements box.**

   You can also choose optimistic concurrency if you're concerned about data conflicts.

10. **With these options chosen, go to the Gridview Tasks menu, and check the Enabling items that you want.**

11. **Save the Web page, and then test it by choosing Debug⇨Start Without Debugging, or pressing Ctrl+F5.**

   If you've done everything right, you now have a fully functional Web application that not only retrieves information, but also allows data editing.

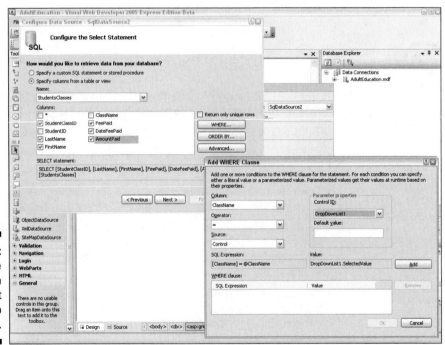

Figure 20-8: Setting the drop-down list's output to help locate data.

12. Configure the look-and-feel of your application, and then deploy the Web site.

I've saved this step for last, and suggest that you do the same. Don't worry about how the application appears until you have all the pieces working together. Figure 20-9 shows the page with some new fonts and styles applied. It's still not done, but it's closer. Don't be surprised if you spend most of your development time working on look-and-feel issues rather than database and application logic tasks.

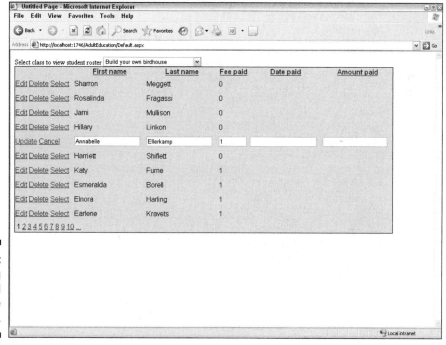

Figure 20-9:
Changing the look and feel of the application.

Chapter 21

Using XML with SQL Server 2005 Express

*F*or many of you reading this chapter, Extensible Markup Language (XML) is something that you've heard of but know nothing about. Others will be somewhat informed, and a significantly smaller proportion will be well versed in this technology.

Regardless of your familiarity with XML, this chapter can help you grasp how you can blend it with your SQL Server 2005 Express database. To begin, I take you on a brief tour of XML, followed by an overview of how you can store this type of information in your database. Finally, you see how to work with XML data after placing it into SQL Server 2005 Express.

What Is This Thing Called XML?

First specified in the late 1990s, XML has mushroomed into a very popular method for storing and working with information. It provides a structured, text-based approach to organizing data. Unlike many earlier file formats and data structures, which were often proprietary, closed, and required special software, you can use any text editor or word processor to create and edit XML information. Many modern applications and tools now support XML as well, including packages such as Microsoft Office and, of course, SQL Server.

XML advantages

When compared with alternate means of representing and interchanging information, XML offers some compelling benefits:

- ✔ **Standards-based:** The XML standard was created and is maintained under the auspices of the Worldwide Web Consortium (W3C). In addition, numerous standards bodies have in turn created their own XML-derived standards from this underlying specification.

- ✔ **Multilanguage:** Today, most commercial applications are hardcoded for more than one language. Global organizations need to track their information regardless of its native language. XML supports Unicode, meaning it can encode information in any language.

- ✔ **Plain text storage:** By storing its information in open, plain text files, rather than locking it inside proprietary formats, XML allows you to apply a broad range of technologies to work with your data.

- ✔ **Robust and easily enforced syntax:** Don't be fooled by XML's openness and ease-of-use; any XML-based information must adhere to very specific syntax and formatting rules. These rules allow XML data to easily interoperate with SQL Server 2005 Express.

- ✔ **Vendor and platform independence:** When choosing a technology standard, the last thing most customers want is to have that standard tampered with by vendors who may not have their best interests at heart. Because of many of the reasons I list here, XML is particularly well suited in protecting you from the vagaries and machinations of hardware and software vendors.

XML has a few relatively minor drawbacks. They chiefly revolve around the somewhat cumbersome nature of supporting non-text information (such as video, music, and other binary data) within an XML document. In addition, some believe that the parsing and manipulation of XML data is too expensive, and leads to degraded performance. Finally, a real-world XML document with many levels of nested data can be very hard to understand by a human reader.

XML structure

What does XML look like? Take a peek at the following small example of a purchase order:

```
<?xml version="1.0" encoding="UTF-8"?>
<PO Identifier="RR89291QQZ" date_generated="2006-30-Dec"
    application="Optimize v4.3">
  <Customer>
    <Name>Soze Imports</Name>
    <Identifier>21109332</Identifier>
```

```
    <reg:Instructions xmlns:reg="http://www.samplenamespace.com/importexport">
        <reg:Restrictions>Not subject to export control</reg:Restrictions>
        <reg:Duties>Not subject to duties</reg:Duties>
    </reg:Instructions>
  </Customer>
  <Creator>Michael McManus</Creator>
  <Product quantity="1" price="9.99">GG2911</Product>
  <Product quantity="6" price="54.94">TK3020</Product>
  <ship:Shipment xmlns:ship="http://www.samplenamespace.com/shipping">
      <ship:ShipDate>6/10/2007</ship:ShipDate>
      <ship:Instructions>Contact Mr. Hockney in receiving</ship:Instructions>
      <ship:Instructions>Fax bill to Mr. Kobayashi</ship:Instructions>
  </ship:Shipment>
</PO>
```

Confused? Don't be: The best way to make sense of an XML document is to look at it line by line, which is what I do next.

```
<?xml version="1.0" encoding="UTF-8"?>
```

This first line is known as the XML declaration, and includes details about the XML version as well as any language encoding. This XML was created to support version 1.0 of the XML standard, and it's encoded with Unicode.

```
<PO Identifier="RR89291QQZ" date_generated="2006-30-Dec"
  application="Optimize v4.3">
...
</PO>
```

I just said to look at XML on a line-by-line basis, and yet now I show you the second and very last lines. The reason I did so is to point out that the entire document is wrapped by the `<PO>` and `</PO>` tags, known as the *start tag* and *end tag*, respectively. Everything between these two tags refers to the purchase order, identified by PO in this case. Tags like this one represent an *element*. You can nest elements as well; in fact, most XML data consists of elements often deeply nested within higher-level elements. In this case, the PO element is the highest-level element. Everything that you see between the start tag and end tag is known as *content*.

What about the `Identifier`, `date_generated`, and `application` entries that are also on this line? These are *attributes*, which are additional details about an element. For example, the purchase order's `date_generated` attribute is set to December 30, 2006. You must enclose all attributes in either single or double quotes.

```
<Customer>
   <Name>Soze Imports</Name>
   <Identifier>21109332</Identifier>
   <reg:Instructions xmlns:reg="http://www.samplenamespace.com/importexport">
      <reg:Restrictions>Not subject to export control</reg:Restrictions>
```

```
      <reg:Duties>Not subject to duties</reg:Duties>
    </reg:Instructions>
  </Customer>
```

Continuing, you now see a nested element known as `Customer`, whose start tag is `<Customer>` and end tag is `</Customer>`. This element itself contains two nested elements, one known as `Name`, and the other known as `Identifier`.

It also contains a nested element known as `Instructions`. This element and those nested within it appear to be a little confusing, though. What's going on? Looking at the XML document listed earlier in the chapter, you may wonder how your computer can keep things straight when handling XML received from different sources. For example, what happens if you receive purchase orders from two different organizations that use different element names and attributes that actually mean the same thing? Conversely, what happens if they use identical element names and attributes that mean different things?

This situation is where namespaces comes to the rescue. Typically available for consultation and review via the Internet, *namespaces* are assemblages of element type and attribute names that help establish order and clear up confusion. By providing a solid point of reference, they also assist when merging smaller subsets of XML documents.

In this case, the document includes a link to a namespace server:

```
<reg:Instructions xmlns:reg="http://www.samplenamespace.com/importexport">
```

By specifying this namespace server, any applications that use this XML document consult the namespace server for details about any elements or attributes prefixed with `reg`. A second namespace server comes up a little later in the XML.

```
<Creator>Michael McManus</Creator>
```

Here's an example of an element that tracks the purchase order's creator. It has no nested elements within; it is, however, nested within the purchase order element itself.

```
<Product quantity="1" price="9.99">GG2911</Product>
<Product quantity="6" price="54.94">TK3020</Product>
```

Now you can see additional elements, both known as `Product`. These elements have their own attributes, `quantity` and `price` in this case.

```
<ship:Shipment xmlns:ship="http://www.samplenamespace.com/shipping">
    <ship:ShipDate>6/10/2007</ship:ShipDate>
    <ship:Instructions>Contact Mr. Hockney in receiving</ship:Instructions>
    <ship:Instructions>Fax bill to Mr. Kobayashi</ship:Instructions>
</ship:Shipment>
```

Finally, the document contains an element known as `Shipment`, which itself contains nested elements called `ShipDate` and `Instructions`. Notice that to clear up confusion with the earlier reference to `Instructions`, a link is included to another namespace server:

```
<ship:Shipment xmlns:ship="http://www.samplenamespace.com/shipping">
```

That's it — you now know how to parse an XML document. As you may imagine, however, bigger or deeper XML documents are harder to understand. Fortunately, many tools on the market help you make sense of this kind of information. For example, Figure 21-1 shows how this document looks inside Microsoft's XML Editor. If this tool looks familiar to you, it should: It's Microsoft Internet Explorer, which happens to be the default application for displaying XML documents in Windows.

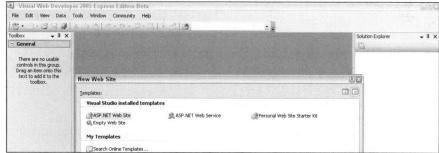

Figure 21-1: An XML document within the XML Editor.

One nice thing about using a specialized XML viewer is that you can expand or collapse various elements. Figure 21-2 shows how I collapsed some of the inner elements. Imagine how useful this technique would be for an XML document containing thousands of lines of detail.

Figure 21-2: A more concise view of an XML document.

Other important XML concepts

Getting up to speed on XML often involves digesting an intimidating alphabet soup of acronyms and other jargon. Earlier in the chapter, I show you some of these concepts, but several remain. However, you don't need to worry: I'm as concise as possible.

XML documents versus fragments

Think of an XML document as a well-formed, fully complete set of XML-based information that happens to have a root element. On the other hand, an XML fragment needs to be well formed, but by definition does not have a root element. For example, look at the following fragment of XML, taken from the sample earlier in the chapter:

```
<Customer>
    <Name>Soze Imports</Name>
    <Identifier>21109332</Identifier>
    <reg:Instructions xmlns:reg="http://www.samplenamespace.com/importexport">
        <reg:Restrictions>Not subject to export control</reg:Restrictions>
        <reg:Duties>Not subject to duties</reg:Duties>
    </reg:Instructions>
</Customer>
```

This snippet is well-formed XML, and it even contains a reference to a name-server, but placing it into context is hard: There's no indication of where it fits in the larger scheme of things.

XML schema

An *XML schema* is a data structure that you define to help provide validation constraints and other details about specific typed XML data (more about that in the upcoming section). You can specify which attributes are mandatory, their formats, permissible quantities, and so on. I show you an XML schema in conjunction with database operations in the "Placing XML into Your SQL Server 2005 Express Database" section.

Typed versus untyped XML

By referencing an existing XML schema collection, a column, parameter, or variable is said to be *typed*. Stand-alone XML that doesn't reference a schema is described as *untyped*. The benefit of typed XML is that SQL Server 2005 Express performs all the data enforcement and validation rules specified in the XML schema.

When should you use XML?

This XML thing looks pretty good, don't you think? You're probably wondering, though, *when* you should put XML to work in your environment. XML is the right tool for the job for many good reasons:

✔ **Standardized file format:** More and more application developers are using XML-based files to hold non database-hosted information. For example, perhaps you're building a software solution that will maintain its own configuration files. In the past, you would have likely designed (and then had to maintain) your own customized text file. With XML, you can leverage a predefined structure, along with all the software necessary to maintain this data.

In fact, many popular applications are now using XML as an alternative to previously proprietary layouts. Microsoft Office is a great example: You can now save Word and Excel documents in XML. Take a look at the following XML fragment, which was created when I built and saved a very simple spreadsheet:

```
<Table ss:ExpandedColumnCount="2"
ss:ExpandedRowCount="4" x:FullColumns="1"
x:FullRows="1">
<Row>
 <Cell><Data ss:Type="String">East</Data></Cell>
 <Cell><Data ss:Type="Number">20110</Data></Cell>
</Row>
<Row>
 <Cell><Data ss:Type="String">West</Data></Cell>
 <Cell><Data ss:Type="Number">43000</Data></Cell>
</Row>
</Table>
```

✔ **Information interchange:** Whether or not you much like XML, you may not even have a choice about whether or not to use it. For example, many organizations interchange data with other enterprises. In an increasing number of cases, this information exchange follows rigid specifications, which are often XML-based.

✔ **Industry standards:** From automotive to zoology, many industry and trade associations have based data storage and communication standards on an XML underpinning. If your enterprise wants to work with information feeds that are built on these guidelines, you need to incorporate XML into your plans.

Placing XML into Your SQL Server 2005 Express Database

In this section, you take a look at the interaction between SQL Server 2005 Express and XML. First, because XML is a built-in data type, you can use it anywhere within the database, Transact-SQL, or any of the supported

Common Language Runtime (CLR) languages. You are faced, however, with a 2GB limitation for any particular XML document. To find out more about integrating CLR with SQL Server 2005 Express, check out Chapter 16.

In this section, I show how to leverage the XML storage capabilities of SQL Server 2005 Express. Before I begin, remember that I keep the examples as straightforward and basic as possible. You can perform some extremely sophisticated data manipulations, using XML, but starting with a solid foundation is a good idea before attempting more advanced operations. These examples highlight an application that tracks shipment and part information.

To get started, just follow these steps:

1. **Launch your favorite SQL editor, and connect to your database server and database.**

   I use SQL Server Management Studio Express, provided by Microsoft via free download.

2. **Decide if you want to create or use an XML schema collection.**

   In this case, I've chosen to create a new XML schema collection, which creates an element known as parts, which itself contains elements known as code, name, and price. It also cites that a given part can have an unlimited number of these nested elements:

   ```
   CREATE XML SCHEMA COLLECTION Parts AS
   N'<?xml version="1.0" encoding="UTF-16"?>
   <xsd:schema
    xmlns:xsd="http://www.w3.org/2001/XMLSchema">
    <xsd:element name="parts">
     <xsd:complexType>
      <xsd:choice  minOccurs="0" maxOccurs="unbounded" >
       <xsd:sequence>
        <xsd:element name="code" type="xsd:string"/>
        <xsd:element name="name" type="xsd:string"/>
        <xsd:element name="price" type="xsd:decimal"/>
       </xsd:sequence>
      </xsd:choice>
     </xsd:complexType>
    </xsd:element>
   </xsd:schema>
   ```

   After your XML schema is in place, you can put it to work and associate it with relevant objects.

3. **Design and create your table.**

   Here's an example of a table:

```
CREATE TABLE Shipments
(
    ShipmentID INTEGER PRIMARY KEY NOT NULL,
    ShipmentDate DATETIME NOT NULL,
    ShippedParts XML
)
```

If you've created an XML schema, you can simply reference it as part of the table creation logic. If I wanted to associate this table with the XML schema collection that I created earlier, all that's necessary is to slightly alter the table definition:

```
CREATE TABLE Shipments
(
    ShipmentID INTEGER PRIMARY KEY NOT NULL,
    ShipmentDate DATETIME NOT NULL,
    ShippedParts XML (Parts)
)
```

You can create indexes on XML columns. You have two types of indexes at your disposal: primary and secondary. A primary index *shreds*, or disassembles, the XML data that is normally stored in binary large object (BLOB) format, making information quicker to find. With the primary index in place, you may then create three distinct types of secondary indexes.

- **PATH:** This contains the Path ID and Value columns from the primary XML index.

- **PROPERTY:** This is made up of the primary key from the underlying table, concatenated with the Path ID and Value columns from the primary XML index.

- **VALUE:** This index is the mirror image of the PATH index. It contains the Value and Path ID columns.

The SQL Server 2005 Express query optimizer chooses the proper secondary index based on the query criteria.

4. **Insert data into your table.**

Here's an example of creating a single row with two XML entries. Normally, this kind of relationship would require you to separate the line item entries into their own table, because it has two entities:

```
INSERT INTO Shipments VALUES(1,'<Root>
<Parts OrderID="1" PurchaseOrderNumber="NSSDJS#1">
<DeliveryDate>2006-12-30</DeliveryDate>
<Items>
    <ShipmentWeight>2.44</ShipmentWeight>
        <LineItem>
            <Name>DentaKit for Adults</Name>
```

```
          <Code>DK-R001</Code>
          <Price>29.95</Price>
     </LineItem>
     <LineItem>
          <Name>Retainer Brite 1 Year</Name>
          <Code>DK-RB1Y</Code>
          <Price>35.00</Price>
     </LineItem>
</Items>
</Parts>
</Root>')
```

Notice how seamlessly the SQL and XML code integrate; embedding XML inside SQL just requires some careful quote mark placement.

Operating on XML-based Information

After you have XML-based data residing in your SQL Server 2005 Express database (the subject of the preceding section), the next logical step is to make use of it. Stay tuned — that's the subject of this section.

As with many other SQL Server 2005 Express technologies, you can take various paths when working with XML data. To keep these examples as straightforward as possible, I explore a limited subset of these options. In particular, I steer away from the potentially confusing subject of namespaces. I also use untyped XML to reduce visual clutter.

To help you locate and modify XML-based information, five data functions are at your disposal. Table 21-1 highlights these methods, along with their purposes.

Table 21-1	XML Data Methods
Method	*Purpose*
exist()	Check to see if XML information exists
modify()	Alter XML data
nodes()	Break up XML data, making it conform to relational structure
query()	Search XML data
value()	Convert XML-formatted information into standard SQL style

For the balance of this chapter, I show you how to use these methods to achieve your goals. I continually refer to the Shipments table that I lay out in the "Placing XML into Your SQL Server 2005 Express Database" section, earlier in this chapter.

Searching for XML data

In this first example, I'm running a basic search against the table, using the query() method from the XML ShippedParts column. Notice that I combine a standard WHERE clause with this method:

```
SELECT ShippedParts.query('/Root/Parts/DeliveryDate')
FROM Shipments
WHERE ShipmentID = 1
```

This query retrieves the DeliveryDate element. To get a list of all the items in the document, here's how the query looks:

```
SELECT ShippedParts.query('/Root/Parts/Items')
FROM Shipments
```

Using the exist() method, you can easily create a query that inspects the XML data and looks for matches:

```
SELECT ShippedParts.query('/Root/Parts/Items/LineItem')
FROM Shipments
WHERE ShippedParts.exist('
   /Root/Parts/Items/LineItem[Name="DentaKit for Adults"]
') = 1
```

This query returns all records that have line items with a product name that corresponds to DentaKit for Adults.

If you want to retrieve XML information and place it in standard SQL format, just use the value() method:

```
SELECT ShippedParts.value('
(/Root/Parts/Items/ShipmentWeight)[1]','decimal(6,2)
')
FROM Shipments
```

In the preceding example, I'm converting the shipment weight element from the ShippedParts XML column into a decimal(6,2).

If you want to cut to the chase and just issue plain old SELECT statements, you must know how SQL Server Management Studio Express displays this information. Just click any column that contains XML, and you see something like what's shown in Figure 21-3.

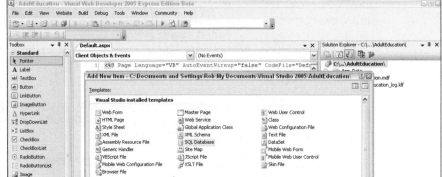

Modifying XML data

Looking at all this nifty XML information is nice, but how easy can you make alterations? Amending data is actually quite easy. Here's a statement that uses the combination of the `modify()` method and the `replace` statement and changes the purchase order number attribute:

```
UPDATE Shipments
SET ShippedParts.modify('
  replace value of (/Root/Parts/@PurchaseOrderNumber)[1]
  with "TVC-15 PR1DA"
')
WHERE ShipmentID = 1
```

The `modify()` method expects you to provide a string that conforms to the XML Data Manipulation Language (XML DML). XML DML extends the standard XQuery language, making data alterations easier to undertake.

When deleting records, you can use the `delete` statement from within the `modify()` method. Here's an example of removing the second line item entry from within the `Items` node:

```
UPDATE Shipments
SET ShippedParts.modify('delete /Root/Parts/Items/*[2]')
WHERE ShipmentId = 1
```

Formatting relational data as XML

What should you do if all your data is locked up in a relational format, yet you want to work with it in an XML format? This is actually quite simple, as I now show you. For the purposes of this example, suppose that you track information about shipping vendors in two important tables. The first table, `Shippers`, holds details about each vendor. The second table, `ShippingLocations`, stores information about each location supported by your vendors. In the next two sample queries, I ask SQL Server 2005 Express to provide a list of all locations for each shipper.

By using the `FOR XML` directive, you can instruct SQL Server 2005 Express to convert the output from a given query into XML. In this first example, I use the `RAW` directive to create basic XML output:

```
SELECT Shippers.ShipperName,
       ShipperLocations.LocationName
FROM Shippers, ShipperLocations
WHERE Shippers.ShipperID = ShipperLocations.ShipperID
ORDER BY ShipperName
FOR XML RAW
```

By using `RAW`, I've asked SQL Server 2005 Express to create generic, non-nested rows that are prefixed with `row`:

```
<row ShipperName="Federales Pesadillas SA de CV" LocationName="El Paso" />
<row ShipperName="Federales Pesadillas SA de CV" LocationName="Phoenix" />
<row ShipperName="Federales Pesadillas SA de CV" LocationName="Los Angeles" />
<row ShipperName="No Questions Asked Delivery" LocationName="Jersey City" />
<row ShipperName="No Questions Asked Delivery" LocationName="Brooklyn" />
<row ShipperName="No Questions Asked Delivery" LocationName="Phoenix" />
<row ShipperName="No Questions Asked Delivery" LocationName="Fresno" />
<row ShipperName="Sumimasen Shipping" LocationName="Seattle" />
<row ShipperName="Sumimasen Shipping" LocationName="Phoenix" />
<row ShipperName="Sumimasen Shipping" LocationName="Los Angeles" />
<row ShipperName="Two Guys and a Truck" LocationName="Brooklyn" />
<row ShipperName="Two Guys and a Truck" LocationName="Jersey City" />
<row ShipperName="Two Guys and a Truck" LocationName="Bronx" />
```

Things get more interesting with the `AUTO` directive, which returns its results in a simple tree:

```
SELECT Shippers.ShipperName,
       ShipperLocations.LocationName
FROM Shippers, ShipperLocations
WHERE Shippers.ShipperID = ShipperLocations.ShipperID
ORDER BY ShipperName
FOR XML AUTO
```

```
<Shippers ShipperName="Federales Pesadillas SA de CV">
  <ShipperLocations LocationName="El Paso" />
  <ShipperLocations LocationName="Phoenix" />
```

```
  <ShipperLocations LocationName="Los Angeles" />
</Shippers>
<Shippers ShipperName="No Questions Asked Delivery">
  <ShipperLocations LocationName="Jersey City" />
  <ShipperLocations LocationName="Brooklyn" />
  <ShipperLocations LocationName="Phoenix" />
  <ShipperLocations LocationName="Fresno" />
</Shippers>
<Shippers ShipperName="Sumimasen Shipping">
  <ShipperLocations LocationName="Seattle" />
  <ShipperLocations LocationName="Phoenix" />
  <ShipperLocations LocationName="Los Angeles" />
</Shippers>
<Shippers ShipperName="Two Guys and a Truck">
  <ShipperLocations LocationName="Brooklyn" />
  <ShipperLocations LocationName="Jersey City" />
  <ShipperLocations LocationName="Bronx" />
</Shippers>
```

This small sample shows how you can format relational data into an XML structure. You have many other options at your disposal, from controlling the layout of the tree to producing an XML schema to handling binary information.

Part VII
The Part of Tens

The 5th Wave   By Rich Tennant

Oh come on— how fatal can it be?

FATAL ERROR

In this part . . .

SQL Server 2005 Express is a great choice for a database platform. It combines entry-level simplicity and price with the power and capabilities of an industrial-strength database engine. And given the broad reach of Microsoft's technologies, a wealth of information is out there about how to make the most of this product.

To begin, I give ten places you can go to get more help about SQL Server 2005 Express. Next, even though your SQL Server 2005 Express experience should go smoothly, you may get befuddled or things can go wrong. To help you get over these obstacles, I catalog ten of the most beneficial troubleshooting tips.

Chapter 22

Ten Sources of Information on SQL Server 2005 Express

In This Chapter

▶ Microsoft SQL Server Web site

▶ Microsoft Developer Network

▶ Wikipedia, newsgroups, and user groups

▶ Magazines and books

▶ Design, administrative, and database generation tools

A s you embark on your SQL Server 2005 Express journey, you can take comfort in the fact that there are many others on the same path. In this chapter, I show you how to leverage some of the abundant resources provided by your fellow SQL Server devotees to help make your trip smoother.

Microsoft SQL Server Web Site

Here's a great place to get started finding more about SQL Server 2005 Express. Aside from the usual market-speak, you find a variety of valuable product and technical details that you can use to further your understanding of not only SQL Server 2005 Express, but all the available database editions. You can find it here:

```
www.microsoft.com/sql/default.mspx
```

Microsoft Developer Network

In an effort to support software developers, Microsoft offers a comprehensive set of services known as the Microsoft Developer Network. In addition to the broad suite of software available for purchase, an extremely content-rich Web site is available to anyone, whether or not they are a subscriber. It contains white papers, technical briefs, and a deep knowledge base that you can search to get answers to your questions. You find it here:

```
http://msdn.microsoft.com/sql
```

You can also get some great help at the Microsoft TechNet Web site:

```
www.microsoft.com/technet/prodtechnol/sql/default.mspx
```

Wikipedia

No, this isn't a misprint: You read correctly. Believe it or not, this Internet-based, open-source encyclopedia (`www.wikipedia.org`) is a great source of information about all technology topics, including relational database theory and practical application. For example, here's a link to a very comprehensive article on database normalization in theory and practice:

```
http://en.wikipedia.org/wiki/Database_normalization
```

Newsgroups

These collaborative spaces are an immense help when you're struggling with a technical problem. Chances are that someone can address your question. In the past few years, Google has done a great job helping to organize and rescue Usenet. It's easier than ever to access these groups via your browser. Here's a link to 27 (at last count) newsgroups focused solely on SQL Server:

```
http://groups.google.com/groups/dir?lnk=gh&hl=en&sel=33606733
```

Alternatively, you can just search Google Groups (`http://groups.google.com`) for groups with SQL Server in their name.

You can also find some great links to SQL Server newsgroups at Microsoft TechNet:

```
www.microsoft.com/technet/community/newsgroups/server/
sql.mspx
```

Magazines

Several well-written magazines are available that provide significant coverage of database topics. Some are database-agnostic, while others focus specifically on this product. These periodicals include

SQL Server Magazine:

www.sqlmag.com

Intelligent Enterprise:

www.intelligententerprise.com/info_centers/database

Databased Advisor:

www.databasedadvisor.com

As an added bonus, many magazines maintain online community message boards, letting you interact with other readers.

User Groups

These gatherings of like-minded individuals are a great place to enhance your understanding of SQL Server 2005 Express. Some groups meet virtually, while others have physical events; some groups span both realms. Two of the better Internet-focused most relevant user groups include the SQL Server Worldwide Users Group (www.sswug.org), as well as the Professional Association for SQL Server (www.sqlpass.org).

On the other hand, if you want to meet and greet your counterparts face-to-face, chances are that an Internet search can point you toward a good candidate user group not too far from you.

Books

While this book helps you get started with SQL Server 2005 Express, many other titles can give you a broader understanding of building high-quality database applications. Try looking for well-regarded books that cover any of these topics; they are all pertinent in the context of SQL Server 2005 Express:

- Relational database design theory and practice
- Best practices for user interface design
- Distributed computing

Database Design Tools

If you're building a simple application, chances are that you won't need to perform any extensive database design and modeling to realize your goals. However, if you face a more daunting task, you're wise to look into specialized tools that focus on this portion of the application development lifecycle. Embarcadero Technologies makes a collection of products that add value throughout the entire process. You find them here:

www.embarcadero.com/products/products.html

Administrative Tools

As I've shown throughout the book, SQL Server Management Studio is a great tool for administering your SQL Server 2005 Express database. However, you may also be interested in one of the third-party tools out there. I've used TOAD for SQL Server by Quest Software; all the major database platforms have versions of this product. You can find it here:

www.toadsoft.com/toadsqlserver/toad_sqlserver.htm

Data Generation Tools

Generating sample data by hand is one of the more tedious tasks you face when building and testing an application for your SQL Server 2005 Express installation. Fortunately, tools on the market can automate this for you, freeing you up to spend your time developing and then tuning your application. I've had great success with the DTM Data Generator, which you find here:

www.sqledit.com/dg/index.html

Blogs

There are some great blogs out there that offer a broad range of information about SQL Server. You'll even find postings from the Microsoft product development teams. Check out the blogs at technet.com and msdn.com:

http://blogs.technet.com

http://blogs.msdn.com

Chapter 23

Ten SQL Server 2005 Express Troubleshooting Tips

. . . .

In This Chapter

▶ Getting a copy of SQL Server 2005 Express

▶ Solving installation, connection, and administration problems

▶ Mastering security difficulties

▶ Resolving data inconsistencies

▶ Setting up automated operations

▶ Simplifying complicated data structures

▶ Developing high quality software

▶ Speeding up a sluggish server

. . . .

As an entry-level database server that is built on the same platform as the entire SQL Server product family, SQL Server 2005 Express combines simplicity with great power and a massive set of features. Naturally, all these capabilities can a bit confusing at times, so this chapter is dedicated to helping you rise above some of the most common predicaments that you likely encounter.

Show Me How I Can Get the Product

If you're ready to get started with SQL Server 2005 Express, all you need to do is follow one of the following two paths:

✔ **Check out Microsoft's Web site.** You find a handy download link for SQL Server at www.microsoft.com/sql.

✔ **Use the enclosed CD.** To make things even easier, a copy of SQL Server 2005 Express is on the CD that comes with this book. Simply insert the disc in your CD drive, and follow the on-screen instructions. You'll be off and running in no time. (Appendix D contains more information about the CD.)

I Can't Install It!

Having some cool new software and not being able to get it installed is not much fun. Luckily, SQL Server 2005 Express usually installs without a hitch. If you do encounter an obstacle, use the following checklist to help get you out of hot water:

1. **Make sure you have sufficient permissions to add or remove software.**

   In general, installing or removing software as an administrator is a good idea. Otherwise, the operating system may block you from making these kinds of changes.

2. **Remove any previous versions of SQL Server 2005 Express via the Add/Remove Programs application within the Control Panel.**

   If you skip this step, the installer probably complains loudly and then keels over. Even though it's tedious, take the time to clean things up before trying to install.

3. **Download and deploy the Windows Installer.**

   If you're running a more modern version of Windows, you likely already have the installer on your system.

4. **Download and install the Microsoft .NET Framework 2.0.**

   SQL Server 2005 Express is built upon this framework; if it's missing, you can't install the database.

If you want more ideas about how to have a good installation experience, have a look at Chapter 2.

I Can't Connect to the Database!

Connection problems are one of the most common complaints about any database server, SQL Server 2005 Express included. Happily, you can usually overcome these complications without too much difficulty. If you can't connect, try one of these remedies:

✔ **Make sure the database server is running:** Unless you request that the SQL Server 2005 Express service launch when your system boots, you simply need to start the service. Chapter 2 tells you all about kicking off the SQL Server 2005 Express service.

✔ **Make sure that you're using the right protocol:** You can use several communications methods to communicate with SQL Server 2005 Express. In order to successfully converse with the database server, you need to make sure that both the client and server are speaking on the right channel with the right setup. In particular — because SQL Server 2005 Express defaults to local connections only — if you want remote access, you must run the SQL Server Surface Area Configuration tool to allow both local and remote connections. You can also choose the protocol for these conversations. Chapter 3 reveals all that you need to know to get the dialogue going.

✔ **Adjust your connection string:** When you connect to SQL Server 2005 Express, you need to specify a connection string that helps locate the database server. Often highly site-specific, even the smallest error in this connection string dooms your conversation from the start. Chapter 4 has all the details about the various flavors of connection string that you're likely to encounter.

Show Me How to Administer My Database

Even though SQL Server 2005 Express is an entry-level database that doesn't require much care and feeding, you still need to periodically handle administrative tasks. Here are two good choices to get the job done quickly and easily:

✔ **SQLCMD utility:** This character-based tool ships with every copy of SQL Server 2005 Express. You can run just about any administrative task by using direct Transact-SQL or one of the hundreds of built-in system stored procedures.

✔ **SQL Server Management Studio Express Edition:** If you have more of a hankering for graphical tools, you want to look at this utility. While a full-featured version ships with the more extensive SQL Server editions, even this entry-level version available for SQL Server 2005 Express lets you perform many administrative chores. And whatever isn't possible, you can always handle with direct Transact-SQL or system stored procedures.

I Can't See My Data!

If you can't seem to locate information that you know is in your database, don't despair: Unless someone has inadvertently deleted data, it's likely still patiently waiting inside your database. In many cases, difficulties like this one really are symptoms of an underlying permission problem.

Because it's built on the enterprise-class SQL Server database platform, SQL Server 2005 Express offers all the security capabilities of its bigger siblings. Unfortunately, all this power can sometimes translate into unforeseen security obstacles. These aren't hard to overcome, but you do need to know how to correctly configure your permissions. Check out Chapter 11 to get a handle on all that you can do with security in SQL Server 2005 Express.

My Data Is Messed Up!

Unless you believe in gremlins or other supernatural entities that descend out of the ether and wreak havoc on your data, chances are that any information problems are due to one of a relatively small number of errors and omissions. Here's what to watch out for:

- **Referential integrity issues:** To help keep all your data synchronized, SQL Server 2005 Express offers referential integrity features. These prevent you or your applications from inadvertently altering rows from one table without making corresponding changes in another table. To get a better idea of how to use referential integrity to your advantage, take a look at Chapter 8.

- **Failure to use transactions:** Transactions help certify that your database interactions happen in logically consistent groups. Without proper transactions, an operation may update one table but fail to do the same for other tables. The result is damaged data integrity. Chapter 12 is designed to help you make the most of transactions.

- **Incorrectly defined columns:** Believe it or not, sometimes database designers choose the wrong kind of data type when setting up their tables. For example, a particular field may need to contain currency amounts, which include decimals. Yet when they write the SQL to create the table, they choose the INTEGER data type for this column. This data type means that SQL Server 2005 Express discards any fractional amounts from that column.

  Another common problem sees database designers not providing enough space for character-based fields. Again, SQL Server 2005 Express cheerfully tosses away any extra data, leading to damaged information and unhappy users.

I Want to Automate Some Operations

SQL Server 2005 Express offers two very helpful features that you can use to help streamline common database tasks:

- **Stored procedures and functions.** Stored procedures and functions are bits of logically grouped application software that you can write in a variety of programming languages, including Transact-SQL, Visual Basic,

Visual C#, and so on. After you create them, you then place these procedures inside the SQL Server engine, where anyone with the right permission can run them. They centralize your application logic, and generally
help performance to boot. If you're curious about stored procedures and
functions, check out Chapter 14.

✔ **Triggers.** Think of a trigger as a very specialized stored procedure, one
that gets run when a certain event happens. For example, you may want
to send an e-mail alert when inventory drops below a certain level.
That's a great use of a trigger; you can probably think of many more that
apply in your organization. You can also use triggers to help you administer your database server, as well as run administrative operations. If
you want to get a better handle on triggers, have a look at Chapter 15.

I Want to Simplify My Data

As a database administrator, making sense of your information can be confusing, especially if your environment sports a substantial number of tables with
complex interrelationships. If you find it difficult, imagine how laborious it is
for your users and application developers. Luckily, none of you has to suffer
in silence. One way to create a more transparent picture of your data is to
take advantage of views.

Think of a view as a window into your information, one that can span the
entire database to retrieve results. By pre-building all the joins and stripping
out any extraneous details, you can make this window much simpler than the
underlying data. The end result is that your users and developers can work
with the view, rather than the base database tables. To see how views can
make things better for your enterprise, take a look at Chapter 10.

I Want to Build Good Software

If you're looking to construct some high quality software, I have good news
for you. A wide range of excellent tools work really well with all the SQL
Server products, including the Express edition. Here are three that you
should look into:

✔ **Visual Studio:** This flagship of Microsoft's development tool product
family is feature-packed, supports several popular programming languages, and you can use it to build the most rich and complex applications. On the other hand, if you don't need all that power, check out the
next products on my list.

✔ **Visual Web Developer 2005 Express:** This entry-level product is
designed and priced so that a large audience can use the technology to

create Web-driven, database-ready applications. In Chapter 20, I show how this product seamlessly works with SQL Server 2005 Express.

✓ **Visual Basic Express:** Visual Basic is an extremely popular programming language, especially for traditional client/server applications. This Express version is aimed at the same audience as Visual Web Developer 2005: Developers who want a low-priced, easier-to-use tool that still offers substantial capabilities.

If you have a different taste in programming languages, don't worry: You can develop software that works with SQL Server 2005 Express in just about any language. In fact, Microsoft offers Express editions of its Visual Studio product for other languages, such as Java, C++, and C#.

My Database Server Is Too Slow!

Before you toss your slow-running database server out the window, you can run a few effortless checks to identify and remedy the source of the headache:

✓ **Are your tables indexed correctly?** Without a doubt, improper or missing indexes cause most of the performance problems that plague the average database application. You need to take the time to make sure that you've placed indexes in the right places. Chapter 10 is a great place to start on the path to good indexing.

✓ **Is there enough memory?** Don't shortchange your database server by denying it the memory it needs to get the job done quickly. You can quickly tell if you're running out of memory by launching the Windows Task Manager, and studying the amount of available physical memory. If this number is approaching zero, you're asking your server to do too much work with too little memory.

✓ **Are there too many users and applications?** Sometimes, no matter how much memory you install, or how well your tables are indexed, you approach the limit of what a database server can handle. There's no hard-and-fast way to tell if you're on the brink, but if you exhaust all your other options and you can't coax any more speed out of your server, you should distribute your workload among multiple servers.

Part VIII

Appendixes

The 5th Wave By Rich Tennant

It started as a little experiment in data compression, and...well... just close the door and call the zoo!

In this part . . .

Now that you know SQL Server 2005 Express backwards-and-forwards, I have just a few more topics to discuss.

To begin, I describe what criteria you should use when determining if the time is right to upgrade to a higher-capacity version of SQL Server. Next, you see how easy you can populate your SQL Server 2005 Express database with information from other sources. You also find a glossary of important relational database and SQL Server 2005 Express terms. Finally, I also relate what you can find on the CD that accompanies this book, as well as how to use it.

Appendix A

Upgrading to SQL Server 2005

In This Chapter

▶ Deciding whether to migrate

▶ Planning to migrate

▶ Completing the migration

SQL Server 2005 Express is an entry-level, yet highly capable database that is built on the mainline SQL Server platform. This architecture offers you a relatively easy upward migration path. After you use SQL Server Express for some time, you may run up against some of its built-in constraints, which gets you thinking about migrating to one of its more powerful siblings.

In this chapter, I show you how to make an informed decision about whether to upgrade or not. Assuming that you elect to follow the upgrade path, you find out how to create a workable plan, as well as how to leverage an excellent utility that makes migrations a snap.

Why Migrate?

For many SQL Server 2005 Express installations, this question never arises. The product will faithfully serve your needs, and there will be no need to look for an alternative. However, a significant number of database administrators find themselves bumping up against some of the product's inherent limitations. Here are a few of these barriers:

- ✔ **Memory:** Even if you fill your server with memory, SQL Server 2005 Express doesn't take advantage of any more than 1GB of RAM. For small to mid-sized applications, this limitation isn't a problem. However, larger solutions may need more.

- ✔ **Database size:** If you're building a solution that needs to hold large amounts of data in a single database, you may not be happy with the 4GB limitation per database in SQL Server 2005 Express.

- ✔ **Multi-processors:** SQL Server 2005 Express takes advantage of only one physical processor-based CPU, regardless of how many are available on your database server. Note that a multi-core CPU still counts as a single CPU.

✔ **Full-text searching:** This feature helps you index and then query large blocks of text-based information. SQL Server 2005 Express doesn't include full-text searching, which means that any searches that you run against large blocks of text-based information aren't as fast as with one of the more full-featured editions. SQL Server 2005 Express with Advanced Services does offer full-text search capabilities, and this edition is also free. See Chapter 18 for details.

✔ **Analysis services:** If your environment contains large volumes of data that needs to be crunched to come up with recognizable patterns, the lack of these analytic services is a significant limitation in SQL Server 2005 Express. However, third-party applications can take up much of this slack. Note, however, that these additional applications may end up costing much more than simply upgrading to a more powerful SQL Server 2005 edition.

✔ **Reporting services:** If your goal is to easily create and distribute reports, you might find the baseline edition of SQL Server 2005 Express too constraining in its capabilities. However, the still-free but more powerful SQL Server 2005 Express with Advanced Services includes a very helpful set of reporting features. Chapter 18 is filled with important details about this impressive edition.

✔ **Automated server administration:** SQL Server 2005 Express is the only edition of this product that does not ship with SQL Server Agent. This sophisticated feature serves as a single point of control for executing a wide variety of tasks. These tasks can be launched based on user interaction, by schedule, or in response to one or more events. If your database environment requires this level of automation, consider upgrading to another edition.

✔ **Database mail:** This capability, not present in SQL Server 2005 Express, lets you create and send e-mail messages directly from the database engine. However, you're still free to embed mail creation logic inside your applications no matter what edition you select.

✔ **Backup/recovery options:** Your data archiving choices are somewhat more reduced for SQL Server 2005 Express than in the more full-featured editions. Despite this restriction, you can still safeguard your information.

Coming Up with a Good Migration Plan

Upgrading your database without a solid migration plan is foolhardy. Luckily, you don't need to do too much work to create a trustworthy strategy. Just take all the following points into consideration as you make your arrangements:

✔ **Data archiving:** By far, this task is the most important to complete during your migration. In addition to preserving your information, backing up your data yields a nice peace-of-mind benefit.

✔ **Migration timing:** Attempting to upgrade your database in the middle of a very hectic workload is not the best idea; you're much better off picking a quiet time to undertake this effort.

✔ **Application compatibility:** In the vast majority of cases, your applications work just fine with the more full-featured SQL Server editions. However, to be safe you should check with your software provider for confirmation.

✔ **Other housekeeping:** This catchall is for those little, but important, responsibilities that are part of any software upgrade. You want to make sure that you update the configuration for components such as your ODBC instance names, scripts, and so on.

✔ **Testing:** Naturally, even the best migration plan won't fly unless you allocate enough time and resources to test your new configuration prior to going live.

Delivering on the Migration

If you've made it this far, you're probably serious about carrying out your database upgrade. In this section, I show you how easily you can get the job done. In fact, this operation can be as simple as backing up your SQL Server 2005 Express database and then restoring it into another edition of the product. Check out Chapter 13 for more on backup and restore. Another approach would be to use SQL Server Management Studio (which ships with all other editions of SQL Server) to simply copy the database between database servers.

However, for the balance of this chapter, I focus on the excellent Import and Export Wizard, which is part of SQL Server Management Studio. Understanding this utility is important; you may find it very useful for other types of data migration, such as importing information from other brands of database server. The one assumption that I make here is that you can connect to both your existing SQL Server 2005 Express database server as well as your new database server.

Your first goal is to create a new database; here's how to proceed:

1. **Start SQL Server Management Studio.**

2. **Connect to the database server that's the destination for your upgrade.**

3. **Right-click the Databases folder, and choose New Database.**

   You're creating a new, empty database and then importing the structure and all data from the existing database.

4. **Fill in all the necessary details about your new database.**

5. **After you finish creating your new database, click OK to confirm your work.**

Your new database is now ready to receive all your data from SQL Server 2005 Express. Just follow these steps to finish the job; you can skip Steps 1 and 2 if you left SQL Server Management Studio running from the previous set of instructions.

1. **Start SQL Server Management Studio.**

2. **Connect to the database server that is the destination for your upgrade.**

3. **Expand the Databases folder.**

4. **Right-click the database you just created, and choose Tasks⇨ Import Data.**

   The SQL Server Import and Export Wizard launches.

5. **From the Data Source drop-down list, choose SQL Native Client.**

   As shown in Figure A-1, there are many other types of connectivity options, which are useful if you're trying to move data among other types of information sources.

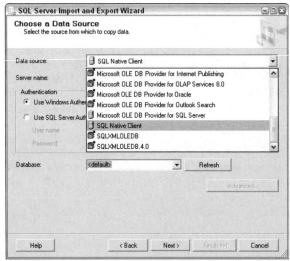

Figure A-1:
Choosing a
data source.

6. **Choose your new database server from the Server Name drop-down list and select either Windows or SQL Server authentication.**

7. **Select your new database.**

   Figure A-2 shows how the Choose a Destination screen appears after you make choices in Steps 5 through 7.

8. **Click Next.**

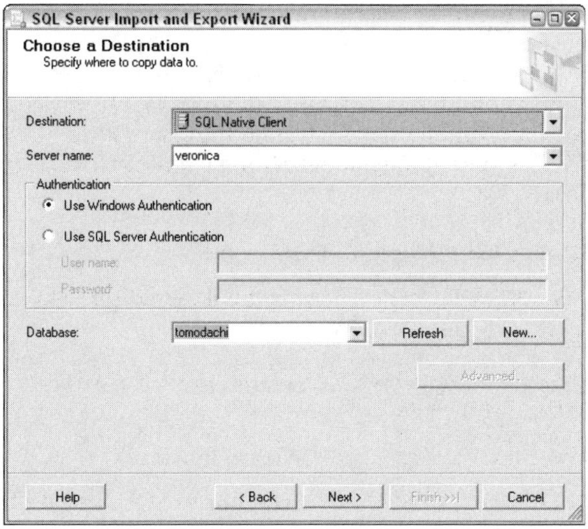

Figure A-2:
Destination
server
details.

9. **On the Specify Table Copy or Query screen, decide whether you want the wizard to copy all data, or if you want to provide a query to restrict the result set. Then click Next to continue.**

   For this example, stick with a full database copy (as I've done in Figure A-3).

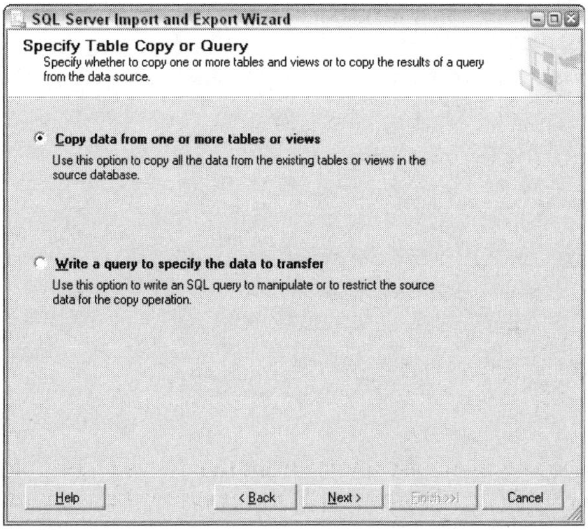

Figure A-3:
Choosing
whether to
copy all
data or
provide a
filtering
query.

10. **On the next screen of the wizard (shown in Figure A-4), pick one or more tables and views to copy, and click Next.**

Because you're upgrading your entire database, choose all tables and views. If your new database already has tables in place, you can edit the field mappings by clicking the Edit button for the tables in question.

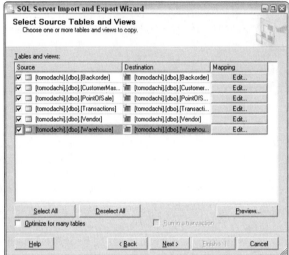

Figure A-4:
Selecting
tables and
views for
import.

11. **Decide if you want to run the job immediately, or save it for later. Click Next to continue.**

For this example, keep going and run the job right now.

After you click Next, the wizard gives you one last chance to change your mind before it starts its work, as you can see in Figure A-5.

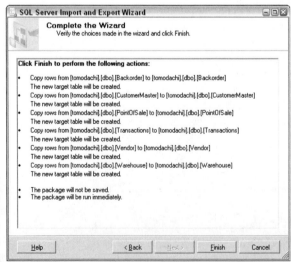

Figure A-5:
Confirming
your
selections.

12. **Verify your choices and click Finish.**

13. **Check for any errors after the job runs.**

    Figure A-6 shows the report that the wizard creates upon completion. No rows have been copied; in this case, my SQL Server 2005 Express source database was empty because my goal was to simply replicate the database structure. In reality, you see accurate row counts for each table.

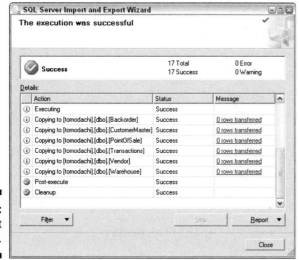

With the migration finished, you have one more important task to complete: Back up your new database so that you preserve your information in a pristine state.

Appendix B

Migrating to SQL Server 2005 Express

- -

- -

There are many good reasons to choose a functionally rich yet low-priced database platform like SQL Server 2005 Express. Regardless of your rationale for making this decision, you can use the information found in this appendix to help guide you through the important process of safely and securely moving your data from its existing locations to your new SQL Server 2005 Express instance. On the other hand, if all you seek is more details on the process of installing your database server, check out Chapter 2.

Getting Ready to Migrate

Although rushing out and upgrading your existing database to SQL Server 2005 Express is tempting, you may regret your haste later. Taking a little time and planning your upgrade properly is much better.

Proper planning prevents poor performance

When performing any type of software upgrade, you never want to put yourself into a position where you have no way backward or forward. A good plan prevents that unpleasant scenario from ever arising. With that in mind, what should you include in your migration plan? While all the following topics may not apply to your enterprise, chances are that many of them are worth considering.

- ✔ **Are your hardware and software sufficient?** SQL Server 2005 Express doesn't require a supercomputer, but it does have some basic hardware and software prerequisites that you want to make sure your environment meets. Chapter 2 addresses these preconditions.

- ✔ **Does SQL Server 2005 Express meet your needs?** In Chapter 1, I highlight some features and limitations of this product; it's worth reviewing before attempting a migration.

- ✔ **What applications are affected?** Make an inventory of those applications that are affected by the upgrade, and check that they work with SQL Server 2005 Express. The odds are that most general-purpose, ODBC-capable solutions can interact with this product. The same can't be said for heavyweight enterprise applications. To be safe, check with the solution provider.

- ✔ **When is the right time to upgrade?** Ideally, you want to perform your upgrade during a period of reduced activity, while also factoring in time to restore your original configuration should things go askew. Juggling a particularly busy workload and a software upgrade at the same time is not fun.

- ✔ **Are there major product differences?** Given that its architecture is based on the powerful SQL Server platform, chances are that SQL Server 2005 Express is more feature-rich and functional than your existing database product. Still, double-checking this assumption is worth your time, especially if your current database has highly specialized features that are necessary for your environment.

- ✔ **Should you work in parallel?** In many cases, working in parallel is the safest way to test a new software configuration. You could assign a group of users to work with SQL Server 2005 Express, manage any problems, and then switch everyone to the new platform after you resolve these issues.

If you go the parallel route, be sure that you keep track of data modifications in both the new and old systems. Otherwise, you run the risk of losing information when the upgrade is complete.

Safeguarding your existing information

As I state in the previous section, the worst possible thing that can happen during an upgrade is to find that you have no way to go back to your older configuration should something go wrong. To prevent that possibility, backing up your current software and information is essential before beginning the upgrade process. If anything goes awry, you now have a way of recovering.

Completing a Successful Migration

With the vital preparation out of the way, you can now perform the migration itself. In this section, I show you how to upgrade from three popular data storage formats:

- ✔ Microsoft Access
- ✔ Microsoft Data Engine (MSDE)
- ✔ Text files

An important point to note is that Microsoft's SQL Server Management Studio offers an excellent Import and Export Wizard that you can use to interchange information among a wide variety of data sources and formats, including the previous formats. I describe how to use this wizard in Appendix A, so I assume that you're using an alternate data migration technology.

Microsoft Access

Up until now, many of you have used Microsoft Access as your database environment. It's a good choice for many entry-level, single-user applications, but a time comes when you need to upgrade to a more powerful and flexible database platform such as SQL Server 2005 Express. Fortunately, making this transition is quite easy.

You may take several iterations to get the import process working correctly. Don't despair: You can keep fine-tuning your import effort until you get it right. Here's what you need to do:

1. **Launch Microsoft Access.**

2. **Make a backup of your existing database.**

3. **Launch the Upsizing Wizard (its initial screen is shown in Figure B-1) by choosing Tools⇨Database Utilities⇨Upsizing Wizard.**

   Depending on the version and configuration of your Microsoft Access environment, you may see some installation messages from your server. These may require you to insert your original program disks for this product.

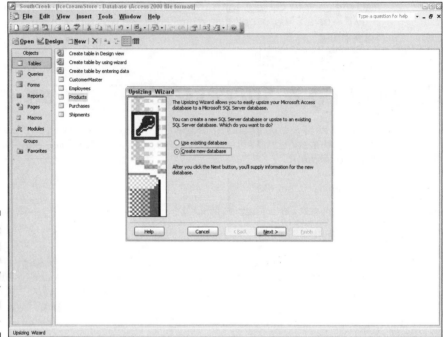

Upsizing Wizard

Figure B-1:
Choosing
to create
a new
database or
load existing
database.

4. **Choose either to create a new database in SQL Server 2005 Express or to use an existing one. Click Next when ready.**

   Although copying the Microsoft Access .mdb file onto your database server is probably faster, it's not essential; you can connect remotely.

5. **Fill in the login details for your SQL Server 2005 Express server, along with the name of the new or existing database you want to populate (see Figure B-2), and then click Next.**

   If you're confused about how to connect to the database server, check out Chapter 4 for some guidance on this topic.

6. **Pick one or more tables to upgrade (as shown in Figure B-3), and click Next.**

   Unless you have a good reason not to, you're smart to upgrade all the tables at one time.

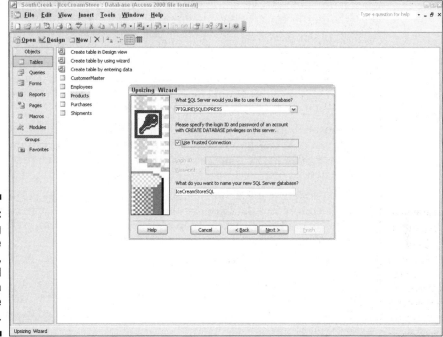

Figure B-2:
Connecting
to the
database,
and
providing a
database
name.

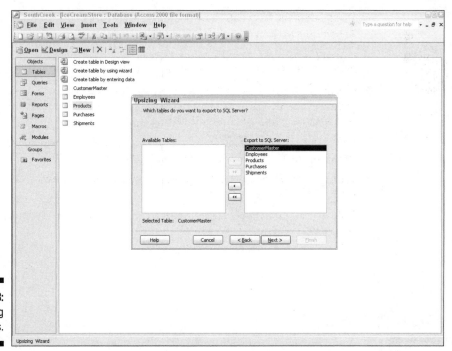

Figure B-3:
Upgrading
all tables.

7. **On the next screen of the wizard (shown in Figure B-4), choose whether to export table attributes as well as data, and click Next.**

Generally, accepting the default values for these settings is a good idea.

If you have any problems during the data migration, you may want to uncheck some of the table attributes in this dialog box. For example, the table relationships setting may cause trouble during the import process. Trial-and-error is definitely the watchword.

8. **Choose whether you want the Upsizing Wizard to create a new Microsoft Access application that will make use of your new SQL Server 2005 Express database. Click Next when you're ready to proceed.**

If you already have an application in place that uses the current Microsoft Access database, let the wizard create a new client/server application. Otherwise, you can choose the No Application Changes option (see Figure B-5).

9. **Click Finish for the wizard to complete its work.**

If everything is okay, you see a series of status messages letting you know that the wizard is doing its job. When complete, the wizard produces a rather lengthy report telling you what happened (a portion of which is shown in Figure B-6).

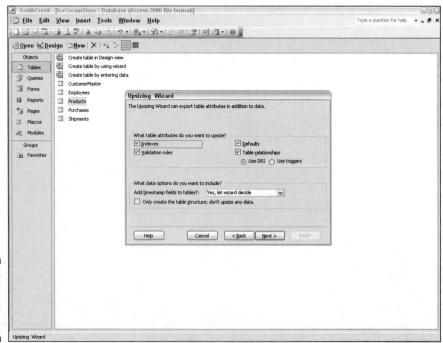

Figure B-4:
Exporting table attributes.

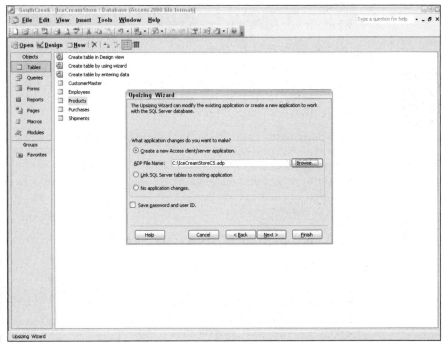

Figure B-5:
Setting
application
properties.

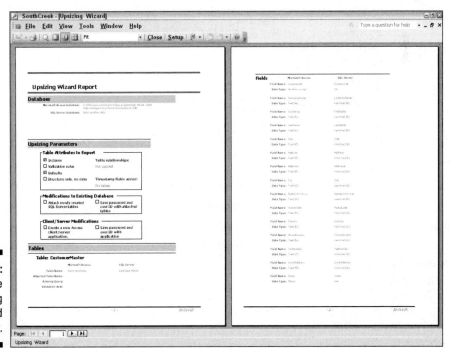

Figure B-6:
The
Upsizing
Wizard
report.

Microsoft Data Engine (MSDE)

Prior to SQL Server 2005 Express, many Microsoft developers took advantage of earlier free database servers, known either as the Microsoft Data Engine (MSDE) or MSDE 2000, depending on the version. Upgrading from these prior packages is quite easy; in fact, if you installed MSDE using an MSI setup, the installation program automatically handles the upgrade for you.

Use the default instance name for your new SQL Server 2005 Express instance if you directly installed MSDE.

On the other hand, if you installed MSDE as part of a larger packaged software installation, just follow these steps to ensure that your database gets moved to the new server.

1. **Install SQL Server 2005 Express using a different instance name than your MSDE instance.**

   Use the Named Instance option to request this alteration.

2. **When SQL Server 2005 Express is installed, detach the database from your earlier MSDE instance.**

3. **Attach the database to SQL Server 2005 Express.**

Alternatively, you can run the SQL Server 2005 Express setup program in custom mode. You can then specify the instance name of your existing MSDE environment, and you'll be asked if you want to upgrade this database to SQL Server 2005 Express.

Text files

If you've been storing your information in text files, you'll find SQL Server 2005 Express to be a much safer and more powerful alternative. However, you must do some work to get your data migrated. Here's what you need to do to make the leap forward:

1. **Decide on a database and table structure for SQL Server 2005 Express.**

   In order to import data, you need a destination. You can elect to create a one-to-one correlation between your text file–based data and its new home in SQL Server 2005 Express. On the other hand, you can choose to create a by-the-book relational database design. In either case, some planning and thought are required on your part.

   To find out more about designing relational databases, have a look at Chapters 8 and 9.

2. **Run the bcp utility, instructing it where to find the data source and destination.**

This feature-rich, command-line application allows data to move between SQL Server 2005 Express and external solutions and file formats. You can feed this utility many parameters and settings to help it gracefully handle your import files; once determined, you can then save the settings in format files. Figure B-7 shows the available settings for this application.

I discuss how to use bcp in more detail in Chapter 9.

3. Alternatively, run one of the many third-party utilities available for data migration.

While the bcp utility is very powerful, you may find it too cumbersome and arcane to be useful. However, the software market abounds in independent tools that do nothing but move information among various formats; one of these tools may make sense for you.

You can even use tools like Microsoft Access and Excel as import utilities, but you have to set up ODBC connections and perform other gymnastics that are handled more naturally by bcp or a specialized, third-party data migration utility.

Figure B-7:
bcp utility
variables.

Wrapping Up Your Migration

If you've made it this far without major complications, congratulations! You're not quite done yet, however. You need to take a few more simple — yet vital — steps to guarantee complete success.

First, backing up your brand-new SQL Server 2005 Express database is essential. Doing so gives you a way out in case anything goes wrong after you start using the database server.

With the backup out of the way, the next order of business is to create an ODBC data source. You can skip this step if you have no applications or tools that use ODBC as their primary communication mechanism with your database. However, odds are you need to complete this step. Here's how to do it:

1. **Launch the Windows Control Panel and then choose Administrative Tools⇨ODBC.**

2. **In the ODBC Data Source Administrator dialog box, click either the User DSN or System DSN tab.**

   Selecting the System DSN tab is generally a good idea; your data source is then visible to other users on your computer.

3. **From the list of drivers, pick either the SQL Native Client or the SQL Server driver.**

   The SQL Native Client is the more current connectivity driver, so I recommend that you select this option.

4. **Enter the name and description of your connection, pick the server, and click Next.**

5. **Choose the authentication method you want, and click Next.**

6. **Choose your default database and click Next.**

7. **Fill in the final settings, and click Finish.**

8. **Test your new ODBC connection.**

   The SQL Native Client offers a very useful feature to help validate that your connection was set up correctly. Just click the Test Data Source button (shown in Figure B-8) to launch this verification utility. Figure B-9 show a successful connection.

With these last steps out of the way, you can now confidently start using your SQL Server 2005 Express database.

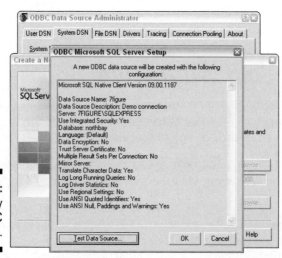

Figure B-8:
Summary
of ODBC
settings.

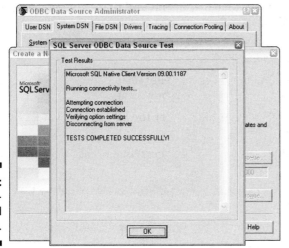

Figure B-9:
A suc-
cessful
connection.

Appendix C

Glossary

Advanced Services: A more capable version of SQL Server 2005 Express. While this edition maintains its sibling's free price point, it includes some advanced technologies such as full-text searching and reporting services.

article: A database object (such as a table, stored procedure, or view) that is contained within a publication. See also *replication*.

assembly: Application logic that is stored in, and managed by, the SQL Server 2005 Express database server, including objects such as triggers, CLR software, and stored procedures. See also *Common Language Runtime (CLR)*.

attribute: Information, contained in the form of name-value pairs, located after the start tag of an XML element. See also *element; content*.

backup: The process of copying your database's information to another form of media, such as tape or disk. A good backup strategy is vital for any production SQL Server 2005 Express environment. See also *full backup; full differential backup*.

backup device: A hardware unit that hosts the media for your database backups. You configure your backup to work with this object. These devices are typically disk or tape drives. See also *backup*.

Business Intelligence Development Studio: Found in the SQL Server toolkit, this environment makes it easy to create and deploy useful reports. See also *reporting services*.

checkpoint: Like any modern relational database management system, SQL Server 2005 Express performs much of its work within high-performance memory. However, to make any data alterations permanent, eventually memory must preserve data onto disk drives. The checkpoint process is how the database server accomplishes this synchronization.

column: Stored within tables, a column contains a particular piece of information. For example, if you're tracking details about a customer, you likely place this data in a table. Within the table, you have columns to monitor things such as name, address, and so on. See also *table*.

Common Language Runtime (CLR): When building a database application, many developers choose to use SQL Server's internal language, Transact-SQL. However, other programming languages (such as Visual Basic, Visual C#, and so on) offer better performance and functionality for certain tasks, such as parsing a string or solving sophisticated mathematical computations, than Transact-SQL. CLR is a Microsoft software development and integration technology that allows you to build software and store it within SQL Server 2005 Express using one of these other languages. In most cases, however, using Transact-SQL will be the right choice.

composite index: This index is made up of two or more columns. See also *column*.

content: All information contained between the start and end tag of an XML element. See also *element; attribute*.

database server: A sophisticated software product that hosts a broad range of data, making it available for many concurrent clients. SQL Server 2005 Express is one example of a database server. Other vendors, such as Oracle and IBM, offer their versions of this type of product.

distributor: A central database server that acts as an administrator and coordinator for replication. See also *replication*.

Document Type Definition (DTD): A specification that describes the structure and format of an XML document. Generally included at the top of the XML document, it helps people and applications better understand and work with the XML-based information. See also *XML*.

element: Surrounded by a start and end tag, this XML-based information may also include attributes and content. Elements may contain other nested, child elements. See also *attribute; content*.

file backup: A type of backup relevant only when there are multiple filegroups. See also *filegroup*.

filegroup: Collections of SQL Server 2005 Express data files. For performance and administrative reasons, you can place user objects into their own, dedicated filegroups. See also *master data file (MDF); file backup*.

first normal form: One of the three normal forms that make up relational database guidelines, this rule states that a table should not have any repeating fields. See also *normalization; second normal form; third normal form*.

foreign key: Information that establishes a relationship between two or more tables. By preventing erroneous data modifications, this association helps preserve data integrity. See also *primary key*.

full backup: As its name implies, this type of backup archives all information within a database. Should the database be lost or damaged, you can restore it to its state as of the time you created the full backup. See also *full differential backup; partial backup; restore*.

full differential backup: Identical to a full backup, with one major difference: A full differential backup archives only information that has changed since the last full backup. This backup can be very handy if only small portions of your database change on a regular basis; by running differential backups you don't need to incur the time and media costs of full backups. See also *backup; full backup*.

full text catalog: The file system-based object that holds the contents of all full-text indexes.

full-text search: The ability, present in SQL Server 2005 Express with Advanced Services, to quickly and efficiently search large quantities of text-based information.

function: A centralized, server-based routine that can be included as part of your Transact-SQL statements. Typically used to streamline logic and reduce the amount of required programming effort, you can build your own functions. You can also take advantage of the many built-in functions offered by SQL Server Express 2005. One difference between functions and stored procedures is that the former must return a value; it's optional with the latter. See also *stored procedure*.

index: An internal database structure, sometimes defined by the database administrator, and sometimes automatically created by SQL Server 2005 Express. Indexes enable speedy access to information, as well as perform integrity and other validations to safeguard data. See also *unique index; composite index*.

isolation level: A configurable setting that affects how a transaction interacts with other SQL Server Express users and processes. Increasingly stringent isolation levels are

Read uncommitted	Snapshot
Read committed	Serializable
Repeatable read	

These isolation levels interact with your application, allowing or denying visibility to modified data depending on the setting. See also *transactions*.

log file: A file system–based, internal database construct that records data and table modifications, and restores information to its previous state should the application rollback a transaction.

logical design: The abstract design and structure of your relational database. Focusing on the high-level objects, and their interrelationships, this design is usually generated during the analysis phase of most projects. It then serves as a guideline for creating the actual implementation of your SQL Server 2005 Express database. See also *physical design*.

master data file (MDF): SQL Server 2005 Express databases contain two types of operating system files: MDF and log files. This class of file stores data, and is dedicated to one-and-only-one database. See also *log file; filegroup*.

named pipes: A communication method between two processes. In the context of SQL Server 2005 Express, this is a means for a database client to communicate with the database server. See also *protocol*.

namespace: A collection of element and attribute names designed to reduce confusion and ambiguity when dealing with database objects as well as XML documents. See also *XML*.

normalization: A series of database design recommendations that dictate how information should be dispersed among tables, as well as how these tables should relate. See also *first normal form; second normal form;* and *third normal form*.

optimizer: The optimizer is an internal technology that is responsible for selecting the most efficient means to accessing or altering information. It uses detailed statistics about the database to make the right decision.

partial backup: An operation that archives a subset of your database, including

Data from the primary filegroup

Any requested read-only files

All read-write filegroups

See also *partial differential backup; full backup; full differential backup*.

partial differential backup: Archives only those portions of the last partial backup that have changed since the partial backup was completed. See also *partial backup; full backup; full differential backup*.

permission: A privilege that you grant to a principle. After it's authorized, the principle may then interact with one or more securables. See also *principal; securable*.

physical design: The actual tables, columns, indexes, and other data structures used to store information in a SQL Server 2005 Express database. Development projects typically progress from a logical database design to a physical database design. See also *logical design*.

primary key: This column, or group of columns, provides a unique definition for a given row. By definition, no two rows in the same table can have the same primary key value. See also *foreign key*.

principal: Any user or process that you can authorize to interact with your SQL Server 2005 Express database. See also *securable*.

procedural language: A general-purpose programming language containing full logic and flow control capabilities. Typically compiled to binary code, these languages can usually handle more complex algorithms at higher performance than interpreted database-centric languages such as Transact-SQL. See also *Common Language Runtime (CLR)*.

protocol: To communicate effectively, client applications and database servers need a commonly agreed-upon approach. A protocol is a communication standard adhered to by both parties that makes these conversations possible. See also *TCP/IP; named pipes*.

publication: A single unit containing one to many articles, available for replication to other database servers. See also *replication*.

publish-and-subscribe: An architecture that allows easy interchange of information among distributed computers and processes. Data may be pushed by a publisher, or pulled by a subscriber. See also *replication*.

publisher: A specific database server that offers information to other databases using replication technology. See also *replication*.

record: A grouping of information typically returned from a query or other database operation. It may consist of data from only one table, or it may be an aggregation of information dispersed among many tables. See also *row*.

recovery model: A preset plan used by SQL Server 2005 Express when archiving and restoring information. See also *backup; restore*.

referential integrity: A set of rules enforced by the database server, the user's application, or both that protects the quality and consistency of information stored in the database.

replication: A process whereby information is published from a database server and sent to one or more subscribers. Data may be transferred proactively by the publisher, or may be requested by the subscribers. See also *publish-and-subscribe*.

reporting services: The collection of technologies, found in SQL Server 2005 Express with Advanced Services, that make it easy to design, develop, and deploy reports for users regardless of their location. See also *Business Intelligence Development Studio*.

restore: The process of reinstating archived information onto your database server. See also *backup; recovery model*.

row: An individual entry from a given table. For example, a table may contain details about thousands of customers; a specific customer's data is in one row. See also *record*.

schema: A group of database objects that make up a given namespace. Objects include tables, views, and statements that grant or revoke access to other securable objects. No two objects in any namespace may have the same name.

second normal form: Data is said to be in the second normal form if it complies with the first normal form, as well as having one or more columns in a table that uniquely identify each row. See also *first normal form; third normal form*.

securable: This represents any type of object that can be given its own security setting. Some examples of securables include tables, views, and users. See also *principal*.

SQL Server Management Studio Express: Provided by Microsoft, this graphical tool lets you perform common database administration tasks as well as run direct Transact-SQL statements.

stored procedure: Centralized, server-based application code. Typically used to standardize business logic and reduce the amount of required programming effort, you can build your own stored procedures, or leverage the many built-in stored procedures offered by SQL Server 2005 Express. One difference between stored procedures and functions is that the latter must return a value; it's optional with the former. *See also Common Language Runtime (CLR); functions*.

Structured Query Language (SQL): Originally developed by IBM, this standards-based language allows access to information stored in a relational database. See also *Transact-SQL*.

subqueries: A nested query that returns information to an outer query, thereby helping the outer query correctly identify results.

subscriber: A database server that collects replicated, published information sent by one or more publishers. See also *replication*.

subscription: An appeal, sent to a publisher, requesting a publication to be sent via replication. See also *replication*.

table: These contain logical groupings of information about a given topic. For example, if you're interested in students and their grades, your application would have at least two tables: One to track details about students, and one to monitor their test scores. See also *column*.

TCP/IP: An abbreviation for *Transmission Control Protocol/Internet Protocol*, this standard protocol makes up the foundation of most computer-to-computer communication across the Internet as well as on local networks.

third normal form: Table data that complies with both the first and second normal forms, and also directly relates to each rows primary key. See also *first normal form; second normal form*.

transactions: To prevent data corruption or other inconsistent results, developers use transactions to logically group sets of related database access statements into one work unit. If something goes wrong during the processing of these statements, it's easy to rollback, or *cancel*, the transaction so that none of the changes take place. On the other hand, if everything completes normally, the transaction ensures that all the alterations are made at the same time.

Transact-SQL: Microsoft's implementation of SQL. It includes a number of enhancements that make it easier to develop powerful database applications. These additions include conditional logic, variables, and error-handling logic. See also *Structured Query Language (SQL)*.

trigger: Stored in and managed by your database server, this software executes when a certain event occurs. These events can range from information creation or modification to structural changes to your database. After the event occurs, the trigger executes, causing a predetermined set of actions to take place. These actions can encompass data validation, alerts, warnings, and other administrative operations. Triggers can invoke other triggers and stored procedures. See also *stored procedure*.

unique index: Sometimes created explicitly by the user, and sometimes created automatically by the database server, by guaranteeing one-and-only-one value for a given table, this structure speeds access to information as well as preserves data integrity. See also *index*.

view: A virtual grouping of one or more tables, often done to reduce complexity while increasing security and reliability. An administrator defines the view, which is then available for developers and users to access instead of working with the underlying tables.

Visual Studio: Microsoft's flagship development environment, supporting a wide variety of programming languages with a full set of professional features and capabilities for the modern software developer. See also *Visual Studio Express*.

Visual Studio Express: An easy-to-learn, integrated collection of software development and data management tools provided by Microsoft. These tools are aimed at entry-level developers, students, and hobbyists.

XML: A standards-based, structured way of representing and working with information in easily readable text files. Consisting of nested elements that contain content and attributes, XML has become the de facto standard for transmitting data among disparate systems. SQL Server 2005 Express supports storing and working with XML data. See also *element; attribute; content*.

XQuery: Designed to interrogate XML-based data, this standards-based query language also has some programming capabilities. See also *XML*.

Appendix D

About the CD-ROM

*I*n Chapter 2, I describe several different ways that you can obtain and install your own copy of the SQL Server 2005 Express software. One of the easiest methods is simply to install the product from the CD that comes with this book.

System Requirements

Make sure your computer meets the minimum system requirements listed. If your computer doesn't match most of these requirements, you may have problems installing or running the contents of the CD:

- A PC with a 600 MHZ Pentium III or faster processor.
- Any of the following Windows operating systems:
    - Windows Server 2003 with SP1
    - Windows Small Business Server 2003 with SP1
    - Windows XP Home Edition with SP2 or later
    - Windows XP Media Center Edition with SP2 or later
    - Windows XP Professional Edition with SP2 or later
    - Windows XP Tablet PC Edition with SP2 or later
    - Windows 2000 Advanced Server with SP4
    - Windows 2000 Professional Edition with SP4 or later
    - Windows 2000 Server with SP4 or later
- The Microsoft .NET Framework 2.0.
- At least 192MB of total RAM installed on your computer. 512MB of RAM is recommended.

- ✔ At least 500MB of available disk space. If you're storing a lot of information in your database, you need more disk space.

- ✔ Administrative privileges on the computer. If you have insufficient permission, Windows blocks any software installation.

- ✔ A CD-ROM drive.

If you need more information on the basics, check out *PCs For Dummies,* by Dan Gookin; or any of the *Windows For Dummies* titles by Andy Rathbone (all published by Wiley Publishing, Inc.).

What You'll Find

The CD contains a free, fully functional copy of Microsoft SQL Server 2005 Express Edition with Advanced Services, including a series of associated programs and utilities listed here:

- ✔ The database server and all supporting files.

- ✔ The character-based SQLCMD utility, through which you can directly enter SQL to work with your database.

- ✔ The bcp utility, which you use to interchange information between SQL Server 2005 Express and other applications.

- ✔ The SQL Server Configuration Manager, which helps you construct and tune your environment.

- ✔ The SQL Server Surface Area Configuration tool, which lets administrators enable or disable protocols, services, and features. This can help improve security.

- ✔ SQL Server Management Studio Express Edition, an easy-to-use yet powerful database administration application.

You can use this database platform alone, or in combination with popular development tools from Microsoft and other vendors. You can even use it as an information repository for office productivity software such as Microsoft Excel, PowerPoint, and other data analysis and business intelligence technologies.

If You Have Problems (Of the CD Kind)

SQL Server 2005 Express installed for me with no problems. I've tested all the scripts and application code. Alas, your computer may differ, and some programs may not install correctly or work properly for some reason.

The three most likely problems are that you don't have administrative privileges, don't have enough memory (RAM) for the programs you want to use, or you have other applications running that are affecting installation or running of a program. If you get error messages like Not enough memory or Setup cannot continue, try one or more of these methods and then try using the software again:

- ✔ **Turn off any antivirus software that you have on your computer.** Installers sometimes mimic virus activity and may make your computer incorrectly believe that virus is infecting it.

- ✔ **Close all running programs.** The more programs you're running, the less memory is available to other programs. Installers also typically update files and programs. So if you keep other programs running, installation may not work properly.

- ✔ **Add more RAM to your computer.** This is, admittedly, a drastic and somewhat expensive step. However, if you're running any of the Windows operating systems I listed earlier in this chapter, adding more memory can really help the speed of your computer and allow more programs to run at the same time.

Index

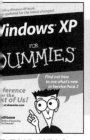

SPORTS, FITNESS, PARENTING, RELIGION & SPIRITUALITY

0-7645-5146-9

0-7645-5418-2

Also available:

- Adoption For Dummies
  0-7645-5488-3
- Basketball For Dummies
  0-7645-5248-1
- The Bible For Dummies
  0-7645-5296-1
- Buddhism For Dummies
  0-7645-5359-3
- Catholicism For Dummies
  0-7645-5391-7
- Hockey For Dummies
  0-7645-5228-7

- Judaism For Dummies
  0-7645-5299-6
- Martial Arts For Dummies
  0-7645-5358-5
- Pilates For Dummies
  0-7645-5397-6
- Religion For Dummies
  0-7645-5264-3
- Teaching Kids to Read For Dumm
  0-7645-4043-2
- Weight Training For Dummies
  0-7645-5168-X
- Yoga For Dummies
  0-7645-5117-5

TRAVEL

0-7645-5438-7

0-7645-5453-0

Also available:

- Alaska For Dummies
  0-7645-1761-9
- Arizona For Dummies
  0-7645-6938-4
- Cancún and the Yucatán For Dummies
  0-7645-2437-2
- Cruise Vacations For Dummies
  0-7645-6941-4
- Europe For Dummies
  0-7645-5456-5
- Ireland For Dummies
  0-7645-5455-7

- Las Vegas For Dummies
  0-7645-5448-4
- London For Dummies
  0-7645-4277-X
- New York City For Dummies
  0-7645-6945-7
- Paris For Dummies
  0-7645-5494-8
- RV Vacations For Dummies
  0-7645-5443-3
- Walt Disney World & Orlando For Dun
  0-7645-6943-0

GRAPHICS, DESIGN & WEB DEVELOPMENT

0-7645-4345-8

0-7645-5589-8

Also available:

- Adobe Acrobat 6 PDF For Dummies
  0-7645-3760-1
- Building a Web Site For Dummies
  0-7645-7144-3
- Dreamweaver MX 2004 For Dummies
  0-7645-4342-3
- FrontPage 2003 For Dummies
  0-7645-3882-9
- HTML 4 For Dummies
  0-7645-1995-6
- Illustrator CS For Dummies
  0-7645-4084-X

- Macromedia Flash MX 2004 For Dun
  0-7645-4358-X
- Photoshop 7 All-in-One Desk
  Reference For Dummies
  0-7645-1667-1
- Photoshop CS Timesaving Technic
  For Dummies
  0-7645-6782-9
- PHP 5 For Dummies
  0-7645-4166-8
- PowerPoint 2003 For Dummies
  0-7645-3908-6
- QuarkXPress 6 For Dummies
  0-7645-2593-X

NETWORKING, SECURITY, PROGRAMMING & DATABASES

0-7645-6852-3

0-7645-5784-X

Also available:

- A+ Certification For Dummies
  0-7645-4187-0
- Access 2003 All-in-One Desk
  Reference For Dummies
  0-7645-3988-4
- Beginning Programming For Dummies
  0-7645-4997-9
- C For Dummies
  0-7645-7068-4
- Firewalls For Dummies
  0-7645-4048-3
- Home Networking For Dummies
  0-7645-42796

- Network Security For Dummies
  0-7645-1679-5
- Networking For Dummies
  0-7645-1677-9
- TCP/IP For Dummies
  0-7645-1760-0
- VBA For Dummies
  0-7645-3989-2
- Wireless All In-One Desk Referenc
  For Dummies
  0-7645-7496-5
- Wireless Home Networking For Dun
  0-7645-3910-8

Notes